History of Books
and Printing

BOOKS, PUBLISHING, AND LIBRARIES
INFORMATION GUIDE SERIES

Series Editor: Harold L. Roth, Director, The Bryant Library, Roslyn, New York

Also in this series:

ACADEMIC LIBRARIES—*Edited by Patricia Gleiberman**

CENTRAL LIBRARIES—*Edited by Ernest Siegel**

HEALTH SCIENCES LIBRARIANSHIP—*Edited by Beatrice K. Basler and Thomas G. Basler*

INDEXING—*Edited by Barbara Preschel**

LIBRARY AND INFORMATION SCIENCE—*Edited by Dorothy B. Lilley and Rose Marie Badough**

MICROFORM PUBLISHING—*Edited by Ralph Folcarelli**

THE PAPERBACK BOOK—*Edited by Frank Culver**

PRESERVATION OF LIBRARY MATERIALS—*Edited by Susan Thompson and Paul Banks**

SCHOOL LIBRARIES AND EDUCATIONAL MATERIALS CENTERS—*Edited by Esther R. Dyer and Pam Berger**

SCIENCE AND TECHNICAL LIBRARIANSHIP—*Edited by Ellis Mount**

SPECIAL LIBRARIES—*Edited by Susan DiMattia**

* in preparation

The above series is part of the
GALE INFORMATION GUIDE LIBRARY

The Library consists of a number of separate series of guides covering major areas in the social sciences, humanities, and current affairs.

General Editor: Paul Wasserman, Professor and former Dean, School of Library and Information Services, University of Maryland

Managing Editor: Denise Allard Adzigian, Gale Research Company

History of Books and Printing

A GUIDE TO INFORMATION SOURCES

Volume 2 in the Books, Publishing, and Libraries Information Guide Series

Paul A. Winckler

Professor of Library Science
Palmer Graduate Library School
C.W. Post Center
Long Island University

Gale Research Company
Book Tower, Detroit, Michigan 48226

Library of Congress Cataloging in Publication Data

Winckler, Paul A
    History of books and printing.

    (Books, publishing, and libraries information guide
series ; v. 2) (Gale information guide library)
    Includes indexes.
    1. Books—History—Bibliography. 2. Printing—
History—Bibliography. I. Title.
Z117.W54   070.5'73   79-13006
ISBN 0-8103-1408-8

To
Mark, Christopher, Karen, Patrick, and Pamela

VITA

Paul A. Winckler received his B.A. from St. John's University in 1948 and the M.L.S. from Pratt Institute Library School in 1950. From New York University he obtained the M.A. in English literature in 1953 and in 1968 a Ph.D. in higher education. He is currently professor of library science at the Palmer Graduate Library School of Long Island University where he regularly teaches courses in the history of books and printing and the history and techniques of book illustration, as well as rare book librarianship.

His professional career includes that of librarian at the Brooklyn (N.Y.) Public Library; librarian in charge of the Brooklyn (N.Y.) Campus Library of St. John's University; library director of the Bryant Library, Roslyn, N.Y., and librarian of Suffolk (N.Y.) Community College. In 1962 he joined the faculty of the Palmer Graduate Library School where he has also served as acting dean.

He is a member of a number of professional and scholarly groups including the William Morris Society of North America, the Typophiles, the Center for Book Arts, the Friends of the Pierpont Morgan Library, and the American Friends of the Gutenberg Museum and also of the Plantin-Moretus Museum. He is a founding member of the Printing Historical Society (England) and the American Printing History Association (serving as a member of the Education Committee) and also of the New York chapter.

In 1972 he prepared a two-part bibliographical essay entitled "Materials and Sources for Teaching the History of Books and Printing," which was published in the JOURNAL OF EDUCATION FOR LIBRARIANSHIP and as a reprint. He is the editor of the READER IN THE HISTORY OF BOOKS AND PRINTING published by Information Handling Services in 1978, as well as the author of articles for various professional publications. Winckler is currently working on a new book entitled A BIO-BIBLIOGRAPHICAL DICTIONARY IN THE HISTORY OF BOOKS AND PRINTING.

CONTENTS

Contents

FOREWORD

The information business, as a field of which books, publishing, and libraries are a part, in its growing complexity and tendency toward specialization, produces a wide range of literature on ever more minute phases. This material, available in unorganized proliferation, makes it difficult, if not impossible, to understand the parameters of any one aspect of the field, to bring into focus the nature of the work being done, or even to understand how things got started and developed.

The Books, Publishing, and Libraries Information Guide Series was started to provide a series of basic research tools to the understanding of the fields the series covers. Each volume is edited by one or more individuals with expertise in the subject matter of the field and in the information sources applicable to the understanding of the problems of the field. Each editor was charged with the responsibility for applying a selection process to the material covering the field so that the practitioner, businessman, government official, librarian, student, and relevant funding agency will have a basic inventory of resources and related information available in the particular area of his interest for fact finding. Each special interest topic is covered in some depth and organized to direct the user to key sources, agencies, and significant organizations which govern the contributions to the intellectual growth of the field.

Harold L. Roth
Series Editor

ACKNOWLEDGMENTS

I would like to thank the board of trustees of Long Island University and the administration at its C.W. Post Center for granting me a sabbatical during which I was able to undertake the compiling and editing of this bibliography.

I also wish to express my appreciation to the administration, faculty, and staff of the Palmer Graduate Library School of Long Island University for their understanding and support during the time I was involved in this work. Of particular assistance were Mrs. Alma Rapp, former librarian of the Palmer Graduate Library School Library, and the present librarian, Mr. T.Y. Lee. A special thanks to my research assistants, Roberta Verdi and Renée Capitanio.

The staff of the New York Public Library and the Pierpont Morgan Library were also helpful in my search for materials.

INTRODUCTION

The advance and progress of civilization was due primarily to the desire and ability of human beings to communicate with each other. In the beginning this was accomplished by the spoken word which, however, could easily be forgotten and misinterpreted. The maxim, "the spoken word passes away, the written word remains," aptly describes the impact of the alphabet and writing, since it is with the written word and later the printed word that men and women were able to record, preserve, and disseminate ideas to their own as well as future generations. During the past five thousand years, graphic communication has evolved through various stages in its recording of the history of civilization. The history of books and printing encompasses all subjects, since it is the one which records all others. Over the years there has been a good deal of interest in the history of the book, resulting in an extensive body of literature.

It is the purpose of this work to fill the need for a practical guide to this extensive literature which will be of value and interest to the student and general reader and can serve as an introduction to further reading, study, research, and enjoyment, and also as a reference source for library educators, librarians, teachers, scholars, experts, historians, bibliographers, bibliophiles, book collectors, publishers, the book trade, and all who are interested in the book. This annotated bibliography does not attempt to be complete or definitive but a contribution to a broad understanding of the field. The annotations are mainly descriptive of the contents of the various items listed rather than a critical overview of the literature. It is my hope that this work will serve as an information guide to the literature of the delightful and fascinating world of the history of the book.

The Contents indicate the scope of this book. In addition to units on general bibliographies and general information sources, a section is devoted to techniques used in graphic communication, containing both historical studies and description of processes, and a unit on the historical evolution of books and printing from the ancient world to modern times. Other units list nonprint media; periodicals and annuals; associations, societies, and clubs; libraries, special collections, and museums; and book dealers.

Introduction

All printed items in this bibliography were examined in the verification of bibliographic data and in the writing of the annotations. A number of nonprint media were also examined but in some cases data were obtained from printed lists or sources. The search for materials involved the checking of a great number of bibliographies and lists, as well as the holdings of library collections. From a seemingly endless number of titles, a selection was made of those items which met the following guidelines: (1) materials of interest to the student and general reader; (2) books which are general in their coverage of each topic; (3) items which have been published mainly in the twentieth century and are currently available; (4) materials which are written or have been translated into English; and (5) a listing of printed books, with a few periodical articles and exhibition catalogs included in the appropriate unit, as well as a section on nonprint media. Each entry contains bibliographical data including author, title, edition, place of publication, publisher, date of publication, pagination, and reprint information. If the original work was examined then that pagination follows the entry, but if the reprint edition was examined then that pagination is listed.

The following subject areas have been excluded as outside the scope of this book: rare books, printer's marks, book plates, book collectors and book collecting, printing as an avocation, printer's trade, the book trade, publishers and publishing, and preservation and conservation of library materials. In some cases these areas may be included if they are part of a work which includes relevant units.

With a few exceptions the following materials have also been excluded: type specimen books; library catalogs; book auction catalogs; bookdealers' catalogs; printer's manuals; biographies, autobiographies, memoirs, and reminiscences; theses and dissertations; and works on individual printers, typographers, illustrators, book-designers, papermakers, bookbinders, and/or presses.

This book has been compiled to fill a gap in the bibliographical literature, and I hope it has accomplished its purpose.

Paul A. Winckler

Section 1

GENERAL BIBLIOGRAPHIES

A general bibliography is one which includes several subjects in an attempt to present an overview of the literature of books about books. The number of general bibliographies is limited, and very few cover the wide span of topics which would encompass the five thousand years of graphic communication. Most of them deal with a specific period or include only a few topics. Several of these bibliographies are also out-of-date and only a few are annotated. A few bibliographies of bibliographies are also included in this section. Some of the specialized bibliographies are included in the appropriate unit.

1   Anderson, Frank J., ed. PRIVATE PRESSWORK: A BIBLIOGRAPHIC APPROACH TO PRINTING AS AN AVOCATION. South Brunswick, N.J.: A.S. Barnes and Co., 1977. 168 p.

> This bibliography is mainly concerned with printing as an avocation serving as a "classified guide to the literature in many areas of printing instruction." It contains units on printing instruction manuals, selecting a press, alphabet and letterforms, type and typography, book design and book production, illustration, history and techniques, bookplates, bookbinding, private presses, printing history, paper and papermaking, libraries and museums, associations, periodicals list, directory of book dealers, and a basic book list. Each entry contains basic data and many are annotated. The material included is of "books which have proved to be useful and of interest to the private press person." It has a list of various suppliers for those who would like to embark on a private-press venture and "who wish to expand their knowledge, improve their skills, or add to their printing experience." The review in FINE PRINT 4 (October 1978): 116, by Stephen Harvard is critical of this work and states: "The book is divided into several topics, each with its book list. Some of these lists are stronger than others, but all are chiefly notable for their lucunae." The reviewer continues: "In the introduction, the author states that in printing, ' . . . perfection is only rarely achieved, and is really the province of Allah and not that of a mere mortal.' Unfortunately, his publishers have

decided to display their mortality to the fullest; they have produced what amounts to a compendium of indifferent printing practices; from broken type to wandering imposition." The book contains a few black-and-white illustrations which are more decorative than relevant. Indexed.

2   ANNUAL BIBLIOGRAPHY OF THE HISTORY OF THE PRINTED BOOK AND LIBRARIES. The Hague: Martinus Nijhoff, 1973. Vol. 1-- , 1970-- . Annual. Pagination varies.

This bibliography was started by the Committee on Rare and Precious Books and Documents of the International Federation of Library Associations as a means of coordinating the individual and separate efforts of publications and research in the area of books and printing. The purpose of this publication is to record "all books and articles of scholarly value which relate to the history of the printed book, to the history of the arts, crafts, techniques, and equipment, and of the economic, social, and cultural environment involved in its production, distribution, conservation, and description." It is international in scope but limited from the beginning of the printed book to the present day and only if the work has been written entirely or partly from a historical point of view. Each annual contains over 2,500 entries. No annotations.

3   Appleton, Tony, comp. A TYPOLOGICAL TALLY: THIRTEEN HUNDRED WRITINGS IN ENGLISH ON PRINTING HISTORY, TYPOGRAPHY, BOOK-BINDING AND PAPERMAKING. Brighton, Engl.: Dolphin Press, 1973. 94 p.

The purpose of this work is to provide "a useful guide to the more notable writings on these subjects." With a few exceptions it does not include bibliographies, booksellers' and library catalogs, or type specimen books. It is divided into three units: printing history and typography, bookbinding, and papermaking, and within each unit the books are arranged alphabetically by author. Appleton gives author, title, place, and date of publication for each item. No annotations.

4   Besterman, Theodore. PRINTING, BOOK COLLECTING, AND ILLUS-TRATED BOOKS: A BIBLIOGRAPHY OF BIBLIOGRAPHIES. 2 vols. Totowa, N.J.: Rowman and Littlefield, 1971.

This is a republishing of the titles found in the units of printing, book-collecting, illustrated books, broadsides and pamphlets, book-production, paper, publishing and bookselling, and special subjects in Besterman's A WORLD BIBLIOGRAPHY OF BIBLIOG-RAPHIES (see below). This is one in a series of books in which the publishers have "gathered together all the titles in some of the major fields" found in A WORLD BIBLIOGRAPHY OF BIBLIOGRAPHIES and reprinted them in a convenient format. Some entries have brief comments.

5   _____. A WORLD BIBLIOGRAPHY OF BIBLIOGRAPHIES AND OF
BIBLIOGRAPHICAL CATALOGUES, CALENDARS, ABSTRACTS, DIGESTS,
INDEXES AND THE LIKE. 4th ed. 5 vols. Lausanne: Societas Bib-
liographica, 1965-66.

> This is an alphabetical subject list of over 117,000 items on
> all subjects. It is particularly useful because of its extensive
> coverage of books and printing, including a number of ap-
> propriate headings such as bookbinding, papyri, paper, illus-
> trated books, alphabet, writing, and printing. Some entries
> have brief comments. The number of entries in each bibliog-
> raphy is given at the end of the citation, in brackets. This
> is the work which the publishers Rowman and Littlefield used
> for the reprint PRINTING, BOOK COLLECTING, AND IL-
> LUSTRATED BOOKS: A BIBLIOGRAPHY OF BIBLIOGRAPHIES
> (see above), and obviously there is duplication.

6   Bigmore, Edward C., and Wyman, Charles W.H., comps. A BIBLIOG-
RAPHY OF PRINTING WITH NOTES AND ILLUSTRATIONS. 2d ed.
3 vols. London: Quaritch, 1880-86. Reprint. New York: Duschnes,
1945.

> This bibliography was "the first of its kind printed in England."
> The material included is limited to their definition of printing
> which includes "typographic, lithographic, copperplate print-
> ing, etc., with the cognate arts of typefounding, stereo-
> typing, electrotyping, and wood-engraving." Paper and book-
> binding are not included. The items are arranged alpha-
> betically by author and most are annotated. The compilers
> felt that their annotations form "as a whole, a valuable col-
> lection of materials toward a future History of Printing." This
> book contains numerous illustrations. Also has a list of pe-
> riodical publications which, at the time, "was the most com-
> plete that has yet been compiled." This is a scholarly work
> and of particular use for nineteenth-century materials on books
> and printing.

7   BOOKS ABOUT BOOKS: AN INTERNATIONAL EXHIBITION ON THE
OCCASION OF THE INTERNATIONAL BOOK YEAR 1972 PROCLAIMED
BY UNESCO. Frankfurt-am-Main, Ger.: Frankfurt Book Fair, 1972.
390 p.

> This is the catalog for the exhibition "Books About Books" and
> "contains 1,395 book titles from 403 publishing houses and
> organizations." Its purpose is to present a picture of "the
> range of books on books presently available throughout the
> world," and it is arranged under the following units: the
> author, copyright, publishing, book production, book distri-
> bution, book promotion, the reader, bibliophily, book and paper
> history, book and art, book statistics, bibliography, documenta-
> tion, audio-visual, library science, and book trade journals.

Most entries have brief annotations and there is an index of authors, editors, and publishers, and a list of abbreviations.

8   DICTIONARY CATALOGUE OF THE HISTORY OF PRINTING FROM THE JOHN M. WING FOUNDATION, THE NEWBERRY LIBRARY (CHICAGO). 6 vols. Boston: G.K. Hall, 1962. 1st supplement, 1970, 3 vols.

A photographic reproduction of the catalog cards of one of the most extensive American libraries of the history of printing. This item is an exception to the listing of library catalogs because of its importance as a major research library on the history of books and printing, and its great bibliographical value. The collection contains more than 23,000 volumes of "books and journals descriptive of the graphic arts, national and regional printing histories, works on papermaking, binding, book design, and illustration ancillary to printing," which constitutes half of the collection, while the other half contains "finely printed or historically significant books." Alphabetically arranged.

9   Gerber, Jack. A SELECTED BIBLIOGRAPHY OF THE GRAPHIC ARTS. Pittsburgh: Graphic Arts Technical Foundation, 1967. 84 p.

The purpose of this work is "to gather in one place a listing of books and articles which represent the latest in graphic arts technology, primarily books from 1950 to 1966, and articles from 1964 to 1966." The major areas of the graphic arts are included from "introductory studies to those which require a rather strong scientific background." This book also has a listing of trade press publications, trade associations, and colleges and universities offering graphic arts programs. The books have brief annotations but not the articles. No index.

10   Hart, Horace. "Bibliotheca Typographica: A List of Books About Books." THE DOLPHIN 1 (1933): 161-94.

This is an annotated listing of 245 items on printing and related subjects arranged under the following headings: the alphabet and writing, type, paper, manuscripts and illumination, printing, bookbinding, bibliography and book collecting. It lists only works in English and is intended for the nonacademic student, collectors, printers, and "for others who have an amateur's interest in this fascinating subject." Substantially this work appeared as BIBLIOTHECA TYPOGRAPHICA IN USUM EORUM QUI LIBROS AMANT: A LIST OF BOOKS ABOUT BOOKS, with an introduction by George Parker Winship (Rochester, N.Y.: The Printing House of Leo Hart, 1933). Indexed.

11   Lehmann-Haupt, Hellmut. ONE HUNDRED BOOKS ABOUT BOOK-
      MAKING: A GUIDE TO THE STUDY AND APPRECIATION OF PRINTING.
      3d ed. New York: Columbia University Press, 1949. Unpaged. Reprint.
      Westport, Conn.: Greenwood, 1976.

        This bibliography is arranged numerically under such headings
        as general works and origin of the book, writing and letter-
        ing, printing history and modern trends, American develop-
        ments, printing practice, printing types and decoration, il-
        lustration, bookbinding and papermaking, and bookmaking
        periodicals, with annotations for each item. Indexed. This
        work first appeared in 1933 as FIFTY BOOKS ABOUT BOOK-
        MAKING, and as a second edition in 1941 entitled SEVENTY
        BOOKS ABOUT BOOKMAKING.

12   National Book League. BOOKS ABOUT BOOKS, CATALOGS OF THE
      LIBRARY OF THE NATIONAL BOOK LEAGUE. 5th ed. Cambridge:
      Cambridge University Press for the National Book League, 1955. 126 p.

        The first edition appeared in 1933 of this classified catalog
        (Bliss) listing the holdings of this particular library. Includes
        material on a wide range of subjects of which some are rele-
        vant including bibliography; documentation; paper and ink
        making; publishing and selling books; reading and readers of
        books; selection, collection, care of; love of books; libraries,
        establishment, services, administration; and English literature.
        Titles include books added to the end of 1953. There is an
        author and subject index, but no annotations.

13   Pratt, R.D. A THOUSAND BOOKS ON BOOKS. London: Merrythought
      Press, 1967. 96 p.

        A "selection of English books on book-making, book-selling,
        and book-collecting." This is not really a bibliography, as
        such, but the listing of the personal selection of the author
        of notes on the books which he collects. The list is arranged
        alphabetically by author and some entries have brief comments
        but most just give bibliographical data. Has a subject index.

14   St. Bride Foundation Institute. CATALOGUE OF THE PERIODICALS RE-
      LATING TO PRINTING AND ALLIED SUBJECTS IN THE TECHNICAL
      LIBRARY OF ST. BRIDE INSTITUTE. London: 1950. 35 p.

        This is a listing of the journal holdings of this special library
        as of that date. According to James Mosley, librarian of
        the St. Bride Library, this listing is still useful since there
        were only a few journals added after 1951.

15 _____. CATALOGUE OF THE TECHNICAL REFERENCE LIBRARY OF WORKS ON PRINTING AND THE ALLIED ARTS. Compiled by R.A. Peddie. London: 1919. 999 p.

> Another exception to the inclusion of library catalogs because this work represents the holdings of one of the major printing libraries of the world and has value as a bibliographical tool. According to James Mosley, this 1919 catalog is still used since it contains the listing of about two-thirds of their collection. Although there is a need of updating this catalog to include items added in the past sixty years, Mosley states that it is hoped "to produce listings in some areas of our collection" . . . "but we have no plans at the moment (1978) to issue a supplementary catalogue covering the whole library."

16 Servies, James A. "A Short-Title List of Books on Printing, etc." Williamsburg, Va.: College of William and Mary, 1962. 39 p. Mimeographed.

> Basically a list of the holdings in the college library, at that time, of items relating to printing and the graphic arts. Alphabetically arranged by author. Gives basic bibliographical information but no annotations or index.

17 Ulrich, Carolyn, and Küp, Karl. BOOKS AND PRINTING: A SELECTED LIST OF PERIODICALS, 1800-1942. Woodstock, Vt.: William Edwin Rudge, Publisher, and New York: New York Public Library, 1943. 244 p.

> This work attempts to serve as "a source of information for the student and to give to those interested in certain specific phases of the field a useful reference tool." It is an extensive listing of periodicals which can be considered "the best and most useful material" in the area of books and printing and related fields, including units on records before the printing press; paleography, illuminating, and calligraphy; the history of printing; the history of bookbinding; printing types; design, layout, and typography; printing practice and shop; illustration and prints; processes of reproduction; paper and papermaking; ink; and materials and practices of binding. This work is still useful because many of these journals are still being published, are available in libraries, and a number have been reprinted. Each entry contains full bibliographical data, including name of journal, dates, place of publication, frequency, indication if indexed or illustrated, and other basic information. It is international in scope and the entries have brief annotations. Appendixes contain material on directories, indexes, yearbooks, associations, organizations, societies, and house organs. Indexed.

18   Webber, Winslow L. BOOKS ABOUT BOOKS. Boston: Hale, Cushman, and Flint, 1937. 168 p.

> Although this is primarily a bio-bibliography for collectors, it does have a few items which deal with the history of the book. This is a listing of "a few of the books and articles on bibliography and collecting which should be of most interest and value to the bookman," with a brief chapter on book collecting and books about books, followed by the bio-bibliography or an alphabetical listing by author with extensive annotations. The final unit is a list of magazine references from 1900 to 1937, arranged chronologically. Has a brief glossary of terms.

19   Williamson, Derek. HISTORICAL BIBLIOGRAPHY. Hamden, Conn.: Archon Books, 1967. 129 p.

> A bibliographical essay on the history of books and printing and the analysis and description of books which contains material on early books and materials, printing, shape and style in writing and typography, the illustration of books, paper and papermaking, the binding of books, and the book trade, as well as on the meaning of bibliography, bibliographer's tools, and bibliography in action. The style is a combination of history and bibliography, in which comments are made on the history of books and printing with references to pertinent books or articles on that event or individual. In addition to listing of entire books on a subject, there are also references to chapters or units in books. Indexed.

20   Winckler, Paul A. "Materials and Sources for Teaching the History of Books and Printing." JOURNAL OF EDUCATION FOR LIBRARIANSHIP 13, part 1 (Summer 1972): 43-71; and 13, part 2 (Fall 1972): 123-36. Reprint. 46 p.

> A listing of items which "could be considered significant and of value in teaching a survey course in the history of books and printing" or for an individual who is interested in knowing more about this subject. Most of the items are of a "general rather than a highly specialized nature." This listing is presented as a bibliographical essay giving full bibliographic data for each item with brief comments. Part 1 includes printed books, divided into various units, such as general reference sources, bibliographies, bibliographical manuals, general surveys of books and printing, and general surveys of the history of the printed book. Part 2 contains a listing of audio-visual materials; exhibition catalogs; dealers' catalogs; sources for original materials, leaves, and rare books; periodicals; special collections; and special events and programs. No index.

Section 2

GENERAL INFORMATION SOURCES

This unit contains a few of the chronologies, dictionaries, and encyclopedias pertaining to the history of books and printing and the graphic arts. Only a few general reference books have been published in this field, and there is a need for new reference sources. Although there are a few dictionaries and chronologies, there is no multivolume English-language encyclopedia on the history of the book, except for pertinent entries in the ENCYCLOPEDIA OF LIBRARY AND INFORMATION SCIENCE (see 25). Some of the general encyclopedias are useful.

21   Allen, Edward M., comp. and ed. HARPER'S DICTIONARY OF THE GRAPHIC ARTS. New York: Harper and Row, 1963. 295 p.

An alphabetical listing of over "6,500 terms currently used by those in the graphic arts industries," which records "the usage of our language by those craftsmen engaged in the various aspects of the graphic arts."

22   AMERICAN DICTIONARY OF PRINTING AND BOOKMAKING. New York: Howard Lockwood and Co., 1894. Reprint. Detroit: Gale Research Co., 1967. 592 p.

A history of the arts of printing and bookmaking "in Europe and America with alphabetically arranged definitions of technical terms and biographical sketches." In the preface to the reprint Robert E. Rusner states: "In spite of . . . Henry L. Bullen's callous comment that Lockwood's DICTIONARY was an 'inaccurate, inexact and contrary publication' most users and readers have acknowledged it as a useful and resonably accurate reference tool." It contains "a storehouse of practical, technical, and historical information, and its biographical accounts of printing contemporaries are in many instances, the single and only source. Printing antiquarians have long found pleasure in its contents, especially in its many illustrations and descriptions of older presses and equipment." The biographical information includes such printers and typefounders as Gutenberg, Baskerville, Caxton, and others.

23   Berry, W. Turner, and Poole, H. Edmund. ANNALS OF PRINTING:
      A CHRONOLOGICAL ENCYCLOPAEDIA FROM THE EARLIEST TIMES
      TO 1950. Toronto: University of Toronto Press, 1966. 315 p.

      Starts with A.D. 105 and the invention of paper, to 1950.
      This illustrated book is a chronological listing of all major
      and significant events in the history of printing. It was
      written for "the student in schools of librarianship, colleges
      of art and printing and technology, for whom an historical
      background to their profession and craft is essential, and the
      non-specialist who is aware of contemporary trends in com-
      munication and in the practice of printing and who wishes to
      look back over its developments." This book is "not aimed
      at completeness: emphasis has been laid upon innovators and
      innovations." Under each year lists facts, short biographical
      data, and comments on the particular event as related to the
      "annals of printing" history. Indexed.

24   Clair, Colin. A CHRONOLOGY OF PRINTING. New York: Frederick
      A. Praeger Publishers, 1969. 228 p.

      Similar to ANNALS OF PRINTING by Berry and Poole (see
      above). This book also starts with A.D. 105 but continues
      through 1967. This chronology is "designed as a compendium
      of information on matters connected with printing, its first
      introduction into Europe and its spread throughout the world;
      being an attempt to set in their chronological order those
      matters most important in the history of the printed book, its
      manufacture, design, and dissemination." It has brief factual
      entries which provide "the widest range of information rather
      than to study any one factor in depth," with a comprehensive
      index which adds to its value.

25   ENCYCLOPEDIA OF LIBRARY AND INFORMATION SCIENCE. New
      York: Marcel Dekker, 1968-- .

      This multivolume English language encyclopedia is devoted to
      a wide range of topics on library science, librarianship, and
      information science. The volumes which have been published
      include a number of entries on the history of books, such as
      Bible (manuscripts), Bible (printed editions), block printing,
      binding, colophons, decoration, design of books, and printers
      and printing, from Gutenberg to the present. In addition
      there are a number of articles on presses, such as Ashendene,
      Eragny, and Golden Cockerel, as well as a number of bio-
      graphical sketches on Aldus, Garamond, Caxton, Estienne,
      Musurus, and others. A detailed analysis of the entries on
      books and printing in this encyclopedia would reveal that
      although not comprehensive, it is extensive. Most entries
      are followed by notes and a bibliography and many are il-
      lustrated.

26   Glaister, Geoffrey A. AN ENCYCLOPEDIA OF THE BOOK. Cleveland:
      World Publishing Co., 1960. 484 p.

> This is an alphabetical glossary of terms "used in papermaking,
> printing, bookmaking, and publishing, with notes on illumi-
> nated manuscripts, bibliophiles, private presses, and printing
> societies." This is a British work, and contains numerous il-.
> lustrations. Appendixes include examples of some type speci-
> mens, Latin place names as used in the imprints of early
> printed books, "The Contemporary Private Press" by John Ryder,
> proof correction symbols, and a short reading list. A second
> edition, GLAISTER'S GLOSSARY OF THE BOOK (Berkeley:
> University of California Press, 1979) is now available.

27   Greenhood, David, and Gentry, Helen. CHRONOLOGY OF BOOKS
      AND PRINTING. Rev. ed. New York: Macmillan Co., 1936. 186 p.

> A chronological listing with brief information on a "broad
> procession of events in the development of the Book" from
> 300 B.C. through A.D. 1935. The purpose of this work is
> "to afford the user of this manual . . . ready access to a
> wide variety of facts which, usually, are obtainable only by
> consulting several volumes, and those not always on one shelf
> or in the same library." Has a list of principal sources con-
> sulted, as well as a chart of the handwriting of western
> Europe, and a conspectus of type designs. Indexed.

28   Haller, Margaret. THE BOOK COLLECTOR'S FACT BOOK. New York:
      Arco Publishing Co., 1976. 271 p.

> This is an exception to items on book collecting and is in-
> cluded because it also contains many facts of value and in-
> terest on the history of the book. It is alphabetically ar-
> ranged with brief entries.

29   Hostettler, Rudolf. TECHNICAL TERMS OF THE PRINTING INDUSTRY.
      4th rev. ed. St. Gall, Switz.: By the author, 1963. 195 p.

> A small book divided into three parts: (1) instructions; (2)
> picture section presented in three languages under the head-
> ings of composition, reproduction, press work, paper, book-
> binding, and tables; and (3) a dictionary in five languages
> (English, French, German, Italian, and Dutch).

30   Peters, Jean, ed. THE BOOKMAN'S GLOSSARY. 5th ed. New York:
      R.R. Bowker Co., 1975. 169 p.

> This is a new edition of an old standard which first appeared
> in serial form in the 12 July 1924 issue of PUBLISHERS'
> WEEKLY and appeared in book form in 1925 under the editorship
> of John A. Holden. Although emphasis is on publishing, this
> book does contain information of value and interest to books and

printing. The brief entries are alphabetically arranged and it
includes a selected reading list.

31   Stevenson, George A.   GRAPHIC ARTS ENCYCLOPEDIA.   New York:
        McGraw-Hill Book Co., 1968.   492 p.

        This work is "designed to provide basic understanding and
        practical guidance in the reproduction of words and pictures.
        As such, deals with (1) the products and tools with which an
        image is formed, (2) the kind of image, and (3) the surface
        or material upon which the image is produced." It is an
        alphabetical listing which attempts to consolidate in one
        volume "all the useful techniques, processes, concepts, and
        methods required in the graphic arts profession," and contains
        numerous illustrations.   There is also a bibliography, list of
        associations and societies, various trade journals, an alpha-
        betically arranged product index, a manufacturer's index,
        and tables.   Indexed.

32   Wijnekus, F.J.M., comp.   ELSEVIER'S DICTIONARY OF THE PRINTING
        AND ALLIED INDUSTRIES, IN FOUR LANGUAGES, ENGLISH, FRENCH,
        GERMAN, DUTCH.   Amsterdam: Elsevier Publishing Co., 1967.   583 p.

        This book is compiled and arranged on an English alphabetical
        base and is a rather comprehensive international dictionary
        of printing trade terms.

Section 3

MATERIALS AND TECHNIQUES
USED IN GRAPHIC COMMUNICATION

In order to obtain an understanding of the history of books and printing, it is essential to have a knowledge of the basic processes and techniques involved in book production. The book of the ancient, medieval, or modern world reveals the time and circumstance in which it was made and the materials needed and the methods involved in its production.

This unit contains a listing of items on the technical aspects of bookmaking and design, as well as on the history of the technique or process. This section contains subunits of general works, surfaces and materials used, the alphabet and writing, type and typography, bookbinding, and book illustration. A great deal has been written on these topics and this listing is a selection of a few items which can serve as an introduction or as a reference source.

GENERAL WORKS

33   Arnold, Edmund C. INK ON PAPER 2: A HANDBOOK OF THE GRAPHIC
      ARTS. New York: Harper and Row, 1972. 374 p.

> A work which examines the printing process and various aspects of written communication, beginning with a historical overview and then examines printing type, printers' terms, hot metal, the electronic era, use of type, various methods of printing, paper, ink, the bindery, and other related topics. It is written in a popular style with numerous illustrations, and each unit has a brief listing of suggested readings. Contains a glossary and index.

34   Brewer, Roy. AN APPROACH TO PRINT: A BASIC GUIDE TO THE
      PRINTING PROCESSES. London: Blandford Press, 1971. 165 p.

> An attempt to present a brief survey of the influences which have shaped "the industry to its present dimensions, and those which are continuing to alter the way in which print is made and used." Brewer examines "the ways in which machines,

equipment, materials, and techniques are changing," containing units on printing processes and the changing scene, use of computers in the printing process, illustration, bindery, paper, and ink, with a concluding chapter entitled "What Happens Next?" There is a two-page bibliography. Indexed.

35   Brunner, Felix. A HANDBOOK OF GRAPHIC ARTS REPRODUCTION PROCESSES. New York: Hastings House Publishers, 1962. 379 p.

This is a "pictorial record of graphic processes from the earliest woodcuts and copperplate engravings down to the very latest example of the art," in a technical guide, in English, German, and French, which explains the printmaking processes for "art collectors, and dealers, librarians, booksellers, publishers, artists, graphic designers, and the printing trade."

36   Craig, James. PRODUCTION FOR THE GRAPHIC DESIGNER. New York: Watson-Guptill Publications, 1974. 207 p.

An attractive and profusely illustrated manual which will enable "a person wishing to understand any area of production to locate the desired information, fast, within the covers of a single book." It includes basic information on typesetting, printing, color printing, inks, paper, imposition, folding, binding, and mechanicals, as well as a glossary of 1,100 entries providing up-to-date definitions and explanations for students, teachers, and professionals. Contains a brief bibliography. Indexed.

37   Curwen, Harold. PROCESSES OF GRAPHIC REPRODUCTION IN PRINTING. 4th ed. Revised by Charles Mayo. London: Faber and Faber, 1966. 171 p.

A practical and useful handbook explaining the various reproduction processes in a work "primarily intended to be of use to those who are engaged in, or intend to engage in making desings for reproductions. . ." and contains many helpful illustrations. Curwen examines the autographic method, photographic reproductions, and bookbinding. There is a sectional index and a bibliography.

38   Davenport, Cyril. THE BOOK: ITS HISTORY AND DEVELOPMENT. New York: Van Nostrand Co., 1908. Reprint. Detroit: Tower Books, 1971. 258 p.

A handy survey of the materials used in book production, including units of early records; tools, books and bookbinding; paper; printing; illustrations; miscellanea; leather; the ornamentation of leather bookbindings without gold; and the ornamentation of leather bookbindings with gold. It contains

seven full-page black and white plates and numerous small
illustrations. Has a listing of books to consult at the end
of each chapter. Indexed.

39   Gaskell, Philip. A NEW INTRODUCTION TO BIBLIOGRAPHY. 3d
printing with corrections. New York: Oxford University Press, 1972.
438 p.

This book aims "to elucidate the transmission of text by explaining the processes of book production" and "attempts for
the first time to give a general description of the printing
practice of the machine-press period." Gaskell provides information on book production: the hand-press period 1500-
1800; book production: the machine press period 1800-1950;
and bibliographical applications. There are three appendixes:
(1) "A Note on Elizabethan Handwriting" by R. B. McKerrow;
(2) Four Specimen Bibliographical Descriptions; and (3) The
Transmission of the Text: Two Examples. Has an extensive
bibliography. Indexed.

40   Hamilton, Edward A. GRAPHIC DESIGN FOR THE COMPUTER AGE.
New York: Van Nostrand Reinhold Co., 1970. 191 p.

An illustrated book on "visual communication for all media"
which is planned for use by anyone who must think or plan
visually, and would like to obtain an insight into visual communications today. There is a chapter on graphic computer
capabilities. It contains black-and-white and color illustrations, as well as a chronology chart, a glossary of computer
terminology, and a bibliography. Indexed.

41   Harrop, Dorothy. MODERN BOOK PRODUCTION. Hamden, Conn.:
Archon Books, 1968. 196 p.

The purpose of this book is "to provide a simple outline of
all the major modern processes involved in the making of
books, periodicals, and newspapers, together with some guidelines to sound design, for the use primarily of students of
librarianship, publishing and printing, practising librarians,
and others interested in the background to the printed material which they handle." Harrop includes units on paper
and papermaking, type, composition, printing surfaces for
illustration, printing in color, from type to printed page,
nonbook forms, special printing methods, book binding by
hand, edition binding, makeup and design, and publishing
for yourself. It has a select bibliography and is illustrated
with sixty-eight black-and-white line drawings and five
plates (three in color). Indexed. A useful introduction to
this topic.

42   Jackson, Holbrook. THE PRINTING OF BOOKS. 2d ed. London:
Cassell and Co., 1947. 285 p.

This book is unique in that the author attempts to examine "the art of printing from the point of view of readers and authors rather than of printers." He examines "the influence of authors on printing, and how that influence has determined the trend of typography." Contains three units: printing for reading, the author and his printer, and occasional papers. There are a number of black-and-white illustrations. Indexed.

43   Jennett, Seán. THE MAKING OF BOOKS. 5th ed. London: Faber and Faber, 1973. 554 p.

Originally published in 1951, this work has established itself as standard and required reading for anyone who would like an overview of the entire process of modern book production. This work examines and explains the "practice and aesthetics of book design and the technologies of printing, binding, process-engraving and the various other trades that contributed their share to the business of turning an author's manuscript or typescript into a book printed and bound and ready for publication." This new edition covers the many changes and new technologies involved in contemporary book production. It contains 209 illustrations and has a selection of books for further reading and reference, and a polyglot glossary of technical terms in English, American, French, German, and Italian. Indexed. An extremely useful source.

44   Karch, R. Randolph. GRAPHIC ARTS PROCEDURES--BASIC. 4th ed. Chicago: American Technical Society, 1970. 409 p.

This book was first published in 1948. It is a how-to-do-it textbook for trainees and apprentices but is also useful for the student and general reader because it explains in simple and basic terms the many and varied processes involved in printing and graphic arts. Profusely illustrated with a glossary of graphic art terms. Indexed.

45   Lee, Marshall. BOOKMAKING: THE ILLUSTRATED GUIDE TO DESIGN/PRODUCTION/EDITING. 2d ed. New York: R.R. Bowker Co., 1978. 440 p.

This book was first published in 1965 and the revised and expanded new edition of this "classic manual" attempts to bring "you right up to date." The revolution in the way books are made necessitates keeping up with "the new electronic technology, new hardware and software, and the new bookmaking skills--from concept to editing, design, and production." This work is intended for those in the field to serve as a practical handbook. However, it can also be of value to all students of book production in its presentation of new developments. There is an expanded section on editing. Illustrated and indexed.

46   McLean, Ruari. MODERN BOOK DESIGN FROM WILLIAM MORRIS
TO THE PRESENT DAY. London: Faber and Faber, 1958. 116 p.

The author presents a brief but useful overview of book design in modern times starting with the revival of printing and
William Morris, the private press movement, and printing in
the twentieth century in the United States and Europe with
the emphasis on printing in England. There is a concluding
chapter entitled "The Future of Book Design." A few illustrations are provided. Indexed.

47   _____. VICTORIAN BOOK DESIGN AND COLOUR PRINTING. 2d
ed. Berkeley and Los Angeles: University of California Press, 1972.
241 p.

A study of "what happened in nineteenth-century book design and printing mainly in England. . . ." McLean examines this little-known period which "is only now coming
into historical focus." The author feels that "more exciting
things happened in book design between 1837 and 1890 than
in any other comparable period in the history of the world's
printing." Has numerous black-and-white illustrations and
sixteen color plates. Indexed.

48   Maddox, H.A. PRINTING: ITS HISTORY, PRACTICE AND PROGRESS.
London: Sir Isaac Pitman and Sons, 1923. 160 p.

This is a useful text for information on the technical aspects
of printing, although now out-of-date for modern developments.

49   Melcher, Daniel, and Larrick, Nancy. PRINTING AND PROMOTION
HANDBOOK. 3d ed. New York: McGraw-Hill Book Co., 1966. 451 p.

A work primarily concerned with planning, production and
use of commercial printing, advertising, and direct mail but
also contains useful information on various aspects of modern
printing procedures. This is a practical manual for anyone
involved in a printing or promotion job because it explains
some of the basic processes of contemporary printing (as of
1966). Divided into an alphabetical encyclopedia and three
appendixes of type faces, a bibliography, postal information,
it also contains some illustrations.

50   Moran, James. PRINTING PRESSES: HISTORY AND DEVELOPMENT
FROM THE FIFTEENTH CENTURY TO MODERN TIMES. Berkeley and
Los Angeles: University of California Press, 1973. 263 p.

This book "deals with the development of the relief printing
press from its inception in the middle of the fifteenth century
until approximately 1940, when it may be said to have
reached its zenith." Moran's book is a most comprehensive

study of the relief or letterpress press and machine in which
he examines the beginning of printing and the wooden press,
with developments of the various metal presses, such as the
Stanhope Press, the Columbian Press, and the Albion Press.
It has many illustrations as well as a bibliography, a general
index, and an index of presses and machines (see also 362).

51   Reed, R., ed. SYMPOSIUM ON PRINTING. Leeds, Engl.: Leeds
Philosophical and Literary Society, 1971. 89 p.

A veritable potpourri of topics, this work contains the papers
presented at a three-day symposium held in 1970 on the subject of "printing and other associated methods of communication." It covers a wide range and variety of subjects including chapters on Caxton to computers, the computer and
literary studies, problems of restoring old books, old books
and their reproduction, the design of type faces, Chinese
prints and printing, television and communication, and storage
and retrieval of information. Illustrated. No index.

52   Rice, Stanley. BOOK DESIGN: SYSTEMATIC ASPECTS. New York:
R.R. Bowker Co., 1978. 256 p.

A book which presents modern problems of book design and
analyzes them as they relate "to the systematic and perma-
nent aspects of complex book design." This book is intended
for "book designers, art directors, and editors" and explains
the processes involved. Contains charts, procedures, and
systems, and is useful for anyone who would like to examine
the technical aspects of contemporary book design problems
and especially as they relate to the new technology.

53   _____. BOOK DESIGN: TEXT FORMAT MODELS. New York: R.R.
Bowker Co., 1978. 224 p.

This is an exception to the inclusion of books which give
type specimens and has been included because it is a companion volume to Rice's BOOK DESIGN: SYSTEMATIC AS-
PECTS (see above). This volume of text format models is
basically a catalog of text typography which contains models
that can be used for a variety of text formats, including lists,
outlines, tables, poems, glossaries, and bibliographies. Each
"type of format is introduced by an explanation of the style
factors to be varied, typographical considerations, and solutions to problems that may arise in paging and structure."
The models in this book "are well suited to the new computer
coding system." A book intended for the practitioner, and
may also be of interest to the advanced student.

54   Smith, Adèle M. PRINTING AND WRITING MATERIALS: THEIR EVO-
LUTION. Philadelphia: By the author, 1901. 236 p.

> Although dated, this illustrated book is still useful as a hand-
> book which provides "in succinct form the leading facts re-
> lating to the history of printing, writing materials, and of
> bookbinding, and the processes by which they are made ready
> for general use." Indexed.

55   Strauss, Victor. THE PRINTING INDUSTRY: AN INTRODUCTION TO
ITS MANY BRANCHES, PROCESSES AND PRODUCTS. Washington, D.C.:
Printing Industries of America in association with R.R. Bowker Co.,
1967. 814 p.

> A detailed study written for "everybody who wants more in-
> formation on the printing industry; it is a book for the in-
> telligent layman." The purpose of the book is "to guide
> you, the reader, to the point where you have sufficient con-
> trol over the subject on which you seek information." This
> is basically a manual to help "understand the language of
> the specialist whom you may meet in working situations."
> Since this book is "planned as an introduction," it assumes
> that "the reader has no knowledge of the subject on which
> he wants information." Strauss includes chapters on printing
> processes and methods, composition for printing, the theory
> and practice of full-color printing, graphic arts photography,
> printing-image carriers, printing presses, presswork, paper
> and other printing stocks, printing inks, binding and finish-
> ing, and art-and-copy presentation. There is a unit of notes
> and references to each chapter, a selective bibliography,
> and a subject index. Illustrated. In spite of the claim that
> this is for the neophyte, it is often rather technical.

56   Turnbull, Arthur T., and Baird, Russell N. THE GRAPHICS OF COM-
MUNICATION-TYPOGRAPHY-LAYOUT-DESIGN. 3d ed. New York:
Holt, Rinehart and Winston, 1975. 462 p.

> A useful and informative textbook which provides information
> on theoretical aspects of graphic communication, verbal ele-
> ments of communication, visual elements of communication,
> design: combining the verbal and visual elements, production
> of graphic communication, and historical background. It
> contains numerous illustrations and a glossary, and bibliog-
> raphy. Examines the new electronic technology as it relates
> to text processing and mass communication. Indexed.

57   Williamson, Hugh. METHODS OF BOOK DESIGN: THE PRACTICE OF
AN INDUSTRIAL CRAFT. 2d ed. London: Oxford University Press, 1966.
433 p.

> A study of such "planning of the printed book's manufacture

as effects its appearance and structure." Includes such topics as the typescript, format, margins, composition, choice of type for the text, text types, principles of text design, color, illustrations, paper, bookbinding, and others. Many illustrations. Each unit has a listing of books and the appendix contains a listing of books and periodicals to supplement those at the end of each chapter. There is also a combined index and glossary.

58   Wilson, Adrian. THE DESIGN OF BOOKS. New York: Reinhold Publishing Corp., 1967. 159 p.

An attractively designed and profusely illustrated book which attempts to "show how the designer goes about preparing his layouts and following the book through the production processes." Wilson includes the art of layout, typography, printing methods, paper, anatomy of the book, binding, and other topics. The author is concerned with how "the typography communicates, the illustrations illuminate, and the binding enhances and preserves the creator's thought." Indexed.

SURFACES AND MATERIALS USED

This unit contains items which deal with the techniques involved in the making of clay tablets, papyrus, parchment, vellum, and/or paper, as well as other materials which have been used in ancient, medieval, and modern times and the materials on which the message was impressed, written, or printed. Some histories are included, tracing the evolution of the materials used during the past five thousand years.

59   Blum, André. ON THE ORIGIN OF PAPER. Translated from the French by Harry Miller Lydenberg. New York: R.R. Bowker Co., 1934. 79 p.

A brief study of paper and its influence on the spread of printing and engraving, with a definition of paper, its invention in China, and manufacture in the Orient, with an examination of the oldest paper mills in Europe and a study of Western papermaking in Spain, Italy, France, and Germany. Blum examines the causes of the slow growth of the paper industry and concludes with a chapter on watermarks and means of dating paper. No illustrations. Contains notes. Indexed.

60   Briquet, Charles M. LES FILIGRANES: DICTIONNAIRE HISTORIQUE DES MARQUES DU PAPIER. 4 vols. Paris: Picard, 1907. Republished 1923. Reprint. New York: Hacker Art Books, 1966. Unpaged.

Although highly specialized, this is included since it is the major dictionary of watermarks containing over 16,000 reproductions of watermarks from their appearance in 1282 until 1600.

It is a standard reference source which is still an important
tool for identification of watermarks. It has a bibliography
and is available on microfilm (see 590).

61   Clapperton, R.H. THE PAPER-MAKING MACHINE: ITS INVENTION,
      EVOLUTION, AND DEVELOPMENT. Oxford, Engl.: Pergamon Press,
      1967. 365 p.

      This book is concerned with the evolution of the papermaking
      machine and presents its history and development in a detailed
      and somewhat technical study. The "main part of this book is
      concerned almost entirely with the evolution of the Fourdrinier
      paper-making machine," and there is a separate unit of bio-
      graphical sketches of some of the papermakers including Robert,
      the Didot family, Fourdrinier, Hall, Dickson, and others.
      Contains many illustrations. Indexed.

62   Day, Frederick T. AN INTRODUCTION TO PAPER, ITS MANUFACTURE
      AND USE. 6th ed. London: Newnes Educational Publishing Co., [1962].
      125 p.

      A brief look at the history of paper, raw materials, paper-
      making by hand and by machine, surface treatment, gummed
      papers, British and international paper sizes, paper as the
      raw material for other industries, and a review of printing
      practices. It contains thirty-six black-and-white illustrations,
      and a glossary of paper and boards.

63   Hardman, H., and Cole, E.J. PAPER-MAKING PRACTICE. Manchester,
      Engl.: Manchester University Press, 1960. 334 p.

      A technical book for the student of paper technology and
      the papermaker which presents "a concise outline of the most
      recent ideas on the various topics which had not already ap-
      peared in the text-books and were therefore only to be read
      in technical publications." Emphasis is on the mechanical
      aspects of papermaking. Has a bibliography. Indexed.

64   Higham, Robert R.A. A HANDBOOK OF PAPERMAKING. London:
      Oxford University Press, 1963. 294 p.

      A book which deals with machine-made paper and its "science
      and technology, as well as papermaking practice," including
      units on fibrous raw materials, stock preparation, paper tests
      and paper testing, the manufacture of wood pulp and a con-
      cluding chapter on the history of papermaking. It has a
      glossary of terms but no bibliography. Indexed.

65   Hunter, Dard. PAPERMAKING: THE HISTORY AND TECHNIQUE OF
      AN ANCIENT CRAFT. 2d ed., rev. and enl. New York: Alfred A.
      Knopf, 1947. 611 p. Reprint. New York: Dover, 1978.

> The first edition was published in 1943. This second edition
> is "a selection of material from the expensive editions, but
> is issued at a modest price." This is a useful "comprehensive
> history of papermaking from its invention in other Oriental
> countries, and its introduction into Europe and development
> there." Hunter examines the early methods of papermaking
> by hand but he also looks at the papermaking machine and
> modern developments. There is a useful chronology of paper-
> making and the use of paper, as well as a map showing the
> journey of papermaking. Contains 317 illustrations and an
> extensive bibliography and notes. Indexed.

66   _____. PAPERMAKING IN PIONEER AMERICA. Philadelphia: Uni-
      versity of Pennsylvania Press, 1952. 178 p. 22 plates.

> An informative work on the beginnings of papermaking, equip-
> ment, and operation of early mills, which also examines the
> work of the papermaker in Pennsylvania, New Jersey, Mas-
> sachusetts, Maine, Virginia, Rhode Island, Connecticut, and
> New York, as well as other states in this early period. There
> is a checklist which is alphabetically arranged by papermaker
> or firm and serves as an index. Has a few illustrations. This
> is based on much of the research and work of Hunter's limited
> and expensive PAPERMAKING BY HAND IN AMERICA (see 72).

67   _____. PAPERMAKING THROUGH EIGHTEEN CENTURIES. New York:
      William Edwin Rudge, Publisher, 1930. 358 p. Reprint. New York:
      Burt Franklin, 1970.

> This book "deals with the same phase of papermaking but in
> a more comprehensive manner than the older work (OLD PA-
> PERMAKING)," and "contains additional text and greater
> variety of illustrative matter." This work is concerned "with
> the early methods of paper fabrication and does not pretend
> to enter into the history of the numerous writing substances
> in use before the advent of paper. . . ." Contains 214
> illustrations. Indexed.

The following is a listing of other works by Dard Hunter supplied by the Institute
of Paper Chemistry. Many of these books are now collector's items and are
rather expensive. They were published in limited editions and contain a number
of specimens of handmade paper which Hunter collected in his world travels.
These books may be of interest to the scholar and the serious student of papermaking.

68   Hunter, Dard. CHINESE CEREMONIAL PAPER. Chillicothe, Ohio:
      Mountain House Press, 1937. 79 p.

69 _____. THE LITERATURE OF PAPERMAKING, 1390-1800. Chillicothe, Ohio: Mountain House Press, 1925. 48 p.

70 _____. OLD PAPERMAKING. Chillicothe, Ohio: Mountain House Press, 1923. 112 p.

71 _____. OLD PAPERMAKING IN CHINA AND JAPAN. Chillicothe, Ohio: Mountain House Press, 1932. 71 p.

72 _____. PAPERMAKING BY HAND IN AMERICA. Chillicothe, Ohio: Mountain House Press, 1950. 326 p.

73 _____. PAPERMAKING BY HAND IN INDIA. New York: Pynson Printers, 1939. 129 p.

74 _____. PAPERMAKING IN INDO-CHINA. Chillicothe, Ohio: Mountain House Press, 1947. 105 p.

75 _____. PAPERMAKING IN SOUTHERN SIAM. Chillicothe, Ohio: Mountain House Press, 1936. 40 p.

76 _____. A PAPERMAKING PILGRIMAGE TO JAPAN, KOREA AND CHINA. New York: Pynson Printers, 1936. 150 p.

77 _____. PRIMITIVE PAPERMAKING. Chillicothe, Ohio: Mountain House Press, 1927. 48 p.

78 Labarre, E.J. DICTIONARY AND ENCYCLOPEDIA OF PAPER AND PAPER-MAKING. 2d ed., rev. and enl. Amsterdam: Swets and Zeit-linger, 1952. 488 p.

> This book attempts to "name and define clearly a number of material things and concepts in the paper field . . ." and developed into an "exercise in comparative philology, as an attempt to ascertain the origin, growth, and methods of variation of the vocabulary of a craft." This is a technical dictionary with brief entries, arranged alphabetically with the main entry in English and foreign-language equivalent and there is an index of each of the seven languages covered: English, French, German, Dutch, Italian, Spanish, and Swedish. Labarre states that this work is not completed but part of a projected one.

79 Leif, Irving P. AN INTERNATIONAL SOURCEBOOK OF PAPER HISTORY. Hamden, Conn.: Archon Books, 1978. 160 p.

> A compilation of over 2,000 entries listing "general histories,

national and regional histories, collections of watermarks, texts on paper history research techniques, and other bibliographies." In FINE PRINT 4 (July 1978): 81-82, John Bidwell's review states that this book is easily "the most extensive compilation to date." However, the reviewer is quite critical of omissions, and of what he refers to as "sloppy bibliography." He concludes that this work does provide "badly needed information" but "leaves plenty of room for something better."

80   Library of Congress. PAPERMAKING ART AND CRAFT. Washington, D.C.: 1968. 96 p.

This is the guide to an exhibition held at the Library of Congress in 1968 which presents a brief survey of the history of papermaking. An informative booklet which is a "convenient and useful introduction to paper and its fabrication" containing many illustrations. There is a brief list of publications on papermaking.

81   Maddox, H.A. PAPER: ITS HISTORY, SOURCES, AND MANUFACTURE. 6th ed. London: Sir Isaac Pitman and Sons, 1947. 180 p.

This is "a popular handbook which will be sufficiently comprehensive to provide a thoroughly good insight into, and understanding of, paper and its manufacture." Primarily for those concerned with papermaking but also for the general reader, although a bit on the technical side. It briefly examines the history of papermaking and materials and processes. Has thirty-seven black-and-white illustrations. No bibliography. Indexed.

82   Mason, John. PAPER MAKING AS AN ARTISTIC CRAFT. London: Faber and Faber, 1959. 96 p.

A basic work which shows the process of the making of paper by hand and which contains information on material preparation for beating, beating to pulp, the mould, the vat, pressing equipment, forming the sheets and couching, separating, wet pressing and drying, sizing, and decorative and straining devices. The stages in the papermaking process are shown through the use of numerous line drawings. There is a note on nylon paper and a brief glossary. Indexed.

83   Norris, F.H. PAPER AND PAPER MAKING. London: Oxford University Press, 1952. 353 p.

A presentation of "all the innumerable aspects of paper manufacture and its ancillary processes in an interesting and easily readable form acceptable to all branches of the industry." Written for the further education of those engaged in the papermaking, paper converting, and allied trades. Although this book is a bit technical, it is a useful survey of the processes. It contains numerous black-and-white illustrations and a glossary of paper and board qualities. Indexed.

84   O'Casey, Ian, and Maney, A.S.   THE NATURE AND MAKING OF PAPYRUS.   Barkston Ash, Engl.: Elmete Press, 1973.   69 p.

An expensive book which examines the papyrus plant, papyrus rolls and codices, scribes and papyri, making papyrus sheets; ancient and modern techniques; practical sheet-making; and the future of papyrus. A beautifully produced book published in a limited edition of 499 copies which provides an intro- duction to this topic with some brief information on the his- torical development of papyri and its importance in the history of books. There is "no one single book available at present which deals with papyrus alone" making this a unique contri- bution on papyrus--a substance which existed longer than any other as the principal surface on which books were written. Contains a sample of genuine papyrus. A useful book for those who would like to know "something about this remarkable plant which played such an important role in history."

85   Reed, Ronald.   THE NATURE AND MAKING OF PARCHMENT.   2 vols. Leeds, Engl.: Elmete Press, 1975.

A study of the nature of animal skins which traces the "de- velopment and use of parchment from the days of ancient Egypt to the medieval period." It has a number of black- and-white line drawings showing the stages in the production of parchment and vellum. A rather expensive book but unique as one of the few monographs on this topic. The nine parch- ment specimens in volume 2 have accompanying commentary.

86   Smith, David C.   HISTORY OF PAPERMAKING IN THE UNITED STATES (1690-1969).   New York: Lockwood Publishing Co., 1970.   693 p.

A study of the history of paper and the paper industry in the United States from the time of the first paper mill to the mid- twentieth century. A useful updating and expansion of the same theme as covered in the earlier book by Lyman Weeks (see 88).

87   Surtermeister, Edwin.   THE STORY OF PAPERMAKING.   Boston: S.D. Warren Co., 1954.   209 p.

One of the best general introductions to the papermaking pro- cess of value "to the casual reader who desires to get a brief, general picture of papermaking operations." There are a few illustrations. No index.

88   Weeks, Lyman H.   A HISTORY OF PAPER-MANUFACTURING IN THE
      UNITED STATES, 1690-1916.   New York: Lockwood Trade Journal Co.,
      1916.   352 p.   Reprint.   New York: Burt Franklin, 1969.

> An examination in "one complete compact narrative (of) all
> the material facts relating to the industry and to present in
> an exhaustive and comprehensive manner, on the purely his-
> torical side, the annals of this branch of American manufac-
> turing from the erection of the first little mill in Philadelphia,
> in 1690, to the opening years of the twentieth century." Il-
> lustrated and indexed.   For twentieth-century developments,
> check the book by David C. Smith (see 86).

THE ALPHABET AND WRITING

Much has been written about the origin and development of the alphabet and
the emergence of a system of writing.   It is probable that around 3000 B.C.
a method was developed whereby the spoken word could be written down.   This
meant that men and women now had the ability to record their ideas and
thoughts, which could be carried from place to place and also preserved for
posterity.   With recorded knowledge, history began.

This unit includes a number of items on the origin of the alphabet, various
writing systems, the book hands, handwriting, calligraphy, and the decipherment
of ancient writings.   David Diringer refers to the study of the alphabet as "a
key to the history of mankind."

89   Anderson, Donald M.   THE ART OF WRITTEN FORMS: THE THEORY
      AND PRACTICE OF CALLIGRAPHY.   New York: Holt, Rinehart and
      Winston, 1969.   358 p.

> A work which deals with the "history and theory of writing"
> and briefly with "working creatively with pen and brush and
> types," and examines the origins of writing; the grand age of
> manuscripts; the origin of modern letter forms; the alphabet in
> types; the twentieth century; form, meaning, and learning;
> and writing: a world art.   Profusely illustrated, with a sec-
> tion of notes, and a rather extensive bibliography.   An ex-
> cellent book for the beginner who is interested in writing and
> it evolutionary development.

90   THE ART OF WRITING: AN EXHIBITION OF FIFTY PANELS.   Paris:
      UNESCO, 1965.   50 p.

> This work contains reproductions and commentaries of some
> of the material contained in these fifty panels prepared by
> UNESCO for an exhibition on "the history of writing from
> its far-off beginnings down to the present day."   The purpose
> of the display was to present a general idea of the gradual

stages in the history of writing and the panels were designed
from a wide variety of examples "for their historical interest,
but also for their content, for the importance of the message
they bring." There is a seven-page essay by M. Cohen entitled "An Outline of the History of Writing," which is an
informative and useful introduction to writing for the general
reader. No bibliography or index.

91   Clodd, Edward. THE STORY OF THE ALPHABET. Rev. ed. New York:
D. Appleton-Century Co., 1938. Reprint. Detroit: Gale Research Co.,
1970. 234 p.

Clodd attempts to fill the gap in the literature because Taylor's
THE HISTORY OF THE ALPHABET (see 111) is "necessarily
charged with a mass of technical detail" and "furnishes only
a meagre account of those primitive stages in the art of
writing." It covers a wide range of topics from the beginnings of the alphabet, memory-aids, picture writing, cuneiform writing, Egyptian writing, Greek papyri, and other topics.
Has a number of line drawings of examples. Indexed.

92   Cohen, Marcel. LA GRANDE INVENTION DE L'ÉCRITURE ET SON
ÉVOLUTION. 3 vols. Paris: Imprimerie National Librarie C. Klinck-
sieck, 1958. 95 plates.

This is a monumental work which is included because of its
value and possible interest to the advanced student. It is
definitely not for the beginner. This work is in French and
provides an in-depth scholarly examination of the invention
of writing and its history. Volume 1 is the text; volume 2
contains an extensive listing of books, with comments, references, and notes to each chapter, as well as an index; volume
3 contains the illustrations.

93   Diringer, David. THE ALPHABET: A KEY TO THE HISTORY OF MAN-
KIND. 3d ed. 2 vols. London: Hutchinson and Co., 1968.

This work was first published in 1948 with a second edition
in 1949, and two reprints in 1953, with amendments. The
purpose of this book "is to provide an introduction to the
fascinating subject of the history of the alphabet." However,
this is a detailed study which is really not "introductory" but
is a source for the student who knows something about the
subject. Volume 1 is the text and volume 2 contains many
illustrations. Part 1 of the text is devoted to nonalphabetic
systems of writing and part 2 to alphabetic scripts. Has a
general bibliography, as well as a bibliography for most of
the units. Indexed.

94 _____. WRITING. Ancient Peoples and Places Series. New York: Frederick A. Praeger Publisher, 1962. 261 p.

> A study of "a subject common to many ancient peoples, namely the communication of thought through distance and time by writing" which contains material on primitive means of communication, analytic scripts of the ancient Near East, the Far East, pre-Columbian America, phonetic scripts, the alphabet, and the diffusion of the alphabet. It includes seventy-eight photographs, some line drawings, and maps with a unit on notes on the plates and a general bibliography. Indexed.

95 Doblhofer, Ernst. VOICES IN STONE: THE DECIPHERMENT OF ANCIENT SCRIPTS AND WRITINGS. New York: Viking Press, 1961. 327 p.

> A study written for the general reader, which attempts to show "the procedure followed in the decipherment of several important scripts and the interpretation of languages, presented in an intelligible manner . . . and to tell the story of the men who deciphered them." It has a few illustrations, a unit of notes, and a bibliography. Indexed.

96 Fairbank, Alfred. THE STORY OF HANDWRITING: ORIGINS AND DEVELOPMENT. New York: Watson-Guptill Publications, 1970. 108 p.

> This book is an excellent source for the beginner which is written in a popular style and in which the author examines the beginnings of writing, writing and various cultures, and a wide range of topics, such as pattern and spacing, pens, ink, paper, vellum and papyrus, the teaching of handwriting, and left-handed writers. It has a list of some books to consult as well as a number of color and black-and-white illustrations. Indexed.

97 Fairbank, Alfred, and Wolpe, Berthold. RENAISSANCE HANDWRITING: AN ANTHOLOGY OF ITALIC SCRIPTS. Cleveland: World Publishing Co., 1960. 104 p. 96 plates.

> The introduction discusses the calligrapher's art as revealed in the humanistic scripts with emphasis on their use and development in the Renaissance which is followed by a section of notes to the plates, and a bibliography. The last unit contains the ninety-six black-and-white illustrations dealing with manuscripts and letters, writing manuals and writing masters, and the revival of italic. A bit specialized. Indexed.

98   Fraenkel, Gerd. WRITING SYSTEMS. Boston: Ginn and Co., 1965.
       134 p.

      This useful handbook is "about writing systems, not about the
       shapes of individual letters or about penmanship, but about
       the systematic attempts man has made to develop the best
       possible means of written communication." The purpose of
       the book is "to increase your understanding of man." It ex-
       amines types of writing, the story of the alphabet, the story
       of decipherment, the history of the phonetic alphabet, spell-
       ing reform, a summary, and a glossary.

99   Gelb, Ignace J. A STUDY OF WRITING: THE FOUNDATIONS OF
       GRAMMATOLOGY. Rev. ed. Chicago: University of Chicago Press,
       1963. 319 p.

      A rather specialized book which the author states attempts to
       "lay a foundation for a new science of writing which might
       be called grammatology," because while "the general histories
       of writing treat individual writings from a descriptive-historical
       point of view, the new science attempts to establish general
       principles governing the use and evolution of writing on a
       comparative-typological basis." This is the first systematic
       presentation "of the history and evolution of writing based
       on these principles." It has ninety-six black-and-white il-
       lustrations, a bibliography and notes to each chapter with a
       separate unit of terminology of writing. Indexed.

100   Gordon, Cyrus H. FORGOTTEN SCRIPTS: THE STORY OF THEIR DE-
       CIPHERMENT. London: Thames and Hudson, 1968. 175 p.

      This is the story of "how forgotten scripts were deciphered
       and lost languages recovered adding two thousand years to
       the documented span of Western civilization." It contains
       a few illustrations. Indexed.

101   Hogben, Lancelot. FROM CAVE PAINTING TO COMIC STRIP: A
       KALEIDOSCOPE OF HUMAN COMMUNICATION. New York: Chanti-
       cleer Press, 1949. 287 p.

      An unusual book written in a very popular style and in a
       format which presents a "panorama of the emergence of man
       as the only literate animal species and a preview of the
       liquidation of illiteracy on a world scale as a prelude to the
       unification of mankind." Contains many illustrations. Indexed.

102   Irwin, Keith G. THE ROMANCE OF WRITING FROM EGYPTIAN HI-
       EROGLYPHICS TO MODERN LETTERS, NUMBERS, AND SIGNS. New
       York: Viking Press, 1956. 160 p.

      This is a popularly written book for the beginner who has little

or no knowledge of the historical development of writing.
Irwin examines the growth of writing from the banks of the
Nile and the libraries of clay, to the developments in Greece
and Rome, and the handmade book of the Middle Ages, down
to the printing of books with movable type and the non-
Roman alphabets. The work contains a number of line drawings but has a limited bibliography. Indexed.

103   Jensen, Hans. SIGN, SYMBOL AND SCRIPT: AN ACCOUNT OF
        MAN'S EFFORTS TO WRITE. 3d ed., rev. and enl. New York: G.P.
        Putnam's Sons, 1969. 613 p.

        A translation from the German by George Unwin of a rather
        detailed survey of early writing and its evolution. This book
        would be useful for a person who has some knowledge of the
        topic. It is profusely illustrated with a brief bibliography of
        general works and extensive footnotes. Has an index of
        scripts, and an index of names and subjects.

104   Lowe, E.A. HANDWRITING: OUR MEDIEVAL LEGACY. Rome: Edizioni
        di Storia e Letteratura, 1969. 38 p. 22 plates.

        A brief study of the history of writing which the author feels
        is "so intimately bound up with the history of the book as
        to be inseparable from it." The particular "forms of letters
        used today both in writing and printing are, for the most part,
        not a direct inheritance from Rome; they are rather the crea-
        tion of the centuries which transmitted, and in transmitting
        modified, that inheritance. They are, in short, the legacy
        of the Middle Ages." This book consists mainly of illustra-
        tions giving examples of various book hands, such as Capi-
        talis Rustica, Uncial, Half-Uncial, Irish Miniscule, Early
        Caroline, Beneventan, and others, and on the opposite page
        a transcription of the facsimile done by W. Braxton Ross, Jr.

105   Mason, William A. A HISTORY OF THE ART OF WRITING. New
        York: Macmillan Co., 1928. 502 p.

        This book deals with a variety of topics including primitive
        picture writing, hieroglyphics, cuneiform writing, alphabetic
        writing, the Greek and Roman alphabets, writing in the
        Middle Ages, and a concluding chapter on the age of print-
        ing. It has a number of illustrations and a rather extensive
        bibliography listing author, title, and date of publication.
        Indexed.

106   Meyer, Hans, ed. THE DEVELOPMENT OF WRITING. Zurich: Graphis
        Press, 1969. 48 p.

        Mainly examples of writing from the letters of the Roman era to modern script, arranged chronologically. Written in German, English, and French. Information is brief but illustrations provide a visual panorama of the evolution of writing and typography including a chart of time sequence of scripts. Brief bibliography.

107   Moorhouse, A.C. THE TRIUMPH OF THE ALPHABET: A HISTORY OF WRITING. New York: Henry Schuman, 1953. 223 p.

An enlarged version of his WRITING AND THE ALPHABET (see below), this book is "to show that the apparently simple art of writing, and especially writing in an alphabetic manner, is one of the world's most original and important intellectual discoveries." Divided into the form of writing, which covers the development of writing; the work of decipherment; pre-alphabetic scripts; the Semitic alphabet and its origin; and the extension of the alphabet. The unit on the use of writing examines the functioning of writing, the historical influence of writing, and writing and the spread of literacy. Moorhouse provides a readable introduction to this rather complicated subject and includes a number of illustrations, and a bibliography which contains a selected number of works in English. Indexed.

108   _____. WRITING AND THE ALPHABET. London: Cobbett Press, 1946. 97 p.

The purpose of this small book is to "set out how writing has developed in its historical forms, especially with reference to the alphabet; and further, what service it gives to mankind." Moorhouse enlarged this work in his THE TRIUMPH OF THE ALPHABET (see above). It contains a few illustrations and a brief bibliography of works in English. Indexed.

109   Morison, Stanley. POLITICS AND SCRIPT. Oxford, Engl.: Clarendon Press, 1972. 361 p.

This is an illustrated study of "aspects of authority and freedom in the development of the Graeco-Latin script from the sixth century B.C. to the twentieth century A.D." which examines the "origins of some of the changes in form that have occurred in the alphabetical medium of Western civilization, written, inscribed, and printed." Illustrated. It contains an extensive list of works consulted. These are the Lyell Lectures, edited and completed by Nicolas Barker. Indexed.

Materials and Techniques

110   Ogg, Oscar. THE 26 LETTERS. 3d ed., rev. New York: T.Y. Crowell, 1971. 294 p.

> Originally published in 1948 with a second edition in 1961, this book is a popular approach to the study of the alphabet and writing, written in an enjoyable and readable style for the beginner. It contains material on before history, and on the Egyptians, the Phoenicians, the Greeks, and the Romans, as well as on the small letters, Caroline and Gothic letters, the invention of type, and printing and the alphabet down to modern developments of computer applications. It has a dictionary index and many illustrations.

111   Taylor, Isaac. THE HISTORY OF THE ALPHABET: AN ACCOUNT OF THE ORIGIN AND DEVELOPMENT OF LETTERS. New ed. 2 vols. London: Edward Arnold, 1899.

> The original edition appeared in 1883 and was one of the first general histories of the alphabet. This book is a pioneer effort filled with technical detail. The purpose of the book is to compile "a brief account of recent discoveries as to the origin of the Alphabet, and its subsequent developments." It is a rather specialized and technical study in spite of the statement that this is "a brief account." It is useful for a view of nineteenth-century research. It contains a general index.

112   Thompson, Tony [Samuel W.]. THE ABC OF OUR ALPHABET. 2d ed. New York: Studio Publications, 1942. 64 p.

> This illustrated book "traces the evolution of our Alphabet through all its various stages," and is written in a popular and basic style. Thompson has a rather unusual format with text superimposed over drawings, which at times makes reading extremely difficult.

113   Tschichold, Jan. AN ILLUSTRATED HISTORY OF WRITING AND LETTERING. New York: Columbia University Press, 1948. 18 p. 70 plates.

> Mainly a book of illustrations of writing and lettering from ancient to modern times, the aim of this work is to "draw attention to the great documents of the penman's craft in the cultures of the past." This is a brief visual survey of the "more circumscribed history of our own writing. . . ." The book has a useful chart on the pedigree of the European styles of writing followed by the list of reproductions, which identifies each plate and then seventy black-and-white illustrations, with brief commentary. A helpful and informative work.

114   Wardrop, James. THE SCRIPT OF HUMANISM: SOME ASPECTS OF
       HUMANISTIC SCRIPT, 1460-1560. Oxford, Engl.: Clarendon Press,
       1963. 57 p. 58 plates.

       Mainly a book of illustrations of the humanistic book hand
       during these one hundred years. Originally the lectures
       given at King's College, Strand, in 1952, which were spon-
       sored by the University of London and were primarily for ad-
       vanced students of paleography. A bit specialized but useful
       for those who are interested in this phase of writing history.
       Indexed.

115   Whalley, Joyce I. WRITING IMPLEMENTS AND ACCESSORIES FROM
       THE ROMAN STYLUS TO THE TYPEWRITER. Detroit: Gale Research
       Co., 1975. 144 p.

       An illustrated description "of all kinds of writing implements
       and accessories from Roman times to the present day." This
       work "traces the development of the pen from the Roman
       stylus and medieval quill to the modern ball-point, by the
       way of the steel-nibbed pen and the fountain pen." Whalley
       provides information on ink, preparation of vellum and paper,
       writing paper, pen knives, pounce pots, paperweights, and
       typewriters. A useful source on a "long-neglected aspect of
       daily life through the ages." Has a bibliography.

TYPE AND TYPOGRAPHY

Type is an extension of writing, producing by mechanical means what had been
handwritten during the thousands of years preceeding the invention of movable
type. That great invention, attributed to Johann Gutenberg, had been known
in the Far East long before its discovery in Western Europe, but the Oriental
languages did not lend themselves to the use of movable type as did the more
simplified alphabetic writing of the West. Around A.D. 1450 Gutenberg per-
fected a machine or mould which was able to make individual type efficiently
and quickly and this process spread from Germany to Italy, France, England
and other countries, in what was the beginning of the technological revolution
of the modern world.

The books in this unit include those which examine the history of typography,
type design, the principles of typography, growth and variety of printing types,
and practical guides to type and typography. Although type specimen books
are not included (except for the work by Hlavsa), many of the items include
examples of type faces.

116   Bennett, Paul A. "On Recognizing the Type Faces." THE DOLPHIN 2
       (1935): 11-59.

       This guide to the identification of type presents briefly the

various type faces and provides a history, giving characteristics and specimens of each. It is a practical, easy-to-read
article of use and interest to the beginner.

117   Biggs, John R. AN APPROACH TO TYPE. 2d ed. London: Blandford
Press, 1961. 136 p.

This book is based on talks to students of the London School
of Printing and the Central School of Arts and Crafts and is
intended as "introductory remarks of the study of type faces."
Biggs examines all aspects of type, the point system, legibility and readability, classification of type faces, kinds of
type, and other topics with the emphasis on the technical
aspects of typography. The book also contains a brief study
of the historical background of writing and typography, and
concludes with a unit on the practical aspects of type. Has
a bibliography, type specimens, and a glossary, and contains
many black-and-white illustrations. A useful introduction to
the topic in a well-organized book which unfortunately lacks
an index.

118   _____. BASIC TYPOGRAPHY. London: Faber and Faber, 1973. 176 p.

An "attempt to examine some of the fundamentals of typographic design that endure through all the vagaries of fashion
in the hope that the student will develop first an analytic
approach to design and second create solutions that grow out
of the nature of the problem instead of trying to impose a
preconceived formula." This book examines the principles,
the mechanics, and the practice of typographic design. It
is profusely illustrated and also has a glossary and a bibliography. No index.

119   Burns, Aaron. TYPOGRAPHY. New York: Reinhold Publishing Corp.,
1961. 112 p.

This book has been planned for the student, professional, and
lay person, and for anyone who wishes to learn more of the
new function of modern typography and the factors that con-
tribute to its development. Has a type-face page index.
Illustrated.

120   Carter, Harry. A VIEW OF EARLY TYPOGRAPHY UP TO ABOUT 1600.
Oxford, Engl.: Clarendon Press, 1969. 137 p.

These are the Lyell Lectures of 1968 given at Oxford University. It includes information on the technicalities of type,
diversity of letter-forms in print, the establishment of common
idioms, Latin and vernacular, and a history of typefounding
and punch-cutting. There is a supplement on italic. Numerous illustrations. Indexed.

121   Craig, James. DESIGNING WITH TYPE: A BASIC COURSE IN TYPO-
       GRAPHY. Edited by Susan E. Meyer. New York: Watson-Guptill
       Publications, 1971. 175 p.

           A practical book which explains the basics of typography.
           This work is meant to be a working tool for the student of·
           typography which tries "to make the subject of typography
           as simple and as interesting as possible, presenting the facts
           in a straightforward manner." The book aims to help students
           develop "an awareness of type and typographic design." It
           has many black-and-white illustrations as well as a bibliog-
           raphy and a glossary. Looseleaf binding. Indexed.

122   Dair, Carl. DESIGN WITH TYPE. Toronto: University of Toronto Press,
       1967. 164 p.

           An earlier version containing part of the material in this
           book was published in 1952 by Pellegrini and Cudahy. The
           "basic principles of design outlined in the original edition
           remain unchanged and reappears here"; however, new in-
           fluences and changes in typography in the decade between
           editions are included in this new work. It is an informative
           study of the nature and uses of type with numerous illustra-
           tions. Has a brief bibliography. Indexed.

123   Day, Kenneth, ed. BOOK TYPOGRAPHY 1815-1965 IN EUROPE AND
       THE UNITED STATES OF AMERICA. Chicago: University of Chicago
       Press, 1966. 401 p.

           First published in 1965 in the Netherlands. This is a col-
           lection of essays by experts on book typography from Belgium,
           France, Germany, Great Britain, Italy, the Netherlands,
           Switzerland, and the United States, examining printing and
           typography in these countries during the nineteenth and twen-
           tieth centuries. Illustrated. No bibliography. Indexed.

124   Denham, Frank. THE SHAPING OF OUR ALPHABET: A STUDY OF
       CHANGING TYPE STYLES. New York: Alfred A. Knopf, 1955. 228 p.

           An examination of changes in taste as reflected in the history
           of typography, with emphasis on its development since the
           Renaissance. Many black-and-white illustrations are provided
           with an appendix on the making of type. Indexed.

125   Dowding, Geoffrey. AN INTRODUCTION TO THE HISTORY OF PRINT-
       ING TYPES: AN ILLUSTRATED SUMMARY OF THE MAIN STAGES IN
       THE DEVELOPMENT OF TYPE DESIGN FROM 1440 UP TO THE PRESENT
       DAY: AN AID TO TYPE FACE IDENTIFICATION. London: Wace and
       Co., 1961. 277 p.

           An illustrated manual which covers both book and display

types. Under each unit contains a grouping of type faces, arranged chronologically, with general introductory comments, a unit on characteristics of that particular type-face, and some other type faces of the same family. The information is brief but helpful in a book "intended simply as an introduction to the subject . . . to familiarize students with the various categories or groups of printing types. We hope that it will also introduce them to wide reading in a fascinating subject." It also contains notes on the 117 illustrations and a bibliography. Indexed.

126   Goudy, Frederic W. TYPOLOGIA: STUDIES IN TYPE DESIGN AND TYPE MAKING WITH COMMENTS ON THE INVENTION OF TYPOGRAPHY, THE FIRST TYPES, LEGIBILITY, AND FINE PRINTING. Berkeley and Los Angeles: University of California Press, 1940. Reprint. Berkeley and Los Angeles: University of California Press, 1978. 170 p.

This work examines the concept of type design of one of the leading U.S. typographers of the mid-twentieth century. Goudy states that "TYPOLOGIA presents more or less graphically my work in type design and describes my own methods of type production." The review by Alexander Lawson in FINE PRINT 4 (July 1978): 81, comments that: "In this book he puts it all down for the record, and it has never been done better. In addition we have the mature thoughts of a great designer of his craft." There are a few black-and-white illustrations. No index. Available in cloth and paperback editions.

127   Hlavsa, Oldřich. A BOOK OF TYPE AND DESIGN. 2d ed. New York: Tudor Publishing Co., 1960. 495 p.

This work was translated by Sylvia Fink and appeared in both Czech and this separate edition in English. Somewhat similar to a type specimen book, but this particular one has been included because it also contains comments on most of the type styles and as such, is a most useful source for a study of the history of typography. A major part of the book "is given to specimens of various typefaces, their design and use, and the basic rules of good composition are also briefly discussed." It is intended for printers, typographers, and all who care for fine books and printing. Indexed.

128   Johnson, A.F. TYPE DESIGNS: THEIR HISTORY AND DEVELOPMENT. 3d ed., rev. London: Andre Deutsch, 1966. 184 p.

The first edition was published in 1934 and a second edition appeared in 1959. This edition presents an introduction to the "study of type design from the invention of the art up to the nineteenth-century." Johnson provides descriptions and history of gothic, roman, italic, script, and other types with forty-three illustrations and a most extensive listing of books, with brief comments, under the heading list of authorities. Indexed.

129 Lawson, Alexander. PRINTING TYPES, AN INTRODUCTION. Boston: Beacon Press, 1971. 120 p.

This book developed out of Lawson's course on printing types given at the School of Printing at Rochester Institute of Technology. Its purpose is to "help the beginner become familiar with the fascinating variety of printer's types." He studies the recognition and identification of type and the nature and history of printing types, as well as nomenclature and type classification. An attractively printed book with many illustrations. No index.

130 Lewis, John. TYPOGRAPHY: BASIC PRINCIPLES, INFLUENCES AND TRENDS SINCE THE 19TH CENTURY. New York: Reinhold Publishing Corp., 1964. 96 p.

A brief illustrated survey of printing in the twentieth century which contains chapters on origins and influences on the form of typographic communication, present-day trends in typographic communication, the mechanics of typography, rules are made to be broken, and notes on typographic styling. There is a short glossary but no index.

131 Morison, Stanley. FIRST PRINCIPLES OF TYPOGRAPHY. Cambridge Author's and Printer's Guides. Cambridge: Cambridge University Press, 1951. 18 p.

This brief essay was originally stated in the fourteenth edition of the ENCYCLOPEDIA BRITANNICA and was reconsidered and entirely rewritten for No. 7 of THE FLEURON and now separately published. This statement by one of the leading exponents of typography of the twentieth century sets forth his principles and rationale on book typography.

132 _____. THE TYPOGRAPHIC ARTS: TWO LECTURES. Cambridge, Mass.: Harvard University Press, 1950. 106 p.

A reprint of two lectures given by Morison--"The Typographic Arts," which was delivered at the Royal College of Art in Edinburgh in 1944, and "The Art of Printing," given at the British Academy in London in 1937. It contains thirty-two illustrations. Indexed.

133   Peignot, Jérôme. DE L'ÉCRITURE A LA TYPOGRAPHIE. Paris: Éditions
        Gallimard, 1967. 242 p.

> A French history of the evolution of writing and typography
> from ancient to modern times which has a useful section of
> biographical sketches of important people in typography, as
> well as a glossary of terms and a brief bibliography. No
> index.

134   Simon, Herbert. INTRODUCTION TO PRINTING: THE CRAFT OF
        LETTERPRESS. London: Faber and Faber, 1968. 120 p.

> A handbook on practical printing which will be of "some
> help to those who wish to acquire practical skills and by so
> doing gain an enduring interest in printing and typography."
> It has chapters on setting type, type and materials, make-up
> and imposition, machine printing, distribution and proof-
> reading, planning and design, graphic and typographic design,
> useful printing paper, and some practical examples, with a
> concluding glossary of printing terminology. The appendixes
> include a listing of where to get supplies (all in England),
> and a select bibliography. Illustrated. No index.

135   Simon, Oliver. INTRODUCTION TO TYPOGRAPHY. 2d ed. Edited
        by David Bland. London: Faber and Faber, 1963. 164 p.

> A work which attempts to "describe as briefly as possible
> from our own experience some of the many fundamentals of
> book-production," with chapters on foundations; rules of com-
> position; choosing the type face; setting the text; the pre-
> liminary pages; appendix; author's notes, glossary, bibliog-
> raphy, and index; illustration; paper; presswork, binding, and
> jacket; and miscellaneous. There is a separate glossary and
> select handlist of books and periodicals as well as numerous
> illustrations and a subject index.

136   Sutton, James, and Bartram, Alan. AN ATLAS OF TYPEFORMS. New
        York: Hastings House, Publishers, 1968. 116 p.

> An oversize book which attempts to "show by illustration
> rather than explaining in words, the main changes in type
> forms over 500 years of printing." More or less a chrono-
> logical arrangement which visually traces the origins and
> evolution of typeforms "not only during recent centuries, but
> by way of medieval writing from the script of Charlemagne
> and by way of the Renaissance calligraphy from the first-
> century inscriptions of Imperial Rome." It contains a short
> bibliography and an index of typefaces. An extremely attrac-
> tive and informative book.

137   Updike, Daniel Berkeley. PRINTING TYPES: THEIR HISTORY, FORMS
      AND USE--A STUDY IN SURVIVALS. 3d ed. 2 vols. Cambridge,
      Mass.: Belknap Press of Harvard University Press, 1962.

      This work has been considered a standard in the study of
      type and typography. Its purpose "is to supply a basis for
      the intelligent appreciation of the best printing types through
      the study of their history, forms, and use." Updike starts
      with the invention of printing, but then goes back to the
      Latin alphabet and its development down to the invention of
      printing and examines type in the centuries that follow as it
      evolved in Germany, Italy, France, the Netherlands, Spain,
      England, and the United States. In the preface to the third
      edition it is stated that this "book did more than provide its
      readers with an unexampled gathering and winnowing of facts;
      it created in them a broadening of historical interest, and
      led them into depths of social and cultural understanding."
      It contains 367 illustrations with extensive notes and an index.

138   Williamson, Hugh. BOOK TYPOGRAPHY: A HANDLIST FOR BOOK
      DESIGNERS. Cambridge: Cambridge University Press for the National
      Book League, 1955. 16 p.

      A pamphlet listing a few books on the development of typo-
      graphy; printers, presses, and typographers; type design, type
      founding, and type specimens; house styles and editorial work;
      methods of typography and composition work; bibliographies;
      and periodicals.

BOOKBINDING

During the past five thousand years the book has had a variety of formats determined mainly by the materials used. The book of the ancient world was the
clay tablet of Mesopotamia and the papyrus roll of Egypt, Greece, and Rome
which existed for several thousand years. It was around 400 A.D. that a major
change took place with the emergence of the codex or book page, gathered in
sequence and bound. During the medieval period the pages of the codex were
parchment or vellum made from animal skins. Although paper was invented in
China around 105 A.D. it was not until the advent of printing with movable
type, around 1450, that the use of paper became dominant in the codex. The
book of the Middle Ages and modern times has been bound in a variety of materials including carved ivory; metal, sometimes gold or silver, and often inlaid
with precious and semi-precious stones; textiles such as velvet, tapestry, or linen;
parchment; leather; decorative papers; buckram; and even plastic. The bound
book lent itself to decoration, especially leather bindings which were often elabo-
rately tooled as a worthy "artistic covering of the codex."

The binding of the codex provided a convenient method for keeping the sections
of the book together and in proper sequence, and also served as a protective

covering for the book. It serves both as a functional item and in the hands of a master craftsman and artist can also become a work of art.

Books on bookbinding include those which trace the history of bookbinding, binding design, and binding styles, and include a group of manuals on the practical how-to-do-it aspect of binding a book by hand and a few items which examine the processes of machine bookbinding. In order to fully understand the history of the book it is essential to know something about the structure or anatomy of the book and its covering. Many of the following books provide this information.

139   Banister, Manly. PICTORIAL MANUAL OF BOOKBINDING. New
       York: Ronald Press Co., 1958. 40 p.

       A book "designed to show, rather than tell you how to bind
       a book." A practical and useful manual which examines
       homemade bookbinding tools, binding for magazine collec-
       tions, binding multistitched magazines, rebinding of books,
       manuscript binding, half-binding in leather, false bands and
       hollow back, the full leather binding, and refinishing the
       book. It contains many line drawings of the various steps,
       but has no bibliography or index.

140   Brassington, W.S. A HISTORY OF THE ART OF BOOKBINDING, WITH
       SOME ACCOUNT OF THE BOOKS OF THE ANCIENTS. New York:
       Macmillan Co., 1894. 278 p.

       This is a somewhat dated but still useful survey for a study
       of the early records and history of bookbinding to the end of
       the nineteenth century.

141   Burdett, Eric. THE CRAFT OF BOOKBINDING: A PRACTICAL HAND-
       BOOK. Newton Abbot, Engl.: David and Charles, 1975. 400 p.

       A useful introduction to bookbinding written for the amateur
       and practitioner who is concerned with present-day trends,
       as well as the design of the earlier periods. It has chapters
       on preparatory work, forwarding, covering, finishing, cover
       design, miscellaneous items, repairs to books, and materials.
       There is a glossary and sources of supply (arranged as a classified
       list by subject and alphabetical by supplier--all are in Eng-
       land), a number of black-and-white photographs and line
       drawings, with eight color plates and a two-page bibliography.
       Indexed.

142   Cockerell, Douglas. BOOKBINDING, AND THE CARE OF BOOKS: A
       TEXT-BOOK FOR BOOKBINDERS AND LIBRARIANS. 5th ed. Rev. and
       reprint. Artistic Crafts Series of Technical Handbooks. London: Sir
       Isaac Pitman and Sons, 1962. 345 p.

       This work was planned as a textbook for workshop practice,

to treat design itself as an essential part of good workman-
ship, and as a kind of vocational stimulus and guide. The
purpose of this book is to "help bookbinders and librarians
to select sound methods of binding books." It contains many
illustrations, a glossary, and an index.

143 Comparato, Frank E. BOOKS FOR THE MILLIONS: A HISTORY OF
THE MEN WHOSE METHODS AND MACHINES PACKAGED THE PRINTED
WORD. Harrisburg, Pa.: Stackpole Co., 1971. 374 p.

A history of bookbinding with emphasis on changes which have
been brought about by the needs for producing books for a
mass audience. This book contains material on the European
tradition in bookmaking, the industrialization of the American
bindery, and modern books and publishing with a list of references and a most extensive bibliography. Indexed.

144 Corderoy, John. BOOKBINDING FOR BEGINNERS. New York: Watson-
Guptill Publications, 1967. 104 p.

A useful paperback which serves as a guide "for the complete
beginner, and explains all you need to know to produce attractive bindings." The book provides step-by-step procedures
and provides the reader with a basic knowledge of how a
book is handbound. It has a number of line drawings, some
black-and-white photographs, and four pages in color with a
list of suppliers and items for further reading. Indexed.

145 Darley, Lionel S. INTRODUCTION TO BOOKBINDING. 1965. Reissue.
London: Faber and Faber, 1978. 118 p.

A practical guide for the beginning bookbinder which contains units on an introduction to bookbinding, examining the
binder's tools, a room to work in, how to make a start, and
the binding process. Other units include making a notebook,
re-binding old books, binding in leather, and machine bookbinding. Darley has a glossary, brief bibliography, and an
index, with a number of pen-and-ink line drawings and a
few plates.

146 Diehl, Edith. BOOKBINDING: ITS BACKGROUND AND TECHNIQUE.
2 vols. New York: Rinehart and Co., 1946. Reprint. Port Washington,
N.Y.: Kennikat Press, n.d.

Diehl has written an extensive study of the history of bookbinding. Volume 1 examines primitive records and ancient
book forms; the book in the Middle Ages, Renaissance, and
modern times; bookbinding styles; national styles of book decoration; and miscellanea. Volume 2 deals with bookbinding
methods and techniques. Contains an extensive listing of

items in the bibliography, together with a list of references, a glossary, and many illustrations. Indexed. This is not for the beginner but useful for the advanced student or book-binder.

147   Gross, Henry. SIMPLIFIED BOOKBINDING. New York: Charles Scribner's Sons, 1976. 176 p.

This book is "organized to guide you through typical binding problems and to show you, step-by-step, how to deal with them." It is a practical manual for the prospective book-binder. Also useful because it presents a detailed outline of the process of hand bookbinding with many illustrations. Provides a list of sources of supply. Indexed.

148   Harthan, John P. BOOKBINDINGS. London: Her Majesty's Stationery Office, 1961. 33 p. 79 plates.

This is mainly a book of illustrations of bookbinding items from the collection of the Victoria and Albert Museum which also has a brief chapter on the development of bookbinding design. There is a section of notes on the list of illustra-tions and a select bibliography. Extremely helpful for a beginner for a visual overview of the history of bookbinding.

149   Hewitt-Bates, J.S. BOOKBINDING. 8th rev. ed. Leicester, Engl.: Dryad Press, 1967. 127 p.

A practical introduction to bookbinding techniques and history, which emphasizes the processes of the craft. Hewitt-Bates provides the teacher with information on the bookbinding pro-cess of value in instruction. The book contains eleven black-and-white plates and numerous line drawings with a very brief bibliography. Indexed.

150   THE HISTORY OF BOOKBINDING, 525-1950 A.D. AN EXHIBITION HELD AT THE BALTIMORE MUSEUM OF ART NOVEMBER 12, 1957 TO JANUARY 12, 1958. Baltimore: Walters Art Gallery, 1957. 275 p. 106 p. of plates.

This is the rather extensive catalog of this exhibit which pre-sented "the story of the artistic covering of the codex." It contains a listing, by number, of the 718 exhibit items, giv-ing data on each, provenance, and bibliography. There is another bibliography of works frequently cited, an index, and illustrations of the items on display. An invaluable survey of these fourteen hundred years of bookbinding history and the binder's art.

151 Hobson, A.R.A. THE LITERATURE OF BOOKBINDING. Cambridge: Cambridge University Press for the National Book League, 1954. 15 p.

> A pamphlet which lists a few items on English, Scottish, Irish, French, Italian, Spanish, Flemish, German, American, and Islamic bindings and also has a brief list of general works and catalogs.

152 Johnson, Pauline. CREATIVE BOOKBINDING. Seattle: University of Washington Press, 1963. 263 p.

> This book examines the potential of bookbinding "as an educative medium as well as an amateur pursuit." This is primarily a manual but is not as concerned with the technical aspects of bookbinding as with its artistic values and possibilities. A how-to-do-it guide which is helpful in explaining the various aspects and range of bookbinding activities. It also has material on the making of portfolios, scrapbooks, memo pads, and other items. Profusely illustrated, it also provides a list of supply sources and a bibliography. Indexed.

153 Lehmann-Haupt, Hellmut, ed. BOOKBINDING IN AMERICA: THREE ESSAYS. Rev. ed. New York: R.R. Bowker Co., 1967. 293 p.

> Includes three major studies on bookbinding: "Early American Bookbinding by Hand" by Hannah D. French, who examines American bookbinding as a craft; "The Rise of American Edition Binding" by Joseph W. Rogers, who studies the transition of bookbinding from craft to industry; and "On the Rebinding of Old Books" by Hellmut Lehmann-Haupt, who looks at the "ethics and aesthetics of rebinding" books. Lehmann-Haupt's essay has a bibliography. Some illustrations. Indexed.

154 Lewis, A.W. BASIC BOOKBINDING. London: B.T. Batsford, 1952. 147 p. Reprint. New York: Dover Publications, n.d.

> A manual which provides "step-by-step instructions in the essential operations involved in the binding of books by hand in cloth and in library style." Geared for the beginner and student of the book crafts, this book includes information on equipment, materials, basic operations, binding of various types of books, end-papers, hollow-backed binding, library style binding, binding single sheets, and lettering a book. A number of black-and-white illustrations and line drawings show the various steps involved in the process. There is a separate appendix on the sequence of operations. Indexed.

155 Perry, Kenneth F., and Baab, Clarence T. THE BINDING OF BOOKS. Rev. ed. Bloomington, Ill.: McKnight and McKnight Publishing Co., 1967. 190 p.

> A useful manual geared for the student of the book crafts on

simple bookbinding techniques providing step-by-step procedures. It also contains information on necessary tools, equipment, materials, and supplies needed to bind a book. Has many illustrations showing the various procedures. Indexed.

156   Robinson, Ivor. INTRODUCING BOOKBINDING. New York: Watson-Guptill Publications, 1968. 112 p.

An "introduction to tools, equipment, and materials of the craft together with sequential demonstration of basic bookbinding skills likely to be within the scope of the average school, college, or similar miscellaneous hand bindery." There are many illustrations of the stages in hand bookbinding, a brief bibliography, and a list of suppliers, mainly British, with a few in the United States. Indexed.

157   Smith, Philip. NEW DIRECTIONS IN BOOKBINDING. New York: Van Nostrand Reinhold, 1974. 208 p.

Mainly a study of the imaginative bookbinding art of Philip Smith and others who are concerned about the close relationship between binding and contents and in new developments in creative bookbinding ideas. This work "reveals the philosophies and techniques underlying the most creative works in a discipline which has recently penetrated the field of art." It has many black-and-white and color illustrations, a bibliography, and an index.

158   Town, Laurence. BOOKBINDING BY HAND FOR STUDENTS AND CRAFTSMEN. 2d ed. London: Faber and Faber, 1963. 297 p.

Based on the author's classes in bookbinding, this book attempts to give "most helpful guidance and instruction to anyone wishing to follow the ancient craft of bookbinding." A work "written primarily with the teaching of bookbinding in schools always in mind, and many of the processes have been modified slightly to fit the needs and ability of children, but without sacrificing the essential methods of the practised craftsman." There are a number of black-and-white line drawings and a brief bibliography. Indexed.

159   Vaughan, Alex J. MODERN BOOKBINDING. New ed. London: Charles Skilton, 1960. 240 p.

First published in 1929 and reprinted several times, this is a practical textbook which describes the operations of letterpress binding and stationery binding, with a section on finishing and design. Illustrated. Indexed.

160   Watson, Aldren A.   HAND BOOKBINDING: A MANUAL OF INSTRUC-
        TION.   New York: Reinhold Publishing Corp., 1963.   93 p.

> An introductory work on how to bind a book by hand. There
> are a number of illustrations on the procedures to be followed.
> It is considered very good for the beginner as a basic text.
> Has an index to suppliers.

BOOK ILLUSTRATION

The clay tablet of ancient Sumer, Assyria, or Babylonia did not lend itself to
illustration because of the nature of the material, even though the earliest human
records on clay were pictographic.   The papyrus roll of ancient Egypt was a
suitable surface for illustration and many were produced in the style of that
time, as seen in the Book of the Dead.   However, it was with the parchment
codex that illustration became an integral part of the hand-produced book in
the thousand years of the medieval period.   The scribe laboriously wrote the
text and the artists and rubricators painted the miniature scenes, decorations,
and initial letters in brilliant colors and often embellished with burnished gold.
This ornamentation and decoration of the book was part of the desire to beautify
the book as an object of devotion.   In modern times this concept changed, and
the purpose of book illustration was to provide a visual interpretation of the contents which would elucidate the text and be a narrative form.

The items in this unit cover a wide range, including those on the history of book
illustration, graphic arts, and the book arts, as well as items on processes and
techniques used, printmaking, and illustration as social commentary.

161   Bader, Barbara.   AMERICAN PICTUREBOOKS FROM NOAH'S ARK TO
        THE BEAST WITHIN.   New York: Macmillan Co., 1976.   615 p.

> A detailed study which attempts to examine "the development
> of picturebooks" for children and to "identify all the picture-
> books published; to examine as many as possible; and, in cer-
> tain instances, to learn of the circumstances of their publica-
> tion."   This book contains many color and black-and-white
> illustrations, with many notes and an extensive bibliography.
> Indexed.

162   Bland, David.   A HISTORY OF BOOK ILLUSTRATION: THE ILLUMI-
        NATED MANUSCRIPT AND THE PRINTED BOOK.   2d rev. ed.   Berkeley
        and Los Angeles: University of California Press, 1969.   459 p.

> A beautifully printed and profusely illustrated survey of the
> history of book illustration which includes chapters on the
> beginnings in roll and codex, medieval illumination in the
> West, Oriental illumination and illustration, from the intro-
> duction of printing until about 1520, from about 1520 to the
> end of the seventeenth century, the eighteenth century, the

nineteenth century, and the twentieth century. Bland contains 404 illustrations of which 23 are in color, as well as an extensive bibliography, and an index. One of the best books for a comprehensive and detailed study of the illustrated book.

163 _____. THE ILLUSTRATION OF BOOKS. 3d ed. London: Faber and Faber, 1962. 200 p.

Bland provides a most useful introduction to book illustration which covers the history of illustration and the processes and their application. This book is "chiefly for students." It has a number of black-and-white illustrations and a short bibliography. It is not as detailed as Bland's A HISTORY OF BOOK ILLUSTRATION (see above), but this is an excellent book for the beginner who might be overwhelmed by the other work. This book is quite readable and most enjoyable combining both the historical and technical aspects of book illustration. Indexed.

164 Bliss, Douglas P. A HISTORY OF WOOD-ENGRAVING. London: J.M. Dent and Sons, 1928. 263 p.

A study of the history of woodcut which examines the beginnings; block books; metal cuts of the "manière criblée"; and early German, French, Italian, Spanish and Netherlandish book illustration, as well as the techniques employed, down to the 1920s. It has 120 black-and-white illustrations and a list of books consulted. Indexed.

165 Chatto, W.A., and Jackson, John. A TREATISE ON WOOD ENGRAVING. 2d ed. London: Henry G. Bohn, 1861. Reprint. Detroit: Gale Research Co., 1969. 664 p.

This is a rather extensive study, of value to the advanced student, on wood engraving including chapters on antiquity of engraving, progress of wood engraving, the invention of typography, wood engraving in connection with the press, wood engraving in the time of Albrecht Dürer, further progress and decline of wood engraving, revival of wood engraving, artists and engravers on wood of the present day, and the practice of wood engraving. Contains many black-and-white illustrations. Indexed.

166 Cianciolo, Patricia. ILLUSTRATIONS IN CHILDREN'S BOOKS. 2d ed. Dubuque, Iowa: Wm. C. Brown Co., Publishers, 1976. 210 p.

Originally appeared in 1970 and now updated and revised, this book is intended for the student of children's literature in becoming "familiar with the varieties of illustrated books that are available to children; to acquire the rudiments of information about the styles of art in the pictures that contemporary artists use in their illustrations; to appreciate the impact that the artist's media have on his creations, and to acquire some insight into the methods that can be used to create in children a keener awareness and an attitude of critical evaluation of the illustrations in the stories that they read." It contains chapters on appraising illustrations in children's books, styles of art in children's books, the artist's media and techniques, and using illustration in the school. It has numerous black-and-white illustrations, an extensive annotated bibliography of illustrated books, and the listing of many references. Indexed. Readable and most informative.

167   Cleaver, James. A HISTORY OF GRAPHIC ART. New York: Philosophical Library, 1963. 282 p.

Cleaver traces "the development of graphic art as a narrative medium from ancient Egyptian tomb painting to the contemporary poster" by examining the many forms and techniques of graphic art, including the roots of book illustration, medieval manuscript books, the invention of printing, copperplate engraving, etching, popular prints, Victorian book illustration, lithography, the poster, private presses, and contemporary graphic art. The work has useful appendixes on methods of printmaking and reproduction, a glossary, a bibliography, and 107 black-and-white illustrations. At one time a supplementary filmstrip set was available but unfortunately the quality was only fair. A readable and helpful source for the beginner. Indexed.

168   Eppink, Norman R. 101 PRINTS: THE HISTORY AND TECHNIQUES OF PRINTMAKING. New ed. Norman: University of Oklahoma Press, 1971. 273 p.

Although this book does not deal specifically with book illustration it is a useful source for information on the range and variety of printmaking and is intended to provide the student with "an understanding of the individual types of prints" and also to make him or her aware of "the extreme versatility of this branch of art." Eppink examines relief, intaglio, mixed media, planographic, stencil, photographic, miscellaneous, and children's processes. Each method is accompanied by a color or black-and-white illustration showing the result of that particular process. There is a selective bibliography. Indexed.

169   George, M. Dorothy. HOGARTH TO CRUICKSHANK: SOCIAL CHANGE
       IN GRAPHIC SATIRE. New York: Walker and Co., 1967. 224 p.

       This book covers the "art from 1720 to about 1830" of graphic
       social satire "before the days of Punch and illustrated jour-
       nalism when prints were engraved and sold separately." In
       the eighteenth century "there was a great vogue for satirical
       prints--political and social" during the "golden age of the
       English engraver." This book contains 201 illustrations of
       which twelve pages are in full color, and includes some of
       the "finest work of the period including that of Hogarth,
       Rowlandson, Gillray, and the Cruickshanks." No bibliog-
       raphy is included but the various chapters have a listing of
       notes; also has an index of artists and a general index.

170   Getlein, Frank, and Getlein, Dorothy. THE BITE OF THE PRINT: SATIRE
       AND IRONY IN WOODCUTS, ENGRAVINGS, ETCHINGS, LITHO-
       GRAPHS AND SERIGRAPHS. New York: Clarkson N. Potter, 1963.
       272 p.

       Using a large number of black-and-white reproductions, this
       book examines the history of the use of prints as social com-
       mentary on the morals and injustice of the times. It contains
       chapters on the bite; the bitten; in the beginning; love and
       death; Albrecht Dürer of Nuremberg; after Dürer; Rembrandt;
       two professionals, Callot and Piranesi; Hogarth; Goya; Daumier;
       Rouault; Käthe Kollwitz; and printmaking today. Has a bib-
       liography for each of the twelve chapters. No index.

171   Hind, Arthur M. A HISTORY OF ENGRAVING AND ETCHING FROM
       THE 15TH CENTURY TO THE YEAR 1914. Boston: Houghton Mifflin
       Co., 1923. Reprint. New York: Dover Publications, 1963. 487 p.

       This is the third and fully revised edition of Hind's A SHORT
       HISTORY OF ENGRAVING AND ETCHING which presents
       "a descriptive survey of the history of engraving on metal
       throughout the various centuries and schools." This work has
       many footnotes and an extensive general bibliography, as well
       as an individual bibliography of particular artists as part of
       the index of engravers. There are 110 black-and-white il-
       lustrations and, of special interest, is the classified list of
       engravers arranged in tabular form under the country giving
       date; medium; master, characteristic, or locality; and en-
       graver's influence by the master in the previous column.

172   _____. AN INTRODUCTION TO A HISTORY OF WOODCUT. 2 vols.
       Boston: Houghton Mifflin Co., 1935. Reprint. New York: Dover
       Publications, 1963.

       An in-depth study of the history of woodcut with emphasis on
       work done in fifteenth-century Europe. Volume 1 includes

processes and materials, general historical survey, the origin
of woodcut, block books, and an examination of book illustration and single cuts in Germany, Austria, and German
Switzerland. Volume 2 is a continuation, examining book
illustration and the single cut in Italy, the Netherlands,
France, French Switzerland, England, Spain, and Portugal.
Bibliographies are included at the end of each chapter or
section, with references to special books cited in the footnotes. It also contains 483 black-and-white illustrations.
The indexes are unique and include designers and engravers
of woodcuts, printers and publishers of books, books illustrated with woodcuts, prints mentioned or reproduced, and
subjects discussed in the text.

173   Hofer, Philip. BAROQUE BOOK ILLUSTRATION. Cambridge, Mass.:
       Harvard University Press, 1951. 43 p. 149 plates.

       A "short survey from the Collection in the Department of
       Graphic Arts, Harvard College Library" which attempts to
       provide an overview of the seventeenth century and the state
       of the baroque in book illustration which the author feels is
       a neglected area of study. It has a very brief text, followed
       by a list and descriptions of the reproductions and concluding
       with the black-and-white illustrations.

174   Holloway, Owen E. FRENCH ROCOCO BOOK ILLUSTRATION. New
       York: Transatlantic Arts, 1969. 115 p. 283 plates.

       A brief study of the work of the French book illustrators of
       the 1700s including Gravelot, Eisen, and Moreau, as well as
       other illustrators of that time. The book is mainly a collec-
       tion of black-and-white plates of book illustration of this
       period. Indexed.

175   Jussim, Estelle. VISUAL COMMUNICATION AND THE GRAPHIC ARTS:
       PHOTOGRAPHIC TECHNOLOGIES IN THE NINETEENTH CENTURY.
       New York: R. R. Bowker Co., 1974. 364 p.

       An investigation into "the nature and practice of visual com-
       munication manifested in the graphic arts practice of nineteenth-
       century America." This work examines photography as a "unique
       medium of expression and its effects upon our notions of art and
       communication" and attempts to reveal "how the graphic arts in-
       fluence how we see, feel, and interpret our world." There are
       many illustrations and the book also contains extensive notes, a
       selected bibliography, and a glossary. Indexed.

176   Kingman, Lee, ed. THE ILLUSTRATOR'S NOTEBOOK. Boston: Horn
       Book, 1978. 153 p.

       This is a selection of essays by artists who "discuss their

philosophy of illustration, the history of illustration, its place in the arts, its place as a means of communication today, and their own experience with various illustration techniques" with the emphasis on children's literature. This book contains articles by Fritz Eichenberg, Lynd Ward, Warren Chappell, Barbara Cooney, Marcia Brown, Ernest H. Shepard, Lee Kingman, and others, with forty-seven color and fifty-five black-and-white illustrations. There is also a list of articles, books, and catalogs suggested for reading and reference. Indexed.

177   Klemin, Diana. THE ILLUSTRATED BOOK: ITS ART AND CRAFT. New York: Clarkson N. Potter, 1970. 159 p.

A book which examines the work of about eighty contemporary book illustrators. It is arranged alphabetically by name of illustrator and shows an illustration of this person's work, with commentary and brief biographical sketch. There are many black-and-white and color illustrations with a separate chapter called "The Art and Craft of Illustration" which examines the various processes. A bibliography and an index are included.

178   Lamb, Lynton. DRAWING FOR ILLUSTRATION. London: Oxford University Press, 1962. 211 p.

This is "not a history of illustration or a survey of what illustrators are now doing" but mainly a statement of the "illustrators main problem and of how he can tackle them in his essential dealings with authors, publishers, blockmakers, and printers. Past and present practice is only touched on where it is relevant to these aims." This book deals with the "theoretical, contractual, and technical aspects of drawing for illustration," and contains a number of black-and-white illustrations. There is also a glossary and an extensive bibliography. Indexed.

179   Leaf, Ruth. INTAGLIO PRINTMAKING TECHNIQUES. New York: Watson-Guptill Publications, 1976. 232 p.

This is a practical guide which presents "a thorough analysis of intaglio printmaking and related techniques." Leaf examines general information, including materials, equipment, tools, paper, presses, and workshop; etching techniques; printing techniques; and other mediums and methods. Useful for the student who wants to know more about the intaglio method since the text and illustrations show step-by-step procedures. Profusely illustrated with both color and black-and-white plates. The volume has an appendix of things every printmaker should know and doesn't know whom to ask, as well as a glossary, list of supplies and suppliers, a bibliography, and an index.

180   Lejard, André. THE ART OF THE FRENCH BOOK FROM EARLY MANU-
       SCRIPTS TO THE PRESENT TIME. London: Paul Elek, [1947]. 166 p.

         Profusely illustrated with black-and-white and full color plates
         showing visually the development and study of the history of
         the book as revealed in France, this book contains introduc-
         tory essays on the various units, followed by the illustrations
         and commentary. In the introduction Philip James states that
         the "full story of the art of the book in France through twelve
         centuries may be read in the admirable essays which precede
         the various sections of this volume." This "book is based on
         the world-famous collection in the Bibliothèque Nationale,
         in Paris." There is a section devoted to manuscripts, which
         is followed by separate chapters examining the French book
         from the fifteenth through twentieth centuries, and a separate
         chapter on bindings. Has a bibliography but no index.

181   Lewis, John. A HANDBOOK OF TYPE AND ILLUSTRATION. London:
       Faber and Faber, 1956. 203 p.

         This book is more concerned with illustration than type. It
         is written from the point of view of the printer who is in-
         volved in the production of illustrated books and the repro-
         duction of oil paintings, water-color drawings, etchings,
         copper engravings, and other illustrations. The emphasis of
         this rather technical book is on reproduction processes and
         the production of illustrated books. It contains a number of
         black-and-white and color illustrations, and an index of sub-
         jects and names.

182   _____. THE TWENTIETH CENTURY BOOK: ITS ILLUSTRATION AND
       DESIGN. New York: Reinhold Publishing Corp., 1967. 272 p.

         A visually exciting book containing many illustrations in color
         and black-and-white which examines modern book illustration
         and design from 1901 to 1967. It is arranged chronologically
         from art nouveau or private press historicism to the paperback
         explosion and the design of the modern book. Indexed.

183   Loche, Renée. LITHOGRAPHY. Craft and Art Series. Geneva: Les
       Éditions de Bonvent, 1971. 128 p.

         This volume is intended to "provide art lovers, visitors to
         museums and exhibitions and collectors with a full description
         of the techniques and history of lithography." It is beauti-
         fully illustrated with fine color and black-and-white plates
         and has a synopsis showing the chronological development of
         lithography as compared to contemporary events on the arts
         and history in general. There is a glossary of technical
         terms, select bibliography, and table of illustrations.

Materials and Techniques

184   MacRobert, T.M.   FINE ILLUSTRATIONS IN WESTERN EUROPEAN
       PRINTED BOOKS.   London: Her Majesty's Stationery Office, 1969.
       23 p.   125 plates.

       This book contains a very brief introduction on illustrated
       books followed by numerous black-and-white illustrations.
       The items included in this work are from the large collection
       in the Victoria and Albert Museum. Has a three-page select
       bibliography.

185   Mayor, A. Hyatt.   PRINTS AND PEOPLE: A SOCIAL HISTORY OF
       PRINTED PICTURES.   New York: Metropolitan Museum of Art, 1971.
       Distributed by the New York Graphic Society, unpaged.

       Arranged more or less chronologically to show the relationship
       of prints to social history. There are many illustrations which
       the author includes as examples and which are arranged by
       illustration number and so indexed.

186   Meyer, Susan E. AMERICA'S GREAT ILLUSTRATORS. New York: Harry N.
       Abrams, 1978.   311 p.

       A look at the American golden age of illustration during the
       end of the nineteenth and early decades of the twentieth
       centuries reflecting the time when "books and periodicals
       provided the major source of public entertainment." Meyer
       examines the work of ten American illustrators who "played
       a crucial role in governing the cultural appetites of the day,"
       including Pyle, N.C. Wyeth, Remington, Parrish, Rockwell,
       Lydendecker, Gibson, Christy, Flagg, and Held. This book
       is profusely illustrated with color and black-and-white illus-
       trations, and contains a general introduction to the times
       followed by separate units on each of the illustrators with
       biographical data and comments on their work and contribu-
       tions. It also contains a selected bibliography. Indexed.

187   Miller, Bertha [Mahony], et al., comps. ILLUSTRATORS OF CHILDREN'S
       BOOKS, 1744-1945. Boston: Horn Book, 1947. 527 p.

       The purpose of this book is "to show that art in children's
       books is a part of all art," and "to invite to further reading
       and study, to wider examination of picture books and illus-
       trated books of the past and present, and to a more conscious
       effort to understanding all that is involved in fine bookmaking."
       It includes material on the history and development of chil-
       dren's book illustration, biographies of illustrators, and ex-
       tensive bibliographies. Indexed.

       The following supplements appeared in 1958 and 1968 to update the basic
       volume and to provide information on trends in children's book illustration.

188   Viguers, Ruth H.; Dalphin, Marcia; and Miller, Bertha
       M., comps. ILLUSTRATORS OF CHILDREN'S BOOKS,
       1946-1956. Boston: Horn Book, 1958. 299 p.

189   Kingman, Lee; Foster, J.; and Lontoft, R.G., comps.
       ILLUSTRATORS OF CHILDREN'S BOOKS, 1957-1966.
       Boston: Horn Book, 1968. 295 p.

190 Pitz, Henry C. ILLUSTRATING CHILDREN'S BOOKS: HISTORY -
TECHNIQUE - PRODUCTION. New York: Watson-Guptill Publications,
1963. 207 p.

This well-known illustrator examines "the development of the
children's picture book; to bring it to the impetuous present;
to evaluate the present moment; and to describe in simple
form the practice and technique that bring the artist's pictorial ideas into finished form on the printed book page." It
is divided into history, techniques and production, and professional practice, and contains many black-and-white and
some color illustrations. A readable and useful book on this
topic. Has a bibliography and an index.

191 _____. A TREASURY OF AMERICAN BOOK ILLUSTRATION. New
York: American Studio Books and Watson-Guptill Publications, 1947.
128 p.

This is mainly a book of illustrations in both black-and-white
and color of a wide range of American artists, most of them
contemporary in 1947. It has units on American illustration,
the artists who illustrate American books, pictures for child-
hood, the growth of book illustration, the book proper, and
book jackets, with some brief comments by the author to the
illustrations. No index.

192 Pollard, Alfred W. EARLY ILLUSTRATED BOOKS: A HISTORY OF THE
DECORATION AND ILLUSTRATION OF BOOKS IN THE 15TH AND
16TH CENTURIES. 2d ed. Books About Books Series. London: Kegan
Paul, Trench, Trübner, and Co., 1917. 254 p.

The first edition appeared in 1893 and this new edition is
basically an introductory sketch to the illustration of books
in the early years. It includes material on rubrishers and
illuminators; the completion of the printed book; and illustration in Germany, Italy, France, Holland, and Spain.
There is a separate chapter on the printed French Book of
Hours. E. Gordon Duff contributed a chapter on early book
illustration in England. There are many black-and-white
illustrations. Indexed.

193   _____. FINE BOOKS. London: Methuen, 1912. Reprint. New Introduction by Michael Pearce. East Ardsley, Engl.: EP Publishing,
1973. 332 p.

A "chronological survey of the development of printing and
illustration" with the emphasis on illustration. This book
discusses the "beginning of printing and printed book-illustration
down to our day," which is 1912. In the new introduction
it is stated that "in a matter of some three hundred pages,
Pollard has been able to survey competently, simply, and
comprehensively enough (in a deceptively easy style), not
only for the collector, but for the amateur and even for the
professional student of bibliography, the main events in the
development of printing and illustration. . . ." Pollard
manages to do this "with scholarship, but without condescen-
sion." The book contains forty black-and-white illustrations,
a select bibliography, and an index. Although dated, this
is still a useful item for information before 1912.

194   Reed, Walt, comp. and ed. THE ILLUSTRATOR IN AMERICA, 1900-
1960. New York: Reinhold Publishing Corp., 1966. 272 p.

A profusely illustrated book which examines the "period during
which illustration became a vital art form in the United States,"
by studying the illustrators of these sixty years. There are
brief units entitled "Is Illustration Art?" and "The Future of
Illustration." The book is arranged decade by decade, and
within each unit the illustrators are listed alphabetically,
including a brief biographical sketch of each illustrator and
a few examples of the artist's work. An excellent overview
of this period in book illustration which contains many illustrations. Has an extensive bibliography.

195   Roger-Marx, Claude. GRAPHIC ART OF THE 19TH CENTURY. Translated from the French by E.M. Gwyer. London: Thames and Hudson,
1962. 254 p.

This is a useful survey of copperplate and wood engraving,
lithography, and other graphic arts during the nineteenth
century. It is profusely illustrated with color and fine black-
and-white plates and contains a list of illustrations and an
index of names.

196   Rumpel, Heinrich. WOOD ENGRAVING. Craft and Art Series. Geneva:
Les Éditions de Bonvent, 1972. 128 p.

A beautifully printed study of the history of woodcut from the
early European period to the present, this work examines both
the historical developments of the woodcut and the process
of making a woodcut and wood engraving. Rumpel includes
many fine color and black-and-white plates and a synoptic

table, arranged chronologically, giving events in the history
of woodcut, the arts, and general matters. A brief glossary
of technical terms, a select bibliography, and a list of illustrations are included. The text is in English, French, and
German.

197   Sandford, Christopher. "The Aesthetics of the Illustrated Book." THE
       DOLPHIN 2 (1935): 82-93.

       A brief look at some principles of book illustration which
       is useful for the beginner who would like to understand the
       concepts of book illustration.

198   Shikes, Ralph E. THE INDIGNANT EYE: THE ARTIST AS SOCIAL CRITIC
       IN PRINTS AND DRAWINGS FROM THE FIFTEENTH CENTURY TO PI-
       CASSO. Boston: Beacon Press, 1969. 439 p.

       Shikes examines the work of over 150 artists "reproducing
       prints and drawings from Western Europe, the United States,
       and Mexico, on subjects of social comment and criticism that
       have been executed over the past five centuries--roughly the
       span of printmaking." The book is illustrated with 405 black-
       and-white plates in this examination of protest art.

199   Simon, Howard. 500 YEARS OF ART AND ILLUSTRATION FROM AL-
       BRECHT DÜRER TO ROCKWELL KENT. Cleveland: World Publishing
       Co., 1942. 476 p.

       This is a useful introduction which may serve "as an impetus
       to further study in the fascinating field of book illustration."
       Mainly a book of black-and-white illustrations showing ex-
       amples of the illustrator's art, with accompanying commentary.
       It is arranged under the past and the present, and by illus-
       trator, in more or less chronological order providing an ex-
       cellent visual survey. Indexed.

200   Slythe, R. Margaret. THE ART OF ILLUSTRATION 1750-1900. London:
       Library Association, 1970. 144 p.

       This is an illustrated study of the various illustration tech-
       niques in use during these 150 years, including the woodcut,
       wood-engraving, etching, engraving, and lithography. There
       is a brief introductory survey of the period. A bibliography
       and an index are included.

201   Strachan, W.J. THE ARTIST AND THE BOOK IN FRANCE. New York:
       George Wittenborn, 1969. 368 p.

       A study of the "livre d'artiste" as seen in the work of the

great painters and sculptors of the school of Paris who "have illustrated books using autographic media" in this "important aspect of twentieth-century French art." It examines the history of the "livre d'artiste" from its conception at the turn of the century down to 1966 with chapters on the making of these books and the ateliers and the autographic process. Strachan includes a glossary and a bibliography with many fine full color and black-and-white illustrations. Indexed.

202   Wakeman, Geoffrey. VICTORIAN BOOK ILLUSTRATION: THE TECH-
       NICAL REVOLUTION. Detroit: Gale Research Co.; and Newton Abbot,
       Engl.: David and Charles, 1973. 182 p.

       This book covers the period from 1837 to 1900 which saw the
       replacement of the autographic method of reproduction by
       photomechanical means. It contains a number of black-and-
       white illustrations, a list of works consulted, and an index.

203   Weber, Wilhelm. A HISTORY OF LITHOGRAPHY. New York: McGraw-
       Hill Book Co., 1966. 259 p.

       An in-depth study of the history of lithography from its origins
       to the present, spanning the nineteenth and twentieth cen-
       turies and including the work of many contemporary artists.
       Weber includes many illustrations, both in full color and
       black-and-white with extensive notes on the text, and a
       four-page bibliography.

204   Weitenkampf, Frank. THE ILLUSTRATED BOOK. Cambridge, Mass.:
       ⌐vard University Press, 1938. 314 p.

       A scholarly work for the advanced student which surveys the
       illustration of books from the fifteenth through twentieth cen-
       turies. It has a few illustrations and an excellent bibliog-
       raphy. Indexed.

205   Weitzmann, Kurt. ILLUSTRATIONS IN ROLL AND CODEX: A STUDY
       OF THE ORIGIN AND METHOD OF TEXT ILLUSTRATION. 2d printing,
       with addenda. Princeton, N.J.: Princeton University Press, 1970. 261 p.

       Originally published in 1947. This book is primarily a meth-
       odological discussion concerning the relation of picture and
       text, and secondarily historical. The work examines the
       general relations between literature and the representational
       arts, the physical relation between the miniature and the
       text, the relation between the miniature and the text with
       regard to content, the relation between text criticism and
       picture criticism, and a concluding chapter on the cycle of
       miniature as the basic unit of the illustrated book. A schol-
       arly and rather technical study for the advanced student or
       scholar. It contains fifty-six pages of illustration. Indexed.

206   Woodberry, George E. A HISTORY OF WOOD-ENGRAVING. New
       York: Harper and Bros., 1883. Reprint. Detroit: Gale Research Co.,
       1969. 221 p.

     In this book the author has "attempted to gather and arrange
     such facts as should be known to men of cultivation interested
     in the art of engraving on wood." He examines wood-engraving
     "in its principal works, as a reflection of the life of men
     and an illustration of successive phases of civilization." Some
     of the black-and-white illustrations in the reprint are fair;
     others, mainly the earlier woodcuts, are good. There is a
     list of the principal works upon wood-engraving useful to
     students. Indexed.

207   Wright, John B. ETCHING AND ENGRAVING: TECHNIQUES AND
       THE MODERN TREND. New York: Studio Publications, 1953. Reprint.
       New York: Dover Publications, 1973. 240 p.

     A handbook for the student, artist, and amateur, this work
     explains the techniques and procedures of the various methods
     of etching and engraving, including line engraving, drypoint,
     etching, soft ground etching, sugar aquatint, deep etch, re-
     lief, combined processes, woodcut, and linocut. It also ex-
     amines the materials needed and the techniques employed.
     Has an index to artists represented. A useful popular guide.

Section 4

THE HISTORY OF BOOKS AND PRINTING

While the previous section was concerned with techniques and materials of book production, this section deals with the history of written and printed books, tracing their evolutionary development in the ancient, medieval, and modern world.

The first unit consists of general works on the history of the book and includes a few items on historical bibliography. The following units present the chronological growth of books and printing, examining the book in the ancient world of Mesopotamia, Egypt, Greece, and Rome. This is followed by histories of the illuminated vellum codex of the medieval period and a listing of some facsimiles of medieval manuscripts. With the invention of printing with movable type, a new era started, and there is a separate unit examining this technological revolution and its impact on books and printing in the Incunabula period (1450-1500) and the Renaissance. This section concludes with two units on printing throughout the world and printing in the New World, bringing the five thousand years of graphic communication down to the computer printing capabilities of today.

GENERAL WORKS

208   Allen, Agnes. THE STORY OF THE BOOK. New York: Roy Publishers, [1971]. 230 p.

      This is a book for young people which provides "a skillful introduction not only to a fascinating subject but to a history of civilization." It is a useful overview of the history of the book for the beginner containing a color frontispiece, twenty full-page, black-and-white illustrations, and many line drawings. No bibliography. Indexed.

209   Binns, Norman E. AN INTRODUCTION TO HISTORICAL BIBLIOGRAPHY. 2d ed., rev. and enl. London: Association of Assistant Librarians, 1962. 388 p.

      An overview of the history of the book which covers a wide

range of topics, including handwriting and the manuscript period; early writing materials; paper; the history of paper-making; block books and the invention of printing with movable type; and the development of printing in Germany, France, Italy, the Low Countries, Spain, and England. There are also units on the introduction of printing into the United States and Canada, the history of the printing press, type families, illustrations, and bookbinding. It contains fifty-three black-and-white illustrations and each unit has some suggested readings. Indexed.

210   Esdaile, Arundell. ESDAILE'S MANUAL OF BIBLIOGRAPHY. 4th rev. ed. by Roy Stokes. New York: Barnes and Noble, 1967. 336 p.

A handy survey of books and printing which examines the parts of a book; papyrus, parchment, vellum, and paper; typography; composition and press work; illustration; binding; landmarks in the development of the book; the collation of books; the description of books; the arrangement of bibliographies; and bibliographical tools. Each unit has a reading list. Indexed.

211   Johnson, Elmer D. COMMUNICATION: AN INTRODUCTION TO THE HISTORY OF WRITING, PRINTING, BOOKS AND LIBRARIES. 4th ed. Metuchen, N.J.: Scarecrow Press, 1973. 322 p.

According to the publisher's blurb this work has been "extensively revised and brought up to date with new materials and fresh viewpoints." Harold Goldstein's review in LIBRARY JOURNAL 98 (1 November 1973): 3237-38, states that this is still a "summative report of the world of librarianship, book printing, and a general overview of the profession," which he feels would be useful for the beginning student as a "basic book on the . . . world of print." It contains some material which is pertinent although a good part of this book is devoted to the history of libraries and librarianship. Each unit has a bibliography, but there are no illustrations; it is also a rather unattractive format. Indexed.

212   Labarre, Albert. HISTOIRE DU LIVRE. Que Sais-je Series. Paris: Presses Universitaires de France, 1970. 128 p.

This is a summary of the history of the book written for a popular audience including material on the origins of the book, the book in ancient Greece and Rome, the book of the Middle Ages, the advent of printing, from the manuscript to the modern book, the book from the Counter Reformation to the Enlightenment, and a concluding chapter on the modern book. It has a brief bibliography, but no illustrations and no index.

The History of Books and Printing

213   Lehmann-Haupt, Hellmut. THE LIFE OF THE BOOK. New York: Abelard-Schuman, 1957. 240 p.

     This is a useful general introduction to the history of the book written in a popular style for young people, which examines "how the book is written, published, printed, sold, and read." It has a few black-and-white illustrations, as well as an annotated list of suggested books for further reading. Indexed.

214   Levarie, Norma. THE ART AND HISTORY OF BOOKS. New York: James H. Heineman, 1968. 315 p.

     This enjoyable book is a "tightly written and relevantly illustrated panorama of fine books from their earliest history to the present day. It traces the history of book design and format against a background of the changing patrons and producers of books, the movements of social and political history, the state of the art, the growth and conflicts of religion, the fresh contacts of trade, and the development of technology." A handsome and readable book which contains reproductions of 176 pages "from books of extraordinary beauty or interest which range in time from ancient Egypt to the 1960's." Unfortunately there are no color illustrations which would have enhanced the reproductions of the medieval manuscripts. It contains a bibliography and an index.

215   McMurtrie, Douglas C. THE BOOK: THE STORY OF PRINTING AND BOOKMAKING. New York: Oxford University Press, 1943. 676 p.

     A revision, updating, and correction of his THE GOLDEN BOOK (1st ed., 1927) which had gone through four editions. Rather than work on another edition, which was the original plan, McMurtrie decided that "the state of knowledge regarding the history of printing and bookmaking had changed considerably during the past ten years," so he started all over again writing "a fresh survey of printing history and practice." THE BOOK has long been a favorite textbook in books and printing courses and is still used today since it is a readable and good introduction to the subject, presenting a chronological coverage of the book from primitive human records to the printer's ideals. It has a number of black-and-white illustrations, and at the end there is an extensive bibliography for each chapter. Indexed.

216   Posner, Raphael, and Ta-Shema, Israel, eds. THE HEBREW BOOK: AN HISTORICAL SURVEY. Jerusalem: Keter Publishing House, 1975. 225 p.

     Appropriate articles on the Hebrew book which are scattered throughout the sixteen volumes of the ENCYCLOPEDIA JUDAICA (1972) have been "gathered, re-edited, and reorganized

to present this fascinating subject to the reader in a form
which is convenient." Examines such topics as writing, the
scroll, the manuscript, the science of the Hebrew book, major
centers, Hebrew printers, love of books, the artistry of the
book, some basic books, and libraries. It is profusely illustrated, has a reading list, but no index. Charles Berlin, in
his review in THE JOURNAL OF LIBRARY HISTORY 13 (Spring
1978): 211-13, states that it is "regrettable that more attention could not have been given to correcting structural flaws
and errors that impair its usefulness," and that "although
this is an attractive, well-intentioned, and useful volume it
is a pity that 'love of the book' did not move the editors
sufficiently to produce a volume more worthy of the bibliographic tradition of its contents."

217   Rider, Alice D. A STORY OF BOOKS AND LIBRARIES. Metuchen,
N.J.: Scarecrow Press, 1976. 173 p.

A basic handbook for "use in the Arts, Social Sciences, and
Humanities courses in high school." Includes material on
man's earliest records; from stones to print-outs; the house of
the tablet; the monks copy and copy and copy; the manuscript
lighted up; libraries in medieval days; China and Gutenberg
give printing to the world; journeys to great book shrines of
the world; and book collecting, an avocation. Each chapter
contains a brief test for students, followed by a list of further readings, and also a list of schoolroom activities, such
as extra-credit projects, to instruct and amuse, group activities, and things to do. No illustrations. Indexed.

218   Vervliet, Hendrik D.L., ed. THE BOOK THROUGH FIVE THOUSAND
YEARS. London and New York: Phaidon, 1972. Distributed in the
United States by Praeger Publishers, New York. 496 p.

A magnificently produced tribute to the book which was is-
sued as part of the celebration of International Book Year in
1972. Although a rather overpowering tome in size and appearance, this book was "not intended for the specialist but
for the educated amateur who wishes to extend his field of
knowledge." It is arranged chronologically under four main
headings: the prehistory of books and printing, the book in
the Orient, the manuscript in the West, and the printed book
in the West, and each unit and subunit has a separate bibliography. This work contains contributions by many scholars
and historians of the book including Diringer, Weitzmann,
Presser, Baudin, McLean, and others. Each chapter "must
clearly be considered as a complete entity and therefore some
omissions and repetitions are inevitable." Vervliet has provided 264 full color illustrations and a number in black and
white, with a list of illustrations. Unfortunately, it has no
index.

219 Winckler, Paul A., ed. READER IN THE HISTORY OF BOOKS AND PRINTING. Englewood, Colo.: Information Handling Services, 1978. 406 p.

> Winckler includes a selection of readings designed to provide an introduction to the evolutionary history of graphic communication through the ages with the emphasis on the role of books and printing in the recording, preserving, and disseminating of ideas and its impact on civilization. The book is divided into four units: overview of books and printing, the materials of books and printing, the hand-produced book, and the printed book. He includes items on surfaces for writing and printing, the alphabet and writing, typography, bookbinding, and book illustration, as well as units on the history of the book in the ancient and medieval world, the Renaissance, and the modern world. Material by Denys Hay, Douglas C. McMurtrie, David Bland, Hellmut Lehmann-Haupt, Otto W. Fuhrmann, John Edwin Sandys, John Rothwell Slater, Robert Escarpit, Joseph Blumenthal, Marshall McLuhan, and others is included. The work has a number of black-and-white illustrations and each unit and subunit has a listing of additional readings. Indexed.

THE BOOK IN THE ANCIENT WORLD

This unit contains a listing of items dealing with early forms of graphic communication of the hand-produced book of ancient Sumer, Assyria, and Babylonia, as well as of ancient Egypt, Greece, Rome, and the Near East.

In addition to items on the history of the book in the ancient world a few deal with paleography and decipherment of ancient writings. This study of "the archeology of the book" has brought new insight and understanding of the life and customs of ancient civilizations.

220 Chiera, Edward. THEY WROTE ON CLAY: THE BABYLONIAN TABLETS SPEAK TODAY. Edited by George G. Cameron. Chicago: University of Chicago Press, 1938. 235 p.

> A study of the many phases of life that have been revealed by the clay tablets of ancient Mesopotamia, this book is a combination of the study of archeology and Assyriology which attempts to present the work of the Assyriologists to outsiders. It provides information on the lives and work of those people who lived in the area of the Fertile Crescent at the dawn of civilization. It is a popularly written book with many illustrations. No index.

221   Deuel, Leo. TESTAMENTS OF TIME, THE SEARCH FOR LOST MANU-
      SCRIPTS AND RECORDS. New York: Alfred A. Knopf, 1965. 590 p.

> An absorbing "book about books and about the scholars who
> searched for and discovered lost manuscripts and who inter-
> preted and deciphered them." Deuel includes information on
> a Renaissance prelude, the permanence of papyrus and clay
> (classics), the ancient Near East, the prevalance of parch-
> ment (the New Testament and Hebrew writs), a profusion of
> silk, bark, and paper (Inner Asia); and the New World. It
> is illustrated, has a bibliography, and an index.

222   Diringer, David. THE HAND-PRODUCED BOOK. New York: Philo-
      sophical Library, 1953. 603 p.

> A very detailed book on a specialized subject which examines
> the book from earliest times to the medieval period, Diringer
> was particularly interested in the various forms taken by the
> earliest books. It contains numerous black-and-white illus-
> trations and there is a listing of items at the end of each
> chapter, as well as a general bibliography. Indexed.

223   Forman, W. and Forman, B. CYLINDER SEALS OF WESTERN ASIA.
      Text by D.J. Wiseman. Illustrations selected and photographed by W.
      and B. Forman. London: Batchworth Press, [1959]. 118 p.

> A book of illustrations of ancient cylinder seals with identifi-
> cation and commentary. These seals were used as marks of
> identification on the tablets of ancient Mesopotamia. The
> items in this book were selected from the collection of the
> British Museum (British Library). It has an illustration of the
> seal in actual size and on the opposite page an enlargement,
> and some introductory chapters on the classification of the
> seals, uses of a seal, technique, inscriptions, and the various
> periods from before 3000 B.C. to 350 B.C. There is a brief
> bibliography but no index.

224   Hussein, Mohamed A. ORIGINS OF THE BOOK: EGYPT'S CONTRI-
      BUTION TO THE DEVELOPMENT OF THE BOOK FROM PAPYRUS TO
      CODEX. Greenwich, Conn.: New York Graphic Society, 1972. 135 p.

> This book aims "to record and illustrate the most important
> phases of the evolution from the papyrus roll to the paper
> codex in Egypt, with its vitality and cultural continuity from
> the early era of the Pharaohs to the Arab Middle Ages in its
> various languages and scripts." This book attempts "to pro-
> vide the reader with an answer to the question about the ori-
> gins of the book by presenting a small selection from an almost
> overwhelming mass of materials." It contains a brief historical
> survey, then a look at the Pharaonic period, the Greco-Roman
> period, the Coptic book, and the book in Islamic Egypt. It is
> beautifully illustrated in color and black and white, with a bib-
> liography, but no index.

225   Kenyon, Frederic G. BOOKS AND READERS IN ANCIENT GREECE
AND ROME. 2d ed. Oxford, Engl.: Clarendon Press, 1951. 136 p.

A study of the methods of book construction from "the date
of Homer . . . until the supersession of papyrus by vellum
in the fourth century of our era." The purpose of this book
is to "show the bearings of the material and form of books
on literary history and criticism, and to consider what new
light has been thrown by recent research on the origin and
growth of the habit of reading in ancient Greece and Rome."
The chapters include the use of books in ancient Greece, the
papyrus roll, books and reading at Rome, and vellum and
codex. It contains nine black-and-white illustrations, some
footnotes, but no bibliography. There is an appendix of il-
lustrative passages from Latin authors. Indexed.

226   Pinner, H.L. THE WORLD OF BOOKS IN CLASSICAL ANTIQUITY.
Leiden, Netherlands: A.W. Sijthoff, 1958. 64 p.

A brief overview of the book in ancient times which includes
material on literary evidence and papyrus discoveries, scrolls
and parchment codices, the Greek book trade, Roman publishers, bookshops in Athens and Rome, and ancient libraries
and bibliophiles. It contains fourteen black-and-white illustrations, a list of source references, but no index.

227   Putnam, George H. AUTHORS AND THEIR PUBLIC IN ANCIENT TIMES.
3d ed., rev. New York: G.P. Putnam's Sons, 1923. 309 p.

A "general introduction to a history of the origin and development of property in literature. . . ." The subtitle
gives the scope which is "A Sketch of Literary Conditions
and of the Relations with the Public of Literary Producers,
from the Earliest Times to the Fall of the Roman Empire."
Includes material on the beginnings of literature in Chaldea,
Egypt, China, Japan, India, Persia, and Judaea, as well as
material on Greece, Alexandria, book-terminology in classic
times, Rome, and Constantinople. There are no illustrations.
It contains a list of principal works referred to as authorities.
Indexed.

228   Thompson, Edward M. A HANDBOOK OF GREEK AND LATIN PA-
LAEOGRAPHY. 3d ed. London: Kegan Paul, Trench, Trübner, and
Co., 1906. Reprint. Chicago: Argonaut, 1966. 343 p.

This is a corrected and revised edition of a work which originally appeared in 1893. Although published over seventy
years ago, the third edition is still recognized as the "standard reference manual on the subject available in the English
language." The author states that this "hand-book does not
pretend to give more than an outline of the very large subject

of Greek and Latin Palaeography." This work is more basic
than Thompson's AN INTRODUCTION TO GREEK AND LATIN
PALAEOGRAPHY (see below), but even so this is not an easy
field to study and both books are rather technical and require
some background. There is a select bibliography and a list
of principal paleographical works used or referred to, and
many illustrations. Indexed.

229   _____. AN INTRODUCTION TO GREEK AND LATIN PALAEOGRAPHY.
Oxford, Engl.: Clarendon Press, 1912. Reprint. New York: Burt
Franklin, n.d. 600 p.

A highly specialized work of value to the advanced student.
This is an enlarged version of Thompson's A HANDBOOK OF
GREEK AND LATIN PALAEOGRAPHY (see above) and follows
the same pattern in its organization. The HANDBOOK was
rewritten in many parts as well as revised, and it is hoped,
gives a "fairly complete account of the history and progress
of Greek and Latin Palaeography. . . ." In the preface to
the reprint of the HANDBOOK it states that the INTRODUC-
TION TO GREEK AND LATIN PALAEOGRAPHY is "more extensive and rich in references" than the HANDBOOK but
specialists agree that the INTRODUCTION "lacks the instruc-
tive value and methodic classification of the HANDBOOK."
Thompson includes many illustrations and an extensive bibliography. Indexed.

230   Turner, E.G. GREEK MANUSCRIPTS OF THE ANCIENT WORLD.
Princeton, N.J.: Princeton University Press, 1971. 132 p.

This is a book "designed to supply the non-specialist classical
scholar with a representative body of material illustrating
Greek manuscripts written in antiquity." It is arranged by
literary genre, has a twenty-seven page introduction, but is
primarily a book containing seventy-three illustrations of
Greek manuscripts with accompanying commentary. There is
no separate bibliography, but some books are listed in the
commentaries, and it also contains a chronological table of
manuscripts, and a paleographical index.

231   _____. GREEK PAPYRI: AN INTRODUCTION. Princeton, N.J.:
Princeton University Press, 1968. 220 p. 2 maps of Egypt.

This book is written for the textual critic, the historian, or
intelligent layman "whose imagination has been stirred at the
idea of making direct contact with the writers of two thousand or so years ago." It is basically a guide "written as
an aid in the use of Greek and Latin papyri," and includes
chapters on writing materials and books, the rediscovery of
papyrus, excavating for papyri, place of origin and place of

writing, how a papyrus text is edited, the persons who owned the papyri in antiquity, papyri and Greek literature, types of papyrus documents, and the principal editions of papyri. Turner includes extensive notes on the chapters and plates, and a general index, a separate index of Greek words, and a few illustrations.

232   Weitzmann, Kurt. ANCIENT BOOK ILLUMINATION. Cambridge, Mass.: Harvard University Press, 1959. 166 p. 64 plates.

This is a history of classical book illumination arranged by genre including chapters on scientific and didactic treatises, epic poetry, dramatic poetry, literary prose texts, and conclusion and outlook. This book attempts to "fill a gap in the history of Hellenistic-Roman art." It has extensive notes and is indexed.

THE MEDIEVAL PERIOD AND THE ILLUMINATED MANUSCRIPT

Probably no time in the history of the book is as exciting as the medieval period and its illuminated manuscripts. During these one thousand years, hand-produced books were executed by monks, scribes, and artists working in the monasteries or workshops. The production of the medieval book was often the work of many people, including those who manufactured the parchment and vellum, the scribes who copied the text, the artists who painted the miniature paintings and initial letters, the rubricators who applied the touches of red and blue to chapter headings and in various parts of the text, the illuminators who applied the burnished gold, and the bookbinders who placed the final product in a binding suitable for its contents. David Diringer states that the talents of many were "combined to create masterpieces which are a delight even to us of the atomic age."

However, in the fifteenth century changes were being felt in Western Europe and a new era in book production was emerging. According to Hellmut Lehmann-Haupt: "It is immensely interesting to observe how the demand of new classes of readers; the rise of universities; the awakening of vernacular literature, together with a revived interest in classical literature and the intimations of reformation in the Church, really preceded the invention of printing. It is quite clearly visible how the makers of books early in the century prepared themselves to meet the new demands even without the printing press, of which they had no knowledge."

The literature on the medieval book is extensive since it includes both the history of books and the history of art. Most of the items in this unit are general histories of the medieval manuscript or of the manuscript in a particular country, region, or during a certain time period. There are also a number of books which are studies of individual manuscripts, but these have not been included except in a few cases in the unit which lists some facsimiles.

233   Alexander, J.J.G. ITALIAN RENAISSANCE ILLUMINATIONS. New
       York: George Braziller, 1977. 119 p.

       These manuscripts reflect the "intellectual, moral, spiritual,
       and artistic rebirth of Europe, the revival of ancient classical
       influences, the rise of a new impulse in culture, in literature
       and in art" which developed in Italy in the early-fifteenth
       century, bringing about a transformation in book illumination.
       This book is beautifully reproduced in full color and gold,
       with some black-and-white illustrations, and consists of a
       general bibliography, and a bibliography on the individual
       manuscripts.

234   _____, ed. A SURVEY OF MANUSCRIPTS ILLUMINATED IN THE
       BRITISH ISLES. 6 vols. Boston: New York Graphic Society, 1975.

       The six volumes under Alexander's general editorship, are
       titled INSULAR MANUSCRIPTS FROM THE 6TH TO THE 9TH
       CENTURY; ANGLO-SAXON MANUSCRIPTS 900-1066; RO-
       MANESQUE MANUSCRIPTS 1066-1190; EARLY GOTHIC
       MANUSCRIPTS 1190-1300; GOTHIC MANUSCRIPTS OF THE
       14TH CENTURY; and LATER GOTHIC MANUSCRIPTS--THE
       15TH CENTURY. These books list "the most important illu-
       minated manuscripts of each century" and provide detailed
       information on each containing a brief introduction, glossary,
       a catalog, and numerous black-and-white and a few color
       plates. There is an index to manuscripts, analysis of the
       manuscripts in the catalog, and a general index.

235   Bradley, John W. ILLUMINATED MANUSCRIPTS. 2d ed. Little Books
       on Art Series. London: Methuen, 1920. 290 p.

       This is an informative book dealing with vellum and other
       materials; writing; and Greek and Roman, Byzantine, Celtic,
       semibarbaric, Carolingian, monastic, Ottonian, Franconian,
       and Gothic illumination. It also includes chapters on the
       development of the initial letter; first English styles; artistic
       education in the cloisters; the golden age of illumination;
       and the rise of national styles with a study of French, English,
       Italian, German, Netherlandish, Spanish, and Portuguese
       illumination and concluding with illumination since the inven-
       tion of printing. One of the most useful features of this
       book is the appendix of manuscripts that may be consulted
       as examples, arranged chronologically in tabular form, giving
       name of the manuscript, where produced, where kept, date,
       and remarks. It contains twenty illustrations and a bibliog-
       raphy. Indexed.

236   Branner, Robert. MANUSCRIPT PAINTING IN PARIS DURING THE
       REIGN OF ST. LOUIS. Berkeley and Los Angeles: University of Cali-
       fornia Press, 1977. 270 p. Plates.

       This book "identifies and provides stylistic histories of the
       many ateliers of illumination active in Paris ca. 1226-1270,
       when potent forces of scholarship and patronage combined to
       spur production of illuminated manuscripts." It contains 438
       illustrations of which 26 are in color.

237   Clark, A.C. THE DESCENT OF MANUSCRIPTS. Oxford, Engl.:
       Clarendon Press, 1918. Reprint. Norwich, Engl.: Fletcher and Son,
       1969. 464 p.

       A rather specialized work which attempts to show "how in-
       ternal evidence furnished by MSS. can be utilized to cast
       light upon the filiation of codices, and in some cases upon
       the archetype from which they are derived; also to apply such
       knowledge to the criticism and emendation of the text." Clark
       includes a good deal of Greek and Latin. This is definitely
       for the advanced student. Indexed.

238   CZECHOSLOVAKIAN MINIATURES FROM ROMANESQUE AND GOTHIC
       MANUSCRIPTS. Introduction by Jan Květ. Mentor-UNESCO Art Series.
       New York: New American Library of World Literature, 1964. 24 p.
       Plates.

       An inexpensive paperback, this work briefly examines the his-
       tory of the artistic developments of manuscript art in the ter-
       ritory of the Czechs and Slovaks. It contains some black-
       and-white illustrations and twenty-eight color plates of ac-
       ceptable quality for a reasonably priced book. There is a
       bibliography and table of contents, but no index.

239   Dain, A. LES MANUSCRITS. Collection D'Études Anciennes. Paris:
       Société D'Édition Les Belles-Lettres, 1964. 196 p.

       This French book examines manuscripts and the problems of
       copying, paleography, the history of texts, and editions. It
       has a few black-and-white illustrations and a rather extensive
       bibliography, but no index.

240   D'Ancona, Paolo, and Aeschlimann, E. THE ART OF ILLUMINATION:
       AN ANTHOLOGY OF MANUSCRIPTS FROM THE SIXTH TO THE SIX-
       TEENTH CENTURY. New York: Phaidon, 1969. 235 p.

       This book is for the student of art and the persone di cultura and
       attempts to be a "Musée Imaginaire" of miniature painting,
       "where each can find what most appeals to his taste." It has a
       brief but useful outline on the development of European miniature
       painting, followed by 146 black-and-white and full color illus-

trations and a separate unit of notes on the plates, and a
short bibliography, concluding with a list of collections. No
index.

241   Delaissé, L.M.J.   MEDIEVAL MINIATURES FROM THE DEPARTMENT OF
MANUSCRIPTS (FORMERLY THE "LIBRARY OF BURGUNDY") THE ROYAL
LIBRARY OF BELGIUM.   New York: Harry N. Abrams, [1965].   216 p.

Delaissé includes fifty color miniatures which gives "a vivid
picture of the manuscript collections in which the Royal Library of Belgium in Brussels so rightly prides itself." It contains commentaries by Delaissé, with a foreword by Liebaers,
and an introduction by Masai. The quality of the reproductions is excellent.

242   Diringer, David.   THE ILLUMINATED BOOK: ITS HISTORY AND PRO-
DUCTION.   Rev. ed.   New York: Frederick A. Praeger Publishers,
1967.   514 p.

This is a major study of the medieval manuscript in which the
author is "mainly concerned with the history of book production" and is limited to "one aspect of illumination, namely,
the meaning of the pictures."   The approach is to "book-
illuminations essentially as a manuscript written in a sort of
pictorial script. . . ."   The work contains numerous illustrations in black-and-white and color and is part of a number which Diringer wrote as companion volumes dealing with
"various aspects of book production in its millenial developments."   These were planned as a "comprehensive, readable,
and up-to-date synthesis of our present knowledge" including
this extensive study of the illuminated book.   There is an
informative introduction, which attempts to define "illumination"
and examines the "elements which influenced book-illumination,"
and is followed by chapters on ancient methods of book illustration; early west-Christian--Byzantine and allied illumination;
Islamic, Hebrew, and Mozarabic illumination; Hiberno-Saxon,
Carolingian, and Ottonian illumination; the Golden Age of
illumination--England; Italy, France--Burgundy, and the Neth-
erlands--Flanders.   Each unit has a bibliography and there is
also a general bibliography.   Indexed.

243   Dupont, Jacques, and Gnudi, Cesare.   GOTHIC PAINTING.   Translated by
Stuart Gilbert.   Great Centuries of Painting Series.   Geneva: Skira,
1954.   215 p.

This book examines the Gothic Age, Italian painters of the
Gothic Age, and court arts.   Although this work emphasizes
miniature painting in the medieval book, it also has a unit
on stained glass and panel painting.   There are many full
color illustrations, an extensive bibliography, and an index of
names and subjects.

244   Formaggio, Dino, and Basso, Carlo, eds. A BOOK OF MINIATURES.
       Translated by Peggy Craig. New York: Tudor Publishing Co., 1962.
       143 p.

> A study of "some of the basic elements that make up the
> long and complex development of this very specialized art,
> whether as technique or as form." This book tries to "give
> a comprehensive idea of what illumination is, and what its
> significance has been, from its earliest phases through its de-
> velopment and to its eventual exhaustion." It contains over
> 130 full-color illustrations but no index.

245   Francastel, P. MEDIEVAL PAINTING. 20,000 Years of Painting Series.
       New York: Dell Publishing Co., 1967. 196 p.

> This is volume 2 in this series which includes frescos, mo-
> saics, and panel painting, as well as medieval illuminated
> manuscript painting. It has a brief introduction, but this is
> mainly a book of small full-color illustrations with accom-
> panying commentary which examines the "history of art from
> the sixth to the fifteenth century." There is no bibliography,
> but it is indexed.

246   Grabar, André, and Nordenfalk, Carl. EARLY MEDIEVAL PAINTING
       FROM THE FOURTH TO THE ELEVENTH CENTURY. Great Centuries
       of Painting Series. New York: Skira, 1957. 243 p.

> This book is divided into two parts: mosaics and mural paint-
> ing by Grabar, and book illumination by Nordenfalk. The
> unit on book illumination covers the following periods: late
> Roman, pre-Carolingian, Ireland and England, Merovingian,
> Carolingian, from Carolingian to Romanesque, Mozarabic,
> Anglo-Saxon in the tenth and eleventh centuries, and Ottonian
> illumination. It contains many full-color illustrations, as
> well as an informative text, and has a rather extensive bib-
> liography. There is an index of manuscripts, index of names
> and places, and a list of colorplates.

247   _____. ROMANESQUE PAINTING: Great Centuries of Painting Series.
       Lausanne: Skira, [1958]. 231 p.

> This is a study of Romanesque art in which Grabar deals with
> mural painting in part 1 and Nordenfalk examines Romanesque
> book illumination in part 2. The unit on book illumination
> includes material on duration and diffusion of Romanesque
> book illumination, principal types of manuscripts, Romanesque
> initial letters, and pictorial styles in the Romanesque minia-
> ture. It is a splendid study of this period with numerous
> full-color illustrations, as well as a bibliography, index of
> manuscripts, index of names and places, and a list of color-
> plates.

248   Harthan, John P. THE BOOK OF HOURS. New York: Thomas Y.
       Crowell Co., 1977. 192 p.

       This book contains an extensive introductory text providing
       "a fresh and wide-ranging discussion of the evolution of the
       Book of Hours, describing contents, decoration, and social
       and devotional meanings." The Book of Hours comprises the
       "largest category of illuminated manuscripts to survive from
       the Middle Ages and the Renaissance." In these books
       "created by scribe and painter, religion, art, and secular
       life were combined to form a unique synthesis." Harthan
       includes many full-color illustrations of pages from various
       books of Hours, with commentary. There is a unit on the
       printed Book of Hours, notes on the text, a select reading
       list, genealogies, and an index.

249   Herbert, John A. ILLUMINATED MANUSCRIPTS. London: Methuen,
       1911. Reprint. New York: Burt Franklin, 1958. 356 p.

       This work attempts "to sketch the history of illumination on
       vellum manuscripts, from classical times down to the decay
       and virtual disuse of the art which resulted inevitably, though
       not immediately, from the introduction of printing; describing
       the main characteristics of each of the most important periods
       and schools, and following the development of the successive
       styles so far as existing materials allow." Herbert has a few
       black-and-white illustrations and a rather extensive select
       bibliography, which contains a list of periodicals, general
       works, and catalogs; reproductions of, or monographs on,
       particular manuscripts; and miscellaneous. There is an index
       of manuscripts, scribes, and illuminators, and a general index.

250   IRISH ILLUMINATED MANUSCRIPTS OF THE EARLY CHRISTIAN PERIOD.
       Introduction by James Johnson Sweeney. Mentor-UNESCO Art Series.
       New York: New American Library, 1965. 24 p. Plates.

       The introduction briefly examines the early Irish gospelbooks
       and the work of the Irish monks, as revealed in the BOOK
       OF DURROW and the BOOK OF KELLS explaining how the
       "intensity, imagination, and freedom of these early Christian
       masterpieces bring them close to the spirit of modern art."
       It has a bibliography, table of contents, but no index. Color
       quality is fair.

251   Lehmann-Haupt, Hellmut. THE GÖTTINGEN MODEL BOOK. Columbia:
       University of Missouri Press, 1972. 102 p.

       A facsimile edition, with translation and commentary, of a
       fifteenth-century illuminator's manual which provided "instruc-
       tions for the compounding of inks and paints that border on
       alchemy and directions for their application that can guide

the hand through the intricacies of ornamentation." The text examines the origin and influence of this model book which was rediscovered in the Göttingen Library. The facsimile is in full color and there are additional black-and-white and color plates. A useful example of an artist's handbook used during this period.

252   Madan, Falconer. BOOKS IN MANUSCRIPT. London: Kegan Paul, Trench, Trübner, and Co., 1893. Rev. ed. 1927. Reprint. New York: Haskell House Publishers, 1968. 208 p.

This book covers the world of manuscripts in a "short introductory essay to their study and use," and contains chapters on materials for writing, and forms of books; the history of writing; scribes and their way; illumination; the errors of scribes and their correction; famous libraries; famous manuscripts; literary forgeries; treatment and cataloguing of manuscripts; and public and private records. It has eight black-and-white illustrations, and three appendixes: public libraries which contain more than four thousand manuscripts; lists of printed catalogues of manuscripts in European languages in the British Museum, the Bodleian Library at Oxford, the Cambridge University Library, and others; and some books useful for the study of manuscripts. Indexed.

253   Meiss, Millard. FRENCH PAINTING IN THE TIME OF JEAN DE BERRY: THE BOUCICAUT MASTER. London: Phaidon, 1968. 384 p.

Primarily a book of black-and-white and color illustrations of the medieval manuscripts executed by the Boucicaut master and his circle, with introductory remarks on the Boucicaut Hours, as well as notes on the text, and a most extensive bibliography. The quality of the illustrations is exceptional. Indexed.

254   _____. FRENCH PAINTING IN THE TIME OF JEAN DE BERRY: THE LATE XIV CENTURY AND THE PATRONAGE OF THE DUKE. 2 vols. London: Phaidon, 1967.

A detailed study of medieval French art during the time of the Duke which provides information on his life and activities as a patron of the arts. This is followed by chapters on the various works which were produced under his patronage. Volume 2 contains 845 black-and-white and color plates. It has notes on the text, an extensive bibliography, and an index.

255   _____. FRENCH PAINTING IN THE TIME OF JEAN DE BERRY: THE LIMBOURGS AND THEIR CONTEMPORARIES. 2 vols. New York: George Braziller, in participation with the Pierpont Morgan Library, 1974.

A monumental study of the medieval illuminated manuscripts

executed by the Limbourg brothers at the end of the fourteenth and beginning of the fifteenth centuries in France,
this work examines in great detail this magnificent period
of French book art. Volume 1 is the text which studies the
Limbourgs and their work and of other artists of that time,
while volume 2 contains 898 black-and-white and color plates.
It has extensive notes and a bibliography, and a general index located in volume 1. All of these books by Meiss are
for the advanced student who would like an in-depth look
at the manuscripts of this time.

256   Meredith-Owens, G.M. TURKISH MINIATURES. London: Trustees of
the British Museum, 1963. 32 p. Plates.

This is a brief look at Islam and painting, characteristics of
the Turkish school, foreign influences, and Turkish artists and
their work. Data on sources for the history of Turkish painting and illustrations of outstanding Turkish manuscripts from
the British Museum collection are also included. It contains
twenty-five color plates, and notes, and a list of suggested
readings.

257   Miner, Dorothy E. THE DEVELOPMENT OF MEDIEVAL ILLUMINATION
AS RELATED TO THE EVOLUTION OF BOOK DESIGN. Baltimore:
Walters Art Gallery, 1958. 20 p.

A reprint from the CATHOLIC LIFE ANNUAL (vol. 1, 1958),
this pamphlet is a brief but informative study of medieval illumination aimed at the general reader. The author presents
an overview of the history of the medieval manuscript com-
menting that the "Middle Ages had set the standards of book
design so high that it never occurred to the early experi-
menters with type to aim for anything short of a beautiful
book." There are a few black-and-white and color illustrations, but no bibliography or index. Most useful for the
beginner.

258   Mitchell, Sabrina. MEDIEVAL MANUSCRIPT PAINTING. Compass
History of Art Series. New York: Viking Press, 1964. 45 p. Plates.

This book contains 45 pages of introductory text, followed by
176 full-color plates and a listing of captions which identi-
fies each illustration. It also has a brief history of the Romanesque, Gothic, and international Gothic schools of illumination, as well as units on René d'Anjou, fifteenth-century
Flemish illumination, and Jean Fouquet and later French illumination, followed by plates illustrating these developments.
Visually an enjoyable book. No bibliography or index.

259   Mütherich, Florentine. CAROLINGIAN PAINTING. Commentaries by
      J.E. Gaehde. New York: George Braziller, 1976. 127 p.

      A study of this period in art history which was "nourished by
      the idea of the rebirth and renewal of cultural life initiated
      by Charlemagne" during which time he "instigated a great
      reform and revival of book learning." This book has a brief
      introduction and a unit with five black-and-white plates, with
      commentaries. This is followed by a selected bibliography
      and a unit on the provenance of manuscripts. The main body
      consists of forty-eight color plates with commentaries. No index.

260   Nordenfalk, Carl. CELTIC AND ANGLO-SAXON PAINTING: BOOK
      ILLUMINATION IN THE BRITISH ISLES, 600-800. New York: George
      Braziller, 1977. 128 p.

      This work examines "the glory of Irish art" as revealed in
      its famous manuscripts THE BOOK OF KELLS and THE BOOK
      OF DURROW. It contains full color and black-and-white
      illustrations. No index.

261   PERSIAN MINIATURES FROM ANCIENT MANUSCRIPTS. Introduction by
      Basil Gray. Mentor-UNESCO Art Series. New York: New American
      Library of World Literature, 1962. 24 p. Plates.

      This is an examination of Persian manuscripts from the fifteenth
      to the eighteenth centuries which gives an "interpretation of
      the theme of each miniature and an analysis of the artists'
      style, composition, and use of color." It contains twenty-
      eight color illustrations and a few black-and-white plates,
      and also a table of contents and a bibliography. A useful
      popular introduction to the topic. No index.

262   Pirani, Emma. GOTHIC ILLUMINATED MANUSCRIPTS. London: Hamlyn
      Publishing Group, 1970. 158 p.

      Translated by Margaret Crosland from the Italian original LA
      MINIATURA GOTICA. The emphasis is on the Italian schools
      of manuscript illumination including units of the Bolognese,
      Florentine, Sienese, Venetian, Lombard, and Neapolitan schools,
      with briefer units on France, Germany, Bohemia, and England.
      Contains sixty-nine color plates.

263   Porcher, Jean. MEDIEVAL FRENCH MINIATURES. New York: Harry N.
      Abrams, 1959. 276 p.

      A study of Romanesque and Gothic illumination in France
      with a number of black-and-white and color illustrations in
      the text, plus ninety full-color plates in a separate unit. It
      has a bibliographical commentary and a list of illustrations.
      Indexed.

264   Putnam, George H. BOOKS AND THEIR MAKERS DURING THE MIDDLE
      AGES: A STUDY OF THE CONDITIONS OF THE PRODUCTION AND
      DISTRIBUTION OF LITERATURE FROM THE FALL OF THE ROMAN EM-
      PIRE TO THE CLOSE OF THE SEVENTEENTH CENTURY. 2 vols. New
      York: G.P. Putnam's Sons, 1896. Reprint. New York: Hillary House
      Publishers, 1962.

            This work encompasses not only the Middle Ages but also the
            early printed book to 1700. It attempts "to present a study
            of certain conditions in the history of the manifolding and
            distribution of books by which the production and effective-
            ness of literature was very largely influenced and determined,
            and under which the conception of such a thing as literary
            property gradually emerged." Volume 1 examines books in
            manuscript and the making of books in the monasteries, the
            libraries of the manuscript period, the making of books in the
            early universities, and the book trade in the manuscript period,
            and it concludes with the early printed book of the Renais-
            sance, the invention of printing, and the printer-publisher of
            Italy. Volume 2 is a continuation with a chapter on the
            early printed book in France, followed by material on Caxton,
            Froben, Erasmus, Plantin, and others, and concluding with
            a unit on the beginning of property in literature. At the
            beginning of volume 1 there is a bibliography of works cited
            or referred to as authorities and an index to both volumes at
            the end of volume 2. No illustrations.

265   Reynolds, L.D., and Wilson, N.G. SCRIBES AND SCHOLARS: A GUIDE
      TO THE TRANSMISSION OF GREEK AND LATIN LITERATURE. 2d ed.,
      rev. and enl. Oxford, Engl.: Clarendon Press, 1974. 275 p. 16
      plates.

            This book was first published in 1968. It is designed as "a
            simple introduction for beginners to a field of classical studies
            which generally remains little known or understood despite its
            importance and intrinsic interest." The work attempts "to
            outline the processes by which Greek and Latin literature have
            been preserved, describing the dangers to which texts were
            exposed in the age of the manuscript book, and showing to
            what extent ancient and medieval readers or scholars were
            concerned to preserve or transmit classical texts." The new
            edition retains "the principal features of the original, a read-
            able text unencumbered by a heavy apparatus of learning . . ."
            The chapters include antiquity, the Greek East, the Latin
            West, the Renaissance, some aspects of scholarship since the
            Renaissance, and textual criticism, and each has extensive
            notes, plus an index of manuscripts, a general index, and
            notes to the plates.

266   Robb, David M. THE ART OF THE ILLUMINATED MANUSCRIPT. South Brunswick, N.J., and New York: A.S. Barnes and Co., 1973. 356 p.

> This is a useful up-to-date study which is a "reasonable comprehensive descriptive and interpretative discussion, in English, of the illuminated manuscript as an art form." It examines the origins and early forms of manuscript illumination, and then discusses Byzantine, Occidental, Carolingian, and Ottonian styles. This is followed by a chapter on the tenth- and eleventh-century illuminated book in non-Germanic countries, the Romanesque, and Gothic, and the fourteenth century with emphasis on the Franco-Flemish style, concluding with a unit on manuscript illumination in the late Middle Ages. There are 216 monochrome illustrations and 30 color plates and each chapter has notes, and there is a separate bibliography. Indexed.

267   Rothe, Edith. MEDIAEVAL BOOK ILLUMINATION IN EUROPE: THE COLLECTIONS OF THE GERMAN DEMOCRATIC REPUBLIC. New York: W.W. Norton and Co., 1968. 307 p.

> Primarily a book of illustrations of medieval manuscripts located in thirty-three libraries in West Germany, which contains illustrations of 160 manuscripts, many of which are here reproduced for the first time. The collections reveal a "rather wide range of material, covering twelve centuries, from 400 to 1600, and representing most of the countries of Europe and a large number of schools." The monochrome and color illustrations are of excellent quality. There is a rather extensive historical commentary, providing a general survey of book illumination in the various periods with notes on the plates, a useful guide to the location of manuscripts, a bibliography, glossary, and index.

268   Salmi, Mario. ITALIAN MINIATURES. New York: Harry N. Abrams, 1954. 214 p.

> An introductory text of eighty pages on the early Middle Ages and the Romanesque, the Gothic era, and the Renaissance as seen in the Italian manuscript book, which is mainly a book of illustrations containing ninety-nine black-and-white and seventy-four color plates. It has a three-page bibliography and a list of illustrations. Indexed.

269   Saunders, O.E. ENGLISH ILLUMINATION. 2 vols. Florence: Pantheon, 1933. Reprint. New York: Hacker Art Books, 1969.

> The brief text examines Celtic illumination, Anglo-Saxon illumination, the Romanesque period, bestiaries, the transition from Romanesque to Gothic, the Gothic period, apocalypses,

East Anglian illumination, and the last phase. It is profusely illustrated, has a fairly extensive bibliography, as well as an index of manuscripts, and a general index.

270   Shaw, Henry. HANDBOOK OF THE ART OF ILLUMINATION AS PRACTISED DURING THE MIDDLE AGES. London: Bell and Daldy, 1866. 66 p.

Although this book was written over one hundred years ago, it is still useful because it is one of the few books providing a "description of the metals, pigments, and processes employed by the artists of different periods." Basically this is a study of the techniques and materials used in the production of the manuscript book containing fifteen full-page illustrations and a few in the text. Other books of this type are A.P. Laurie's THE PAINTER'S METHODS AND MATERIALS, which is not included in this bibliography because it is mainly concerned with subjects other than book painting, and Thompson's THE MATERIALS AND TECHNIQUES OF MEDIEVAL PAINTING (see below).

271   Thompson, Daniel V. THE MATERIALS AND TECHNIQUES OF MEDIEVAL PAINTING. London: Allen and Unwin, 1956. Reprint. New York: Dover Publications, n.d. 239 p.

A study of "medieval paint technology" which "describes these often jealously guarded recipes, lists of materials, and processes." Although this book examines painting in general, during the medieval period, it has a good deal of information on book painting in particular, with chapters on carriers and grounds, binding media, pigments, and metals. It has no bibliography or illustrations. Indexed.

272   Tinker, Edward L. "The Glory That Was Persia." THE DOLPHIN 4 (Fall 1940): 31-38.

This is a brief outline of "Arabian, Mongolian, and Iranian Arts that flourished in the Persian manuscript book" presenting a useful introduction to "a period in art and bookmaking that has not been as widely known as it should be." It has a few illustrations.

273   Turner, D.H. EARLY GOTHIC ILLUMINATED MANUSCRIPTS IN ENGLAND. London: Trustees of the British Museum, 1965. 32 p. Plates.

A popularly written pamphlet, Turner "describes and illustrates English illumination during a particular period of its history," namely from 1220 to 1285. There are four color plates and sixteen in black and white, and a ten-item bibliography. No index.

274   Unterkircher, Franz. A TREASURE OF ILLUMINATED MANUSCRIPTS:
        A SELECTION OF MINIATURES FROM MANUSCRIPTS IN THE AUSTRIAN
        NATIONAL LIBRARY. New York: G.P. Putnam's Sons, 1967. 264 p.

        This is a "brief introduction to the pictures and their original
        environment" of the treasures of this library containing sixty
        examples in full-color, ranging from the eighth century to
        the late illuminations of the sixteenth century, with extensive
        comments on each item. Indexed.

275   Walters Art Gallery, Baltimore. ILLUMINATED BOOKS OF THE MIDDLE
        AGES AND RENAISSANCE: AN EXHIBITION. Baltimore: 1949. 85 p.
        Plates.

        This is the catalog for the exhibition held at the Baltimore
        Museum of Art from 27 January to 13 March 1949, organized
        by the Walters Art Gallery in cooperation with the Baltimore
        Museum. The exhibit was held with a view "to widening the
        public experience in this field." The catalog is arranged
        chronologically, starting with a Psalter of the eighth century
        and ending with a calligraphic specimen of Friar Didace done
        at Paris in 1647. Each entry has a bibliography of relevant
        materials. It contains materials on loan from private and
        public sources.

276   Weitzmann, Kurt. LATE ANTIQUE AND EARLY CHRISTIAN BOOK IL-
        LUMINATION. New York: George Braziller, 1977. 127 p.

        A study of book illumination of the Greco-Roman period which
        was borrowed by the early Christians who developed the "then
        prevailing style of illumination" and adopted it to "their new
        subjects along classical lines." It has examples of such fa-
        mous manuscripts as THE COTTON GENESIS, THE VIENNA
        GENESIS, THE ROSSANO GOSPELS, THE VATICAN VERGIL,
        and others. It is illustrated with forty-eight color plates and a
        few in black and white and has a selected bibliography.

277   _____. STUDIES IN CLASSICAL AND BYZANTINE MANUSCRIPT IL-
        LUMINATION. Edited by Herbert L. Kessler. Chicago: University of
        Chicago Press, 1971. 346 p.

        This is a selection of twelve essays by Professor Weitzmann
        revealing various aspects of his contributions to an under-
        standing of ancient and medieval art and especially in his
        "detailed examination of manuscript illumination." There are
        320 black-and-white illustrations, some which are rather
        small, with extensive notes, and a bibliography. For the
        advanced student. Indexed.

278   Weitzmann, Kurt, et al. THE PLACE OF BOOK ILLUMINATION IN
       BYZANTINE ART. Princeton, N.J.: Art Museum, Princeton University,
       1975. Distributed by Princeton University Press, 184 p.

       This book contains the four lectures given at a symposium in
       April 1973 at Princeton University as a tribute to Professor
       Weitzmann on his retirement from the department of art and
       archeology. It includes the opening address by Weitzmann,
       entitled "The Study of Byzantine Book Illumination, Past,
       Present, and Future," "The Monumental Miniature" by William
       C. Loerke, "The Role of Miniature Painting in Mural Decora-
       tion" by Ernst Kitzinger, and "Toward a History of Palaeo-
       logan Illumination" by Hugo Buchtal. It has many black-
       and-white illustrations and a number of footnotes, but no
       bibliography. Indexed.

279   Welch, Stuart C. IMPERIAL MUGHAL PAINTING. New York: George
       Braziller, 1978. 120 p.

       This book studies the manuscripts made for the Mughal Em-
       perors of India and members of their immediate family during
       the sixteenth and seventeenth centuries. "Mughal patrons
       and artists doted on the world and its inhabitants. No pains
       were spared to record them realistically in life-oriented pic-
       tures of remarkable artistry." This book has forty plates in
       color and gold, as well as a few black-and-white illustrations.

280   _____. PERSIAN PAINTING. New York: George Braziller, 1976.
       128 p.

       The exquisite world of the Persian miniatures is studied in
       this book with "dazzlingly colorful miniatures" which "depict
       court life and mythological adventures." Color and black-
       and-white plates are included.

281   Williams, John. EARLY SPANISH MANUSCRIPT ILLUMINATION. New
       York: George Braziller, 1977. 119 p.

       This is a study of the manuscripts produced from the seventh
       through eleventh centuries in Spain, showing the influence of
       the many cultures which affected Spanish culture and art--
       Visigoth, Jewish, Berber, and Arabic, and which are all
       mingled with the Romanized Celt-Ibernian population. There
       are a number of Mozarabic manuscripts (the term given to
       Christians living in Spain under Moslem rule). These particular
       manuscripts present "a strange vision of the world with strong,
       deep colors that cover the picture with vibrant bands of green,
       red, yellow, and violet, providing the background for the
       monsters, tempests, human figures of every description--all
       displaying an incredibly virile mysticism, evoking a new idea,

the antithesis of the Classic, which was to influence the art
of the later Middle Ages throughout Europe, but which was
anticipated in Spain by nearly two centuries." Williams has
a selected bibliography and forty plates in color and black
and white.

FACSIMILES OF MEDIEVAL MANUSCRIPTS

The following unit contains a selection of some facsimiles of medieval manuscripts which would be of interest to the student and general reader. An examination of these books will give an idea of the beauty of these hand-produced
masterpieces. In addition to containing reproductions of the original manuscripts,
these books usually contain a study and analysis of the manuscript itself.

282   THE BELLES HEURES OF JEAN, DUKE OF BERRY. Introduction and
        commentaries by Millard Meiss and Elizabeth M. Beatson. New York:
        George Braziller, 1974. 268 p.

        This is an example of one of the magnificent manuscripts
        which was executed in the early-fifteenth century by the
        Limbourg brothers for the duke of Berry. There is an intro-
        duction by Meiss and commentaries by Meiss and Beatson and
        also, notes on the introduction and commentaries. It con-
        tains 127 full-color and gold reproductions of the pages in
        actual size and 30 black-and-white plates of the remaining
        miniatures which are "generally less important." John Plummer
        has a chapter on observations on the make-up and decoration
        of the manuscript. There is a unit on the provenance and
        binding, as well as a bibliography and other manuscripts by,
        or closely related to, the Limbourgs.

283   THE BELLES HEURES OF JEAN, DUKE OF BERRY, PRINCE OF FRANCE.
        New York: The Cloisters, Metropolitan Museum of Art, 1958. Unpaged.

        This work contains a brief introduction by James J. Rorimer
        on the manuscript and its history. There are thirty-two full-
        color plates with commentary. THE BELLES HEURES is a
        "rich compendium of brilliant small paintings and ranks among
        the great masterpieces of the Middle Ages."

284   THE BENEDICTIONAL OF ST. ETHELWOLD. Introduction and notes by
        Francis Wormald. New York: Thomas Yoseloff, 1959. 31 p.

        A study of this Anglo-Saxon masterpiece of the tenth century
        which is now in the British Library, London. The book was
        made for St. Ethelwold, Bishop of Winchester. There is a
        brief commentary by Wormald on the text and the illuminator's
        technique, as well as eight color plates.

285   BOOK OF HOURS. By Simon Marmion. San Marino, Calif.: Huntington Library, 1976. 40 p.

> This is a full-color facsimile of this medieval manuscript, now in the Huntington Library, which was executed around 1460-65 by the French miniature artist, Simon Marmion as a book for private devotion. It has an introduction by James Thorpe who also provides a brief commentary on each painting.

286   THE BOOK OF HOURS OF CATHERINE OF CLEVES. Introduction and commentaries by John Plummer. New York: Pierpont Morgan Library, 1964. 83 p. 2 color plates and 30 black-and-white reproductions.

> A study of this manuscript which was executed for Catherine of Cleves around 1440 by an unknown Dutch master, containing a brief introduction, commentaries on the plates, and a few illustrations. (See also 295, THE HOURS OF CATHERINE OF CLEVES).

287   THE BOOK OF KELLS. With a study of the manuscript by Françoise Henry. New York: Alfred A. Knopf, 1974. 226 p.

> The purpose of this facsimile "is to show the illustrations and decoration of the Book of Kells in colour." This edition includes "all the full page illustrations in the manuscript and a representative selection of the ornamentation that is to be found on the text pages." This work contains ninety-three full pages and six half pages reproduced in color. The text by Henry is very informative and gives a detailed account of the history, background, and description of this "most splendid manuscript of the early Middle Ages." Indexed.

288   THE BOOK OF KELLS. 5th ed. Described by Sir Edward Sullivan. London: Studio Publications, 1952. 111 p.

> This work is not as attractive or as well printed as the facsimile published by Knopf (see above). There is a foreword by J.H. Holden, Principal, Wolverton College of Art, with some of the pages of the BOOK OF KELLS reproduced.

289   THE BOOK OF KELLS: A SELECTION OF PAGES REPRODUCED. Introduction and notes by G.O. Simms. Dublin: Dolmen Press and the Library of Trinity College, 1968. 32 p.

> This is a compact introduction to the BOOK OF KELLS but with only a few illustrations, and a brief bibliography.

290   THE CLOISTERS APOCALYPSE: AN EARLY FOURTEENTH-CENTURY MANUSCRIPT IN FACSIMILE. 2 vols. New York: Metropolitan Museum of Art, 1971.

> The first volume is the facsimile reproduction of the book in

The Cloisters, in New York City, while the second volume contains text material of "what is known of the manuscript's history, the text of the manuscript in English, and comments on each of its illustrations."

291　THE DOUCE APOCALYPSE. Introduction and notes by A.G. Hassall and W.O. Hassall. New York: Thomas Yoseloff, 1961. 32 p.

A brief study of this picture-book which illustrates the Book of Revelation of St. John the Divine, this work contains fourteen color and black-and-white plates from this thirteenth-century English manuscript, and a number of references.

292　THE FARNESE HOURS. Introduction and commentaries by Webster Smith. New York: George Braziller, [1976]. 167 p.

This manuscript, now in the Pierpont Morgan Library, was completed in 1546 by Giulio Clovio having been commissioned by Allesandro Cardinal Farnese and was "once the most famous of all illuminated manuscripts." The book contains an introduction followed by the plates and commentaries and units of notes to introduction, notes to commentaries, description of binding and collation of folios, other manuscripts illuminated by Clovio, and a selective bibliography. A beautifully printed copy of this Italian manuscript in full color and gold, with the slipcase and binding adapted from the original manuscript binding.

293　A FIFTEENTH CENTURY ITALIAN PLUTARCH. Introduction and notes by Charles Mitchell. New York: Thomas Yoseloff, 1961. 40 p.

A study of this fifteenth-century Plutarch which is in the British Library, London, and contains "select lives of famous men in humanistic Latin translation, and is brilliantly illuminated with historiated initials and narrative scenes of the north Italian courtly style of the Renaissance." It contains ten color reproductions and extensive notes.

294　THE GRANDES HEURES OF JEAN, DUKE OF BERRY. Introduction and legends by Marcel Thomas. New York: George Braziller, 1971. 183 p.

A magnificent facsimile, in color and gold, of this folio masterpiece of French illumination of the early-fifteenth century, having been completed and presented to the duke of Berry in 1405.

295　THE HOURS OF CATHERINE OF CLEVES. Introduction and commentaries by John Plummer. New York: George Braziller, [1966]. 359 p.

There is more extensive coverage of this manuscript than the

BOOK OF HOURS OF CATHERINE OF CLEVES (1964) published by the Pierpont Morgan Library (see 286). This book
contains 160 full-color reproductions of the two incomplete
parts of this book in the Guennol Collection, New York,
and the other in the Morgan Library with a commentary for
each page. The appendixes include a unit on format and
contents of the volumes, detailed reconstruction of manuscript,
calendar, and selective bibliography. The master of Catherine
of Cleves "played a substantial role in the history of art while
enriching our artistic substance with this matchless masterpiece from which he takes his name."

296   THE HOURS OF ÉTIENNE CHEVALIER. By Jean Fouquet. Introduction
and legends by Claude Schaefer. New York: George Braziller, 1971.
128 p.

This manuscript was completed by Fouquet sometime between
1452 and 1456 and is without doubt "among the greatest
masterpieces of fifteenth-century painting--a view shared
today by art historians of every nationality." The "richness
of these illuminations seem inexhaustible. . . ." THE HOURS
OF ÉTIENNE CHEVALIER "indicate the great importance of
Fouquet's Italian journey for his art" but he always remained
a French artist because "all of French civilization--not only
her art, but her soil and humanity, nourished Fouquet's sen-
sibility, imagination, and thought." This book which is
beautifully reproduced in full color and gold, has a brief
preface by Charles Sterling which investigates the place of
this manuscript in fifteenth-century French art. Each plate
is accompanied with a commentary and there are separate
notes to the preface, introduction, and legends, as well as
a selected bibliography, list of exhibitions, and a title index
of the plates.

297   THE HOURS OF JEANNE D'ÉVREUX, QUEEN OF FRANCE. New York:
The Cloisters, Metropolitan Museum of Art, 1957. 28 p. Facsimile of
48 characteristic pages.

This book was completed in 1325 by Jean Pucelle for Jeanne
d'Évreux, as a gift for her husband Charles IV of France.
"For the excellence of its drawing and the originality and
vitality of its decoration, the Book of Hours of Jeanne d'Évreux
is acknowledged an outstanding example, a masterpiece of
the developed Gothic courtly art of France." The original
contains 209 folios and this reproduction includes all of the
full-page pictures. There is a single page showing the size
of the original which reveals the "minuteness and exquisite
delicacy of the painting, decoration, and writing of the
original." The rest of the plates are reproduced at one-and-
a-half times their actual size. The book was painted in

grisaille or shades of black and white, with occasional high-
lights of color. The border designs depict the wonderful
drolleries and grotesques so popular in the Middle Ages. This
small book contains a twelve-page introduction by John J.
Rorimer, followed by the list of reproductions, with some
comments, and then the facsimile pages.

298   THE HUNGARIAN ILLUMINATED CHRONICLE [CHRONICA DE GESTIS
       HUNGARORUM]. New York: Taplinger Publishing Co., 1969. 200 p.
       Facsimile.

       This book contains four studies on this illuminated chronicle
       examining the period, its history and description, sources and
       arrangement of the text, and description and interpretation
       of the illustrations. This is followed by an English translation
       and appendixes. The final unit is the full-color facsimile.

299   KING RENÉ'S BOOK OF LOVE [LE CUEUR D'AMOURS ESPRIS]. Intro-
       duction and commentaries by F. Unterkircher. New York: George
       Braziller, 1975. 14 p. Plates.

       This facsimile contains sixteen color reproductions of King
       René's allegorical romance of the heart as love's captive in
       a manuscript considered the "crowning achievement not only
       of French book illumination, but of book illumination in
       general. The painter was not satisfied merely to represent
       objects and figures in glowing color, he created a palpable
       atmosphere which gives life to everything contained on the
       page, whether nature's mood by day or night, or the charac-
       ters in the story." There are various manuscripts extant of
       LE CUEUR D'AMOURS ESPRIS and this particular one is the
       copy in the Austrian National Library which was probably
       completed in the "latter half of the 1460s." The original
       consists of 127 parchment pages. The facsimile edition has
       a brief introduction, followed by the plates and commentaries,
       and a one-page bibliography.

300   A KING'S BOOK OF KINGS: THE SHAH-NAMEH OF SHAH TAHMASP.
       Introduction by Stuart C. Welch. New York: Metropolitan Museum of
       Art, 1972. Distributed by the New York Graphic Society, Greenwich,
       Conn. 199 p.

       This is "one of the jewels of Iranian art" which was com-
       pleted in the second quarter of the sixteenth century. This
       facsimile contains many full-color and black-and-white illus-
       trations of this sumptuous manuscript.

301   THE MASTER OF MARY OF BURGUNDY: A BOOK OF HOURS FOR ENGEL-
       BERT OF NASSAU. Introduction and legends by J.J.G. Alexander. New
       York: George Braziller, 1970. Unpaged.

       A gem of a book of this beautiful medieval manuscript which

captures the color and brilliance of the original. This medieval manuscript is "outstanding among the many fine books illuminated in the Netherlands in the late-fifteenth century." This manuscript "from which a selection of pages is here reproduced" was done sometime between 1477 and 1490 and reveals "the technical accomplishment and the imaginative originality of the artist, who is known as the 'Master of Mary of Burgundy,'" which "has already made him one of the best known and most admired of medieval illuminators." This facsimile is reproduced "as nearly as possible actual size." There is a brief introduction to the house of Englebert of Nassau, followed by a selective bibliography and subject index to the plates. The concluding unit is the facsimile of the original in the Bodleian Library, Oxford.

302   THE MIRACULOUS JOURNEY OF MOHAMET. (MIRAJ NAMEH). Introduction and commentaries by Marie-Rose Séguy. New York: George Braziller, 1977. 158 p.

This is a fifteenth-century manuscript of the "mystical legend describing the marvelous visions that marked the stages of that miraculous ascension in the course of which, one night, the founder of Islam reached the Throne of God."

303   OLD TESTAMENT MINIATURES: A MEDIEVAL PICTURE BOOK WITH 283 PAINTINGS FROM THE CREATION TO THE STORY OF DAVID. Introduction and legends by Sydney C. Cockerell. New York: George Braziller, [1969]. 209 p.

This book contains full-color reproductions of forty-six leaves from an imperfect copy in the Pierpont Morgan Library, New York, with additional reproductions of two leaves from the Bibliothèque Nationale, Paris, and another in the collection of Dr. and Mrs. Peter Ludwig, Aachen, Germany. The book contains material on the book and its history, a selected bibliography, notes to the plates, and the plates with commentaries.

304   THE ROHAN BOOK OF HOURS. Introduction and notes by Jean Porcher. London: Faber and Faber, 1959. 32 p.

This French manuscript was produced in the early-fifteenth century and was probably executed in Paris for Yolande of Aragon, Duchess of Anjou and Queen of Sicily. It is considered one of "the masterpieces of medieval art." The name Rohan was given to this work because, early in its existence, it came into the possession of the Rohan family. This edition contains a text concerning this manuscript and eight color plates with notes.

305   THE ROHAN MASTER: A BOOK OF HOURS. Introduction by Millard Meiss. Introduction and commentaries by Marcel Thomas. New York: George Braziller, 1973. 247 p.

> A beautiful facsimile, in color and gold, this fifteenth-century French manuscript has been described as "one of the most surprising masterpieces of French art." It contains introduction 1 by Meiss on the art of the Rohan master and the manuscript, the problem of the patron, and the career of the illuminator. Introduction 2 by Thomas is concerned with the physical make-up of the book. Both introductions have notes. This is followed by the plates and commentaries by Thomas containing 127 full-color reproductions of "the sumptuous illustrations of the ROHAN HOURS" which "has rightly made it one of the most famous manuscripts of the first third of the fifteenth century. In its richness, its variety, its originality, the illustrations are truly exceptional." The appendix has a list of plates, list of related manuscripts and iconographic documents cited, and a selected bibliography.

306   THE TICKHILL PSALTER AND RELATED MANUSCRIPTS. Introduction by Donald D. Egbert. New York: New York Public Library, 1940. 232 p. 112 p. of plates.

> This book contains a brief study of the Tickhill Psalter followed by the black-and-white facsimile of this "treasure" of the Spencer Collection of the New York Public Library. This manuscript is "one of the outstanding Gothic masterpieces that have survived to the present day" having been produced in England in the early years of the fourteenth century. This is an unfinished manuscript and in studying its pages the reader can see the processes and procedures involved in manuscript production. The frontispiece is in color. Indexed.

307   THE TRÈS RICHES HEURES OF JEAN, DUKE OF BERRY. New York: George Braziller, [1969]. 29 p. 139 full-color plates.

> This magnificent manuscript was executed by the Limbourg brothers in the early-fifteenth century on commission for the duke of Berry and has become "one of the most famous of all works of art." The introduction and legends are by Jean Longnon and Raymond Cazelles, with a preface by Millard Meiss. The original is in the Musée Condé, Chantilly, France.

308   THE VIENNA GENESIS. Introduction and notes by Emmy Wellesz. New York: Thomas Yoseloff, 1960. 39 p.

> This is a brief study of an important Greek illustrated Old Testament manuscript which is one of the "main sources for the study of late classical book illustration. Its date is in

question but scholars have placed it somewhere in the fourth century A.D." This work probably originated in one of the eastern provinces of the Byzantine Empire. It contains eight color plates and notes.

309   THE VISCONTI HOURS. Introduction by Millard Meiss. Introduction and commentaries on the plates by Edith W. Kirsch. New York: George Braziller, 1972. 262 p.

This beautifully printed book is "the preeminent Italian example of the numerous surviving Book of Hours produced during the late Middle Ages, mainly in countries north of Italy, for the private devotional use of wealthy lay persons." The original is now in the National Library, Florence, Italy. Each plate has an accompanying commentary, and there is also information on the provenance and format of the Visconti Hours, related manuscripts discussed in the text, notes, and a bibliography. "Those who contemplate the pages of this book will find in them one of the gayest, most spontaneous, and most fanciful talents of Western illumination."

310   THE WINCHESTER PSALTER. Commentaries by Francis Wormald. London: Harvey Miller and Medcalf, 1973. 128 p.

An extensive study of this twelfth-century English manuscript called either THE WINCHESTER PSALTER or THE PSALTER OF HENRY OF BLOIS, and which is now in the British Library, London. This book contains a section on the history of the manuscript and plates in color and black-and-white, with comments and description of the plates.

311   THE YORK PSALTER IN THE LIBRARY OF THE HUNTERIAN MUSEUM, GLASGOW. Introduction and notes by T.S.R. Boase. New York: Thomas Yoseloff, 1962. 32 p.

This is a study of the notable twelfth-century English Psalter which contains one black-and-white, eight color plates, and a list of eighteen references.

THE INVENTION OF PRINTING WITH MOVABLE TYPE AND THE INCUNABULA PERIOD

For one thousand years the hand-produced manuscript dominated book production. There was little need for any other means of producing books because, although slow and tedious, this method was adequate to meet the demands of a limited reading public. According to Denys Hay, "the rising literacy of the fifteenth century was to make many more readers, so many more that the printing press was invented." A new interest in education and reading emerged which necessitated a method for producing books for an ever-growing reading public; thus the production of the hand-written and hand-decorated manuscripts of the medieval period would no longer suffice. With Gutenberg's invention of a machine or mould for making movable type and the application of this method to the printing press, the book could now be produced in quantity and at less cost than the time-consuming work of the scribes. According to S.H. Steinberg, "as 'adventure and art' Gutenberg described his epoch-making invention . . . and 'adventure and art' have ever remained the characteristics of the printed book, from its inception in the mind of the author to the finished product in the bookseller's shop and on the book-lover's shelves."

The period from the invention of printing with movable type, around 1450-1500 A.D., is called the Incunabula Period or "the cradle of printing." It is a time of great activity and experimentation in the mechanical aspects of the art and craft of printing. The techniques developed during this time were to be used by printers for the next three hundred years until the mechanization of the printing press and book production with the Industrial Revolution at the beginning of the nineteenth century.

This unit lists some of the books which examine this important period in the history of the book. There is an exception to the listing of items on individual printers with a few on Johann Gutenberg.

312   Besterman, Theodore. EARLY PRINTED BOOKS TO THE END OF THE
        SIXTEENTH CENTURY: A BIBLIOGRAPHY OF BIBLIOGRAPHIES. 2d
        rev. ed. New York: Rowman and Littlefield, 1969. 344 p.

        This work deals "specifically with the period to 1600/1640"
        and contains 2,389 entries. It has units on block books and
        books printed from type, which includes in addition to bib-
        liographies of bibliographies, general, select, and specialized
        bibliographies and library catalogs, with the special bibliog-
        raphies further divided by subject and country. There is an index
        to authors, subjects, printers, booksellers, printing-places, and
        public and private libraries. The number of items in each
        bibliography is indicated in brackets.

313   Bühler, Curt. THE FIFTEENTH-CENTURY BOOK: THE SCRIBES, THE
        PRINTERS, THE DECORATORS. Philadelphia: University of Pennsyl-
        vania Press, 1960. 195 p.

        This book contains the substance of three lectures given in
        April 1959 as part of the Rosenbach Fellowship in Bibliog-
        raphy, and examines the period of transition from the manu-
        script of the Middle Ages to the printed book of the modern
        age. In these lectures the author examines "the story of
        book production in that century and of the truly amazing de-
        velopment in the printing industry within a short span of fifty
        years." According to the author, the fifteenth century was
        one of the "most curious and confused periods in recorded

history, containing within it elements of both the old and the new, the last flowering of the mediaeval world and the beginning of our own modern age." It has a few black-and-white illustrations and extensive notes. Indexed.

314   Butler, Pierce. THE ORIGIN OF PRINTING IN EUROPE. Chicago: University of Chicago Press, 1940. 155 p.

The author states that "the origin of printing itself was but the first stage in the development of books as we know them. To understand the modern book one should know something of its history and comprehend the gradual process whereby it emerged from the pen-written medieval manuscripts." The work contains chapters on the cultural import of typography, the technological basis of typography, the earliest extant monuments of printing, the tradition of the printing offices, and the evidence of the manuscripts, and is intended "for the general reader" and "addressed to laymen." It has bibliographical notes, an index, and a few illustrations.

315   De Vinne, Theodore L. THE INVENTION OF PRINTING: A COLLECTION OF FACTS AND OPINIONS. New York: Francis Hart and Co., 1876. 556 p. Reprint. Detroit: Gale Research Co., 1969.

In its time this was a useful study and description of prints and playing cards, the block books of the fifteenth century, the legend of Coster, and the work of Johann Gutenberg and his associates. There are a number of reproductions of early types and woodcuts, and a listing of authorities consulted. It is still useful but other sources have replaced it. Indexed.

316   Fontana, John M. MANKIND'S GREATEST INVENTION AND THE STORY OF THE FIRST PRINTED BIBLE. Brooklyn, N.Y.: John M. Fontana, 1964. 112 p.

This popular edition, written for students, tells the story of Johann Gutenberg and the invention of printing with movable type, as well as a discussion of the work on the planning and production of the first printed Bible. It includes material "on notable printers of the incunabula" and is illustrated with black-and-white line drawings and a few photographs. No index.

317   Gerulaitis, Leonardas V. PRINTING AND PUBLISHING IN FIFTEENTH-CENTURY VENICE. Chicago: American Library Association, 1976. 190 p.

This book is based on the author's doctoral dissertation at the University of Michigan. It is an attempt to "evaluate humanism's penetration into social levels below the aristocratic and patrician elite and to ascertain the cultural atmosphere

among the bourgeoisie and its guiding lights." This is a
study of a "few, selected problems" in an analysis of the
"reading public's taste as reflected by the incunabula, the
books printed before the end of the fifteenth century." Three
chapters examine "the social context of the early Venetian
printing industry" and two chapters are devoted to a study
of the books which were selected for printing. The author
selected Venice for this study and analysis because "it was
the largest center of incunabula production not only in Italy
but also in Europe." It contains a number of charts and
tables and an extensive bibliography, but no illustrations.
Indexed.

318   Haebler, Konrad. THE STUDY OF INCUNABULA. New York: Grolier
       Club, 1933. Reprint. New York: Kraus Reprint Corp., 1967. 241 p.

       Translated from the German edition of 1925 by Lucy E. Osborne
       but with some revisions made by the author in 1932, this
       book attempts to provide "preliminary information on this
       special branch of bibliography"--the study of incunabula,
       the make-up and printing of the book, and its contents. No
       illustrations. Indexed.

319   Lehmann-Haupt, Hellmut. GUTENBERG AND THE MASTER OF THE
       PLAYING CARDS. New Haven: Yale University Press, 1966. 83 p.

       In this book the author put forth the thesis "that Gutenberg's
       creative dream included the mechanical reproduction of book
       illumination and ornamentation, rivaling the highest achieve-
       ments of medieval liturgical manuscript production." This is
       based on the close resemblance between a large number of
       miniatures painted in Mainz and the earliest known engravings
       by the so-called "master of the playing cards." There is a
       separate pull-out comparative chart showing newly discovered
       connections between the first engraved playing cards and the
       miniatures of the fifteenth century. The book contains a
       number of illustrations in support of Lehmann-Haupt's thesis.
       Indexed.

320   McMurtrie, Douglas C., ed. THE INVENTION OF PRINTING: A BIB-
       LIOGRAPHY. Chicago: Club of Printing House Craftsmen, 1942. Re-
       print. New York: Burt Franklin, n.d. 413 p.

       This book "is the product of the first attempt, within the past
       half century to compile a comprehensive bibliography of pub-
       lished materials on the invention of printing with movable
       types, which is widely and properly recognized as one of the
       great events in the history of civilization." It lists a total
       of 3,228 titles, of which 2,026 are separate or independent
       publications, either books or pamphlets, which were prepared

as an activity of the Works Progress Administration (WPA) of
Illinois and the Chicago Public Library Omnibus Project.
Unfortunately this book is hard to read since it uses type-
writer script and is poorly arranged. It contains a useful
key to locations and has an author index. No annotations.

321   Peddie, Robert A. FIFTEENTH CENTURY BOOKS. London: Grafton
        and Co., 1913. Reprint. New York: Burt Franklin, 1969. 89 p.

        This is a brief guide to the identification of incunabula which
        lists "all the important works dealing with the subject." It
        has material on "the printer or the place of publication of
        a book, all the available authorities will be found and set
        out, as also those dealing with type, illustration, water-
        marks, and all the other minutiae which go to make up the
        study of the fifteenth century book." A useful sourcebook
        of this period.

322   Scholderer, Victor. JOHANN GUTENBERG: THE INVENTOR OF
        PRINTING. London: Trustees of the British Museum, 1963. 32 p.
        Plates.

        Scholderer provides a handy pamphlet with a few color and
        black-and-white illustrations on the life and work of Guten-
        berg. This is one of the few exceptions to the listing of
        books on individual printers but since the invention of print-
        ing with movable type is so closely related to the man, it
        has been included. It has a unit of selected literature.

323   Schulz, Ernst. THE STUDY OF INCUNABULES: PROBLEMS AND AIMS.
        Translated from the German by Glenys Waldman, edited by Rudolf Hirsch.
        Biographical introduction by Bernhard Bischoff. Philadelphia: Philobiblon
        Club, 1977. 29 p.

        This is an updated version of Schulz's AUFGABEN UND
        ZIELE DER INKUNABELFORSCHUNG published in 1924. The
        thesis of this essay is that "the study of incunabula should
        not be restricted to purely typographic minutiae but should
        be incorporated into broader fields, e.g., the intellectual his-
        tory of the fifteenth century, the study of changing literary
        attitudes and reading tastes, the establishment of critical
        texts, and the like." A useful companion to Peddie's FIF-
        TEENTH CENTURY BOOKS (see 321).

324   Stillwell, Margaret B. THE BEGINNING OF THE WORLD OF BOOKS
        1450 TO 1470. New York: Bibliographical Society of America, 1972.
        112 p.

        This is a chronological survey "of the texts chosen for printing
        during the first twenty years of the printing art," which is

really a bibliographical study of value as a reference source. The main section contains a listing of 215 books and broadsides printed during these twenty years, but it also has a number of supplementary sections and appendixes. Indexed. Can be used with Gerulaitis' PRINTING AND PUBLISHING IN FIFTEENTH-CENTURY VENICE (see 317) which examines incunabula production in that particular city.

325   Wilson, Adrian. THE MAKING OF THE NUREMBERG CHRONICLE. Amsterdam: Nico Israel, 1976. 253 p.

A beautifully printed work which is the "first book in English on the entire production of an early illustrated book, from concept to distribution." THE NUREMBERG CHRONICLE was printed in 1493 by Anton Koberger and is considered one of the most profusely illustrated books ever printed. This book contains many of the woodcuts from the CHRONICLE, with a few in full color, and shows the layout of a number of pages and on the opposite page the final printed version. A wonderful analysis of the problems of book production in the late-fifteenth century. Has a bibliography. Indexed.

326   Winship, George Parker. GUTENBERG TO PLANTIN: AN OUTLINE OF THE EARLY HISTORY OF PRINTING. Cambridge, Mass.: Harvard University Press, 1926. Reprint. New York: Burt Franklin, 1968. 86 p.

This is a brief survey which "aims to be a statement of facts which have in most cases long been established, with as much of the newer conclusions drawn from these facts as seems to the author reasonably certain of eventual acceptance." It is useful for the general reader. There are a few black-and-white illustrations, but no index.

327   _____. JOHN GUTENBERG. Chicago: Lakeside Press, 1940. 38 p.

This is a lecture given at the University of Pennsylvania on 14 February 1940 when the author was the Rosenbach Fellow in Bibliography. It was undertaken to celebrate the five-hundredth anniversary of the invention of printing. The lecture attempts "to present a closeup picture of a man and a book that have, between them, cut quite a figure in the world." Presents a basic introduction to the topic. No illustrations.

328   _____. PRINTING IN THE FIFTEENTH CENTURY. Philadelphia: University of Pennsylvania Press, 1940. 158 p.

Examines early developments of printing in chapters which include John Gutenberg and the invention of printing, 1400-60; printing in Germany, 1456-80; printing at Rome and Venice,

1467-1500; the spread of printing over Europe, 1470-1539; and specialization, 1470-91, which looks at university presses, business, and bookshops. It has a few illustrations but no index.

THE BOOK IN THE RENAISSANCE

According to John Rothwell Slater, "printing did not make the Renaissance, the Renaissance made printing." The invention of printing with movable type provided the means whereby the ideas and concepts of the humanists were recorded and disseminated to an ever-growing reading public. This period saw the search for manuscripts and the collecting, copying, and diffusion of these manuscripts to the printed page. Frederick Artz states that the "humanists restored the whole surviving heritage of Greek and Latin literature, edited all of it, and, later brought out printed editions of the whole" and thus "brought back into the mainstream of western civilization the whole body of still extant Greek and Latin literature."

The process of printing with movable type meant that the printers could now produce books in quantity. Using as their models the manuscripts of earlier times the printers brought out editiones princeps of many of these books. From Mainz the knowledge and skill of the printer spread, first to Italy, then France, and eventually throughout western Europe and the world. The scholar-printers of this time were involved in the problem of language, textual criticism, and accuracy of text, and their work reveals a high degree of scholarship and concern for textual matters.

This unit contains a few books which deal specifically with the development of printing and its impact on the Renaissance.

329   Artz, Frederick B. RENAISSANCE HUMANISM, 1300-1550. Kent, Ohio: Kent State University Press, 1966. 103 p.

> Although this book does not deal specifically with printing, it is useful as background material to the times. It is a readable and informative examination of the medieval background; the early and later Renaissance in Italy; the trans-alpine Renaissance in Germany, the Low Countries, England, France, and Spain; and an interesting concluding chapter on the significance of Renaissance humanism. To understand the history of the book during this period it is essential to know something of the cultural, artistic, and intellectual history of this important period. This book provides a useful introduction to Renaissance humanism for the general reader. There are notes to the text, arranged by chapter, and an index.

330   Geanakoplos, Deno John. BYZANTIUM AND THE RENAISSANCE:
      GREEK SCHOLARS IN VENICE. Hamden, Conn.: Archon Books, 1973.
      348 p.

      This identical work appeared first in 1962 under the title
      GREEK SCHOLARS IN VENICE, published by Harvard Uni-
      versity Press. This book provides a useful insight into the
      "dissemination of Greek learning from Byzantium to Western
      Europe" by examining the background of Byzantium and Venice,
      the relationship between Crete and Venice, and the Greek
      colony in Venice, as well as the life and work of such dis-
      seminators as Michael Apostolis, Marcus Musurus, Desiderius
      Erasmus, and others, with a concluding chapter on the con-
      tributions of the Greek scholars. A scholarly but readable
      work, this is well documented with many footnotes, an ex-
      tensive bibliography, and a few illustrations. Indexed.

331   Goldschmidt, E.P. MEDIEVAL TEXTS AND THEIR FIRST APPEARANCE
      IN PRINT. London: Bibliographical Society Transactions No. 1, 1943.
      Reprint. New York: Biblo and Tannen, 1969. 144 p.

      A rather specialized work which examines the various me-
      dieval texts and traces their textual history through various
      editions. Indexed.

332   _____. THE PRINTED BOOK OF THE RENAISSANCE. 2d ed. Am-
      sterdam: van Heusden, 1966. 93 p. 8 plates.

      This book contains the author's reflections "on the Renais-
      sance movement as it expresses itself in the Book, and on
      the important part which the Book must have played in dis-
      seminating the appreciation of the new art forms among a
      wide European reading public. . . ." It contains three lec-
      tures on type, illustration, and ornament, with thirty-two
      figures in the text plus the black-and-white plates. Indexed.

333   Kenney, E.J. THE CLASSICAL TEXT: ASPECTS OF EDITING IN THE
      AGE OF THE PRINTED BOOK. Berkeley and Los Angeles: University
      of California Press, 1974. 174 p.

      This book is an attempt to "sketch between one pair of covers,
      and that not at great length, the history of the editing and
      criticism of classical texts from 1465 to the present day. . . ."
      This is "a short book on a very large theme." The method
      used was by "selective illustration" and the author states that
      this book will "succeed or fail in its object primarily on the
      merits of the selection." The book contains an appendix on
      "conservation and the apparatus criticus." There is also a
      unit of "works cited by author or short title" and an index
      arranged by passages, persons, and topics.

334   Proctor, Robert. THE PRINTING OF GREEK IN THE FIFTEENTH CEN-
       TURY. London: Oxford University Press for the Bibliographical Society,
       1900. 217 p.

       For the student with some knowledge of the topic, this is a
       useful, detailed, and scholarly study. The author examines
       the "history of Hellenic culture in Italy up to the time when
       the printing press began its work" in this "general survey of
       the early Greek press, touching on the principal groups of
       types, their relation to the writing hand on which they were
       based, the special difficulties which the printers had to over-
       come, and their methods and techniques, where they differ
       from the usual practice of the time." Proctor examines Greek
       printed books from 1476 to the end of the fifteenth century,
       and Greek printing in Germany, the Netherlands, France,
       Spain, and England. Illustrated with numerous examples of
       Greek printing. Indexed.

335   Sandys, John Edwin. A HISTORY OF CLASSICAL SCHOLARSHIP. 3d
       ed. 3 vols. Cambridge: Cambridge University Press, 1920. Reprint.
       New York: Hafner Publishing Co., 1967.

       A major work which examines the history of scholarship from
       the Athenian age in Greece of 600 B.C. to the nineteenth
       and twentieth centuries in Europe and America. He examines
       the materials of scholarship produced by the scribes of the
       ancient and medieval world and the printers of the modern
       world, as well as "the lives and works of individual scholars."
       It contains extensive footnotes and has some black-and-white
       illustrations. Each volume has an index.

336   Slater, John Rothwell. PRINTING AND THE RENAISSANCE: A PAPER
       READ BEFORE THE FORTNIGHTLY CLUB OF ROCHESTER NEW YORK.
       New York: William Edwin Rudge, 1921. 36 p. Reprint. New York:
       Battery Park Book Co., 1978.

       A brief but helpful look at the relationship between printing
       and the Renaissance, which studies the work of Gutenberg,
       as well as Aldus, Estienne, Froben, Koberger, and Caxton.
       Slater believes that "each of these printers stands for a dif-
       ferent aspect of the art of printing" but "taken together the
       books issued from their presses at the end of the fifteenth and
       the beginning of the sixteenth century form a sort of com-
       posite of the Renaissance." Has a few illustrations, but no
       index.

337   Taylor, Isaac. HISTORY OF THE TRANSMISSION OF ANCIENT BOOKS
       TO MODERN TIMES TOGETHER WITH THE PROCESS OF HISTORICAL
       PROOF OR A CONCISE ACCOUNT OF THE MEANS BY WHICH THE
       GENUINENESS OF ANCIENT LITERATURE GENERALLY, AND THE AU-

THENTICITY OF HISTORICAL WORKS ESPECIALLY ARE ASCERTAINED INCLUDING INCIDENTAL REMARKS UPON THE RELATIVE STRENGTHS OF THE EVIDENCE USUALLY ADDUCED IN BEHALF OF THE HOLY SCRIPTURES. New ed., rev. and enl. London: Jackson and Walford, 1875. Reprint. New York: Haskell House Publishers, 1971. 401 p.

> This rather lengthy title is an annotation in itself and states the contents. This book is an example of mid-nineteenth century scholarship and thought "on the process of historical proof" and especially as it relates to classical literature. No illustrations and no index.

PRINTING THROUGHOUT THE WORLD

After the introduction of printing with movable type it spread from Germany to other countries in western Europe and eventually throughout the world.

This unit contains material which traces the history of the book after the incunabula period and the Renaissance down to the present day, revealing the tremendous growth which took place from the wooden presses of the early-sixteenth century to printing in the twentieth century. In these five hundred years the press grew from a handcraft operation to the mechanical and computerized printing of today. Until around 1800 the printing processes were basically the same as that developed by Gutenberg. However, with the Industrial Revolution a major change took place in the mechanization of all aspects of book production, and as a result, production increased and the book entered the technological age.

The following are some of the materials dealing with the history of the printed book from about 1550 to the present day. Most of these items are surveys of these years of printing history, but in a few cases items on the history of printing in a particular country or region are included.

338   Aldis, Harry G. THE PRINTED BOOK. 2d ed., rev. and brought up-to-date by John Carter and E.A. Crutchley. Cambridge: Cambridge University Press, 1941. 141 p.

> A useful introductory study of the history of the printed book which includes the advent of printing; the spread of the art; the fifteenth-century book; the scholar-printers of the sixteenth century; English books, 1500-1800; the modern book; the construction of a book; illustrations; bookbinding; and the handling and mishandling of books. Aldis has an appendix on the development of type faces and includes a list of books for further reading, an index, as well as a few illustrations.

339   Brumfield, Brian, ed. DO BOOKS MATTER? Leeds, Engl.: Dunn and
        Wilson, 1973. 86 p.

        This book contains the papers of a conference held on 27
        April 1972 at the National Film Theatre by the Working
        Party on Library and Book Trade Relations. The theme was
        to study the whole value of books in our present society and
        was selected as part of the celebration of International Book
        Year. The seminar was promoted jointly by the Working
        Party and the National Book League, and included contribu-
        tors such as: H.R.H. The Duke of Edinburgh, Angus Wilson,
        Marshall McLuhan, George Steiner, Asa Briggs, Arthur Garrett,
        and Richard Crossman. The conference wanted to "highlight
        the conflict between scientific and technical developments
        in the world of mass media, and the everlasting value of
        the book not only for its content, but as a permanent physical
        object." The conclusion of the conference was that books
        do matter! A look at the book today in a thought-provoking
        volume.

340   Bennett, Paul A., ed. BOOKS AND PRINTING: A TREASURY FOR
        TYPOPHILES. Rev. ed. Cleveland: World Publishing Co., 1963.
        430 p.

        This is "a collection of over forty articles, poems, excerpts,
        and essays by the foremost practitioners of the art of book-
        making. This is a treasury of wisdom and wit to delight
        typophiles and bibliophiles, and to present a new and en-
        lightening view to those whose knowledge of books has been
        limited to their editorial content." The purpose is "that of
        informing on matters typographic, and on books, their print-
        ing and some of the fascinating steps along the way." This
        material was selected to "appeal to collector, printer, typog-
        rapher, and student," and includes items by McKerrow, Warde,
        Dwiggins, Ransom, Pollard, Grabhorn, Jackson, Gill, Goudy,
        De Vinne, Rogers, Updike, Ogg, and others. It covers the
        "history, theory, and art of creative book design." There
        are a few illustrations. Indexed.

341   Blumenthal, Joseph. ART OF THE PRINTED BOOK, 1455-1955: MAS-
        TERPIECES OF TYPOGRAPHY THROUGH FIVE CENTURIES FROM THE
        COLLECTIONS OF THE PIERPONT MORGAN LIBRARY, NEW YORK.
        New York: Pierpont Morgan Library, 1973. 192 p.

        This is the catalog for the exhibition held at the Morgan Li-
        brary from 11 September to 2 December 1973, of books which
        "illustrate the highest achievements in printing in the western
        world." The exhibit was assembled by Joseph Blumenthal and
        includes 112 books which he considers "represent the peak of
        elegance and accomplishment during the five hundred years
        to 1955." Blumenthal states that "after consultation with

respected colleagues, the collection as a whole seems thoroughly
representative of the heritage of the book." There is an informative essay on the great printers and their books, followed
by 125 duotone illustrations, and a selective bibliography.

342   Bouchot, Henri. THE BOOK: ITS PRINTERS, ILLUSTRATORS, AND
       BINDERS FROM GUTENBERG TO THE PRESENT TIME. New York:
       Scribner and Welford; and London: H. Grevel and Co., 1890. Reprint.
       Detroit: Gale Research Co., 1971. 393 p.

       This reprint is from the London edition. According to the
       editor H. Grevel, "the first edition of M. Henri Bouchot's
       fascinating volume, LE LIVRE, translated and enlarged by
       Mr. E.C. Bigmore, under the title THE PRINTED BOOK,
       having become exhausted, I have availed myself of the oppor-
       tunity to subject the work to a careful revision." This re-
       vision appeared under the title THE BOOK . . . which is
       a chronological study of the printed book from its beginnings
       to the nineteenth century. There are separate chapters on
       a variety of topics including bookbinding, libraries, the art
       of describing and cataloguing incunabula, and others. Has
       a Latin-English and English-Latin topographical index of the
       principal towns where early printing presses were established
       and a general index. It contains 172 reproductions of "early
       typography, book illustrations, printer's marks, bindings, nu-
       merous borders, initials, head and tail pieces, and a frontis-
       piece." Although dated, it is still useful.

343   Brown, Horatio F. THE VENETIAN PRINTING PRESS 1469-1800: AN
       HISTORICAL STUDY BASED UPON DOCUMENTS FOR THE MOST PART
       HITHERTO UNPUBLISHED. New York: G.P. Putnam's Sons; and Lon-
       don: J.C. Nimmo, 1891. Reprint. Amsterdam: van Heusden, 1969.
       463 p.

       This reprint is from the London edition of 1891. The book
       is divided into two parts; "first, an historical study of the
       Venetian Printing Press from its origin down to the fall of
       the Republic, based, in a large degree, upon the documents
       which form the second part of the book." This is primarily
       a chronological study of the Venetian Press, rather than a
       history of printing in Venice. It contains twenty-two repro-
       ductions of early printed books, and a list of the more im-
       portant works referred to in this book. Specialized and for
       the advanced student. Indexed.

344   Carter, John, and Muir, Percy H. PRINTING AND THE MIND OF MAN:
       A DESCRIPTIVE CATALOGUE ILLUSTRATING THE IMPACT OF PRINT ON
       THE EVOLUTION OF WESTERN CIVILIZATION DURING FIVE CENTURIES.
       New York: Holt, Rinehart, and Winston, 1967. 280 p.

       This work originated in the exhibition entitled "Printing and the Mind of Man" which was held at the British Museum and at Earls Court, in London, in 1963, and is an expansion of the original catalog. It provides a listing and information on a number of the more significant and important books printed during these five centuries. There is an introductory essay called "Fiat Lux" by Denys Hay. The main body of the work is arranged chronologically with a commentary on each item listed. It is beautifully printed with numerous illustrations. The exhibition and this catalog "presented an opportunity . . . of illustrating to the printing industry its own historical evolution and of reminding the general public what western civilization owes to print." Indexed.

345   Carter, Thomas F. THE INVENTION OF PRINTING IN CHINA AND ITS SPREAD WESTWARD. 2d ed. Rev. by L. Carrington Goodrich. New York: Ronald Press Co., 1955. 293 p.

The first edition appeared in 1925 published by Columbia University Press. This book examines the development of papermaking and printing in China and studies "the possible line of descent from Chinese to European printing." The review of the first edition in THE TIMES LITERARY SUPPLEMENT 27 (August 1925) states that Carter "does not attempt to demonstrate the exact route by which printing reached Europe; he shows rather that there were numerous possible channels, and leaves us with a strong impression that along some or all of them penetration must inevitably have taken place." Nelson A. Crawford in his review in THE NATION (7 October 1925) states "Professor Carter finds the transmission of paper across Asia into Northern Africa, and then to Spain by means of the Moors, unquestionable. Also there is every probability that European block-printing, first found in playing cards and image prints, came from China. There is only a mere possibility that the movable type of China and Korea, not so important there because of the form of the languages-- actually influenced European typography. Carter believes, however, that reports of travelers as to the great diffusion of books in the Orient must have been a marked incentive to typographical inventions in Europe." This book has chapters on the background of printing in China, block printing in China, the westward course of block printing, and printing with movable type. There are a few black-and-white illustrations. Each chapter has notes and an extensive bibliography, and there is a chronological chart on paper and printing and a list of words in English and Chinese.

346   Cave, Roderick. THE PRIVATE PRESS. London: Faber and Faber, 1971. 376 p.

In this work the author has "attempted to show some of the

different sorts of press which have been owned or operated by amateurs who have worked outside the conventional book trade channels in the past five hundred years." It contains eighty-three black-and-white illustrations and has an extensive bibliography and an index. It is much wider in scope and coverage than Franklin's THE PRIVATE PRESSES (see 354).

347   Chappell, Warren. A SHORT HISTORY OF THE PRINTED WORD. A New York Times Book. New York: Alfred A. Knopf, 1970. 244 p.

This is a presentation of "the aesthetic and technical considerations basic to the art and process of printing." Chappell examines prologue to the discovery of printing with movable type, the alphabet, and the processes of type cutting and casting. The chapters which follow are mainly chronological from Gutenberg to developments of twentieth-century graphic technology. Written in a popular and lucid style to "inform the layman and give pleasure to the typophile." There are many illustrations but no bibliography. Indexed.

348   Clair, Colin. A HISTORY OF EUROPEAN PRINTING. New York: Academic Press, 1976. 526 p.

This is an illustrated account which traces "the main outlines in the development of the craft of printing in Europe from the time of Gutenberg to the present day." Clair examines the development of printing in various European countries. "All the major innovations and printers are considered chronologically and in detail," although emphasis is on the fifteenth and sixteenth centuries. Clair includes many black-and-white illustrations and appendixes which include a chronological list of the establishment of presses in Europe--fifteenth century, and when and where the first books were printed, arranged alphabetically by city or town. Indexed.

349   _____. A HISTORY OF PRINTING IN BRITAIN. New York: Oxford University Press, 1966. 314 p.

This general history which emphasizes the technical developments starts when printing comes to England, successors to Caxton, and then chronologically down to printing in the twentieth century. It has a few illustrations and a section of notes, and an index.

350   _____, ed. THE SPREAD OF PRINTING. 11 vols. Amsterdam: Van- gendt and Co., 1969-73. Distributed by Abner Schram, New York.

This is a series of individual monographs devoted to the history of printing outside Europe in which each volume deals with a separate country or region. Included is the history of early printing in Canada; the Caribbean area; Malta; Greenland; Indonesia; New Zealand; Mauritius, Madagascar, and the Seychelles; India, Pakistan, Burma, and Ceylon; Australia; Iceland; and others. This series was most useful for an understanding of the history of the book in these areas which are generally not included in other histories and it definitely filled a gap in printing literature. Therefore, it is unfortunate that the series has been discontinued.

351   Ede, Charles, ed. THE ART OF THE BOOK: SOME RECORD OF WORK CARRIED OUT IN EUROPE AND THE U.S.A. 1939-1950. London and New York: Studio Publications, 1951. 214 p.

A look at developments in fine printing in Czechoslovakia, France, Germany, Great Britain, Holland, Italy, Scandinavia, Spain, Switzerland, and the United States in the areas of type design and lettering, printing the text, illustration and graphic reproduction, commercial binding and hand binding. It is a useful survey of book production in this eleven-year period, with many reproductions and, an index to the examples under artists, designers, and firms.

352   Escarpit, Robert. THE BOOK REVOLUTION. London: Geroge G. Harrap and Co.; and Paris: UNESCO, 1966. 160 p.

A translation from the French of the 1965 work LA REVOLU-TION DU LIVRE "with several minor modifications prepared by the author." Escarpit looks at books in the world today and examines the transformation that books are undergoing, showing how "things change swiftly . . . in the world of books." Although this work is a useful insight into the contemporary world of books, many of the major changes in book production have taken place after 1968 and so swift are the changes that even Escarpit is now a bit out-of-date. There are notes for each chapter but no index.

353   Febvre, Lucien, and Martin, Henri-Jean. THE COMING OF THE BOOK: THE IMPACT OF PRINTING, 1450-1800. Translated by David Gerard. Edited by Geoffrey Nowell-Smith and David Wootton. Atlantic Highlands, N.J.: Humanities Press, 1976. 378 p.

A translation of L'APPARITION DU LIVRE which appeared in 1968 published by Éditions Albin Michel. Febvre died before the book was finished and it was completed by his collaborator and disciple Henri-Jean Martin. This was the last book conceived by the French historian Febvre, which attempts to be not only a study of the technical preconditions but also of the "social pressures which shaped the epoch-making transition from the manuscript to the printed page in Europe." This is primarily a cultural history which traces the way by

which the advent of movable type "changed the way in which
men could think, by transforming the fundamental tool of the
scholar's craft and carrying the printed word into domains
hitherto untouched by the challenge of new ideas." This book
shows "how revolutionary the impact of printing actually was
in early modern Europe." The chapter on the book as a
force for change is a revealing study of how the book "played
a central role in the diffusion of knowledge of classical
literature at the beginning of the century and later in the
propagation of Reformation doctrine; it helped to fix the vernacular language and encouraged the development of national
literatures." There are extensive notes but no separate bibliography. Indexed.

354   Franklin, Colin. THE PRIVATE PRESSES. Chester Springs, Penn. Dufour
       Editions, 1969. 240 p.

       A study of the history of the private presses from the Daniel
       Press, the Kelmscott, and Ashendene, down to the period at
       the end of World War II when the author believes the private
       press movement ended. It has a unit on collecting private-
       press books and a select bibliography of private presses with
       a list of some recent auction prices and there are a few black-
       and-white illustrations. Indexed.

355   Grannis, Chandler, ed. HERITAGE OF THE GRAPHIC ARTS: A SE-
       LECTION OF LECTURES DELIVERED AT GALLERY 303, NEW YORK
       CITY UNDER THE DIRECTION OF DR. ROBERT L. LESLIE. New York:
       R.R. Bowker Co., 1972. 291 p.

       Contains twenty-two lectures selected from the many which
       have been offered in the Heritage of the Graphic Arts Lec-
       ture Series and which are presented "roughly in chronological
       order in terms of subject matter." There is material on
       Morris, Goudy, Koch, Ransom, Cleland, Gill, Morison,
       Mardersteig and others, as well as lectures on typography.
       No index.

356   Haas, Irvin. A BIBLIOGRAPHY OF MATERIAL RELATING TO PRIVATE
       PRESSES. Chicago: Black Cat Press, 1937. 57 p.

       This is a list of items pertaining to private presses and not a
       checklist of private press publications. It contains units on
       books about individual private presses, arranged by name of
       press; designers and publishers of private press books, arranged
       alphabetically by person's name; books containing data about
       private presses; reviews of private press books; catalogues and
       lists of collections, exhibitions, and auctions of private press
       books; bibliographies and histories referring to private presses;
       and articles in periodicals regarding private presses. Indexed.

The History of Books and Printing

357 Handover, P.M. PRINTING IN LONDON FROM 1476 TO MODERN
TIMES. Cambridge, Mass.: Harvard University Press, 1960. 224 p.

These are the lectures offered at the St. Bride Institute,
London, of interest to a wide-ranging audience from the
scholar to the printer and from the bibliographer to the
youngest apprentice. The chapters examine the book trade
in the sixteenth and seventeenth centuries; the Bible patent;
the periodical press in the sixteenth, seventeenth, and eigh-
teenth centuries and in modern times; jobbing; and the decline of printing in London. This book is more concerned
with the technical aspects than the historical. It contains
fifteen plates and numerous illustrations with notes and an
index to books and periodicals, as well as a general index.

358 Lewis, John. ANATOMY OF PRINTING: THE INFLUENCES OF ART
AND HISTORY ON ITS DESIGN. New York: Watson-Guptill Publications, 1970. 228 p.

A unique and unusual book which studies "the interaction
between the printing press and the artistic, religious, and
economic backgrounds of the Western World" in which printing "revealed itself as a reflection of the art, architecture,
and fashion of its time, showing the fluctuations of style in
these background changes." It is illustrated with 219 black-
and-white and color plates and has a bibliography (arranged
by chapters), and an index.

359 McLuhan, Marshall. THE GUTENBERG GALAXY: THE MAKING OF
TYPOGRAPHIC MAN. Toronto: University of Toronto Press, 1962.
294 p.

McLuhan's modern classic is "intended to trace the ways in
which the forms of experience and of mental outlook and ex-
pression have been modified, first by the phonetic alphabet
and then by printing." Not easy reading but provocative.

360 MacRobert, T.M. PRINTED BOOKS: A SHORT INTRODUCTION TO
FINE TYPOGRAPHY. 2d ed. London: Her Majesty's Stationery Office
for the Victoria and Albert Museum, 1971. 54 p.

This originally appeared in 1957. It contains a six-page introduction to fine printing and black-and-white illustrations
of some of the printed books from the sixteenth to the twentieth centuries and includes a brief select bibliography.

361 Meynell, Francis, and Simon, Herbert, eds. THE FLEURON ANTHOLOGY.
Toronto: University of Toronto Press, 1973. 359 p.

THE FLEURON was a periodical which was published from
1923 to 1930 and was devoted to fine printing and the practice,

theory, and history of typography. This anthology is a selection of some of the articles which appeared in that journal.
This book is beautifully printed with many color and black-
and-white illustrations and includes such contributors as Oliver
Simon, Holbrook Jackson, D.B. Updike, W.A. Dwiggins,
and others writing on a wide range of typographic subjects.
No index.

362 Moran, James. PRINTING PRESSES: HISTORY AND DEVELOPMENT
FROM THE FIFTEENTH CENTURY TO MODERN TIMES. Berkeley and
Los Angeles: University of California Press, 1973. 263 p.

This is a study of the technical problems of the printing press
and its progress in Germany, France, Great Britain, the
United States, and other countries. It is a look at "the
societal impact of continuous technical breakthroughs in the
dissemination of knowledge. . . ." There is a bibliography,
general index, and index of presses and machines, and many
black-and-white illustrations. It is also available as a paperback. (See also 50.)

363 _____, ed. PRINTING IN THE 20TH CENTURY: A PENROSE AN-
THOLOGY. New York: Hastings House, Publishers, 1974. 332 p.

This is a collection of thirty-six reprints from the PENROSE
ANNUAL covering the years from 1895 to 1973 including a
wide range of topics from process of magazines and book illustration to electrostatic printing. Profusely illustrated.
Indexed.

364 Morison, Stanley. FOUR CENTURIES OF FINE PRINTING. 4th ed.
New York: Barnes and Noble, 1960. 254 p.

This book has a brief historical introduction by Morison, but
this is primarily a book of illustrations, containing "192 facsimiles of pages from books printed at presses established between 1463 and 1924." In some cases the illustrations are
quite small and much detail is lost. However, this is still
a helpful visual history of type design and style in book
typography. It originally appeared in a folio edition, in
1924, and this is the cheaper edition for students.

365 Morison, Stanley, and Day, Kenneth, eds. THE TYPOGRAPHIC BOOK,
1450-1935: A STUDY OF FINE TYPOGRAPHY THROUGH FIVE CEN-
TURIES. Chicago: University of Chicago Press, 1963. 66 p. Plates.

Mainly a book of illustrations, this work contains 337 plates
of "examples drawn from Presses of Western European countries and America," which are arranged chronologically. This
is an updating of Morison's FOUR CENTURIES OF FINE PRINT-
ING (see above) in a more attractive format.

366   Morison, Stanley, and Jackson, Holbrook. A BRIEF SURVEY OF PRINT-
       ING: HISTORY AND PRACTICE. New York: Alfred A. Knopf, 1923.
       87 p.

           This is a brief overview of printing history presenting a sur-
           vey from its beginnings to the English Revival of Printing,
           and the revival in France and Germany. It includes chap-
           ters on printing in America, a short history of printing types,
           decoration in printing, notes on printing practice, and a
           short dictionary of printing terms. Eight illustrations, plus
           examples of type are also included. No index.

367   Norton, F.J. ITALIAN PRINTERS, 1501-1520. London: Bowes and
       Bowes, 1958. 177 p.

           Although a bit specialized, this book attempts "to bring to-
           gether essential information about the identifiable presses
           which were functioning in Italy in the years 1501 to 1520."
           The material is "arranged in alphabetical order of places and
           under them, of printers . . ." It has a chronological list
           of places of printing and a map of places of printing, and
           is followed by the text. There is also an index of printers.

368   Orcutt, William Dana. THE BOOK IN ITALY DURING THE FIFTEENTH
       AND SIXTEENTH CENTURIES SHOWN IN FACSIMILE REPRODUCTIONS
       FROM THE MOST FAMOUS PRINTED VOLUMES. New York: Harper
       and Bros., 1928. 220 p.

           This is a history of the book in Italy from its beginnings to
           the year 1599, arranged by cities and towns, and containing
           128 illustrations in color and black-and-white. Orcutt was
           a prolific author of books on printing, but most of his works
           are reminiscences of his experiences as a book collector and
           bibliophile and are not fully cited in this bibliography. These
           include THE ART OF THE BOOK (1914), IN QUEST OF THE
           PERFECT BOOK (1926), THE KINGDOM OF BOOKS (1927),
           MASTER MAKERS OF THE BOOK (1928), and THE MAGIC
           OF THE BOOK (1930).

369   Oswald, John Clyde. A HISTORY OF PRINTING: ITS DEVELOPMENT
       THROUGH FIVE HUNDRED YEARS. New York: D. Appleton and Co.,
       1928. 404 p.

           An overview of printing history consisting of twenty-nine
           chapters, including such topics as cradle books; John Guten-
           berg of Strasbourg and Mainz; Fust and Schoeffer; Anthony (Anton)
           Koberger, the first captain of the printing industry; the early
           printers in Cologne, Italy, and Venice; Aldus Manutius, great
           printer, publisher, and editor; Froben and Erasmus; the early
           printers in France; William Caxton and his contemporaries;
           from William Caslon to William Morris; early printing in

America; fine printing; private presses; paper; and the evolution of the printing press. It contains numerous black-and-
white and a few color illustrations, with a three-page bibliography. Indexed.

370   Peddie, Robert A., ed. PRINTING: A SHORT HISTORY OF THE ART.
       London: Grafton and Co., 1927. 390 p.

       A series of essays, by specialists, providing in a "concise and
       handy form" a "general comprehensive survey of the develop-
       ment of printing in many lands from its invention to com-
       paratively recent times" [1927]. Has an index of printers
       and places.

371   Plomer, Henry R. A SHORT HISTORY OF ENGLISH PRINTING 1476-
       1900. 2d ed. English Bookman's Library Series. London: Kegan Paul,
       Trench, Trübner, and Co., 1915. 330 p.

       The first edition covered the period from 1476 to 1898. This
       work examines the history of printing in England from William
       Caxton to William Morris. It is now out-of-date but still
       useful. Many illustrations. Indexed.

372   Pottinger, David. PRINTERS AND PRINTING. Cambridge, Mass.: Harvard
       University Press, 1941. Reprint. Freeport, N.Y.: Books for Libraries,
       1971. 143 p.

       Pottinger examines the invention of printing, the development
       of printing, the printer's tools, the evolution of type design,
       characteristics of a good book type, and the design of books
       and attempts to simplify the topic of "what is really a very
       complicated subject and to provide, as it were, a series of
       pages on which they could later hang more detailed infor-
       mation." There is a unit of further reading. There are only
       six illustrations. Indexed.

373   PRINTING AND THE MIND OF MAN: CATALOGUE OF THE EXHIBI-
       TION AT THE BRITISH MUSEUM AND AT EARLS COURT, LONDON,
       16-27 JULY, 1963. London: F.W. Bridges and Sons, and the Associa-
       tion of British Manufacturers of Printer's Machinery, 1963. 125 p. 32
       color and black-and-white plates. PRINTING AND THE MIND OF
       MAN: AN EXHIBITION OF FINE PRINTING IN THE KING'S LIBRARY
       OF THE BRITISH MUSEUM, July-September 1963. London: Trustees of
       the British Museum, 1963. 62 p. 16 black-and-white plates.

       This is the original two-part catalog of these exhibitions
       which was organized in "Connexion with the Eleventh Inter-
       national Printing Machinery and Allied Trades Exhibition."
       It was expanded and printed in a larger and more attractive
       format in PRINTING AND THE MIND OF MAN by Carter

and Muir (see 344). The purpose of the main exhibition at Earls Court was to assemble "the latest machinery, equipment, materials, and services available to the many crafts practised and processes employed in the printing and allied trades," and it was also felt that this would be an excellent opportunity to mount an exhibit which would offer "a survey of the history of printing through five hundred years as one of the most important applied arts of the Western world thus demonstrating, by means of a multiple display, the printing industry's debt to its historical past and the debt of civilization to typography." The catalog is mainly a listing of important items in the exhibit giving bibliographical information, as well as a brief comment on its place and importance in illustrating the history of western civilization "and the means of the multiplication of literary texts since the XV century." Both sections are indexed.

374   Ransom, Will. PRIVATE PRESSES AND THEIR BOOKS. New York: R.R. Bowker Co., 1929. 493 p.

This work is the pioneer study of the private press movement although updated with Cave's THE PRIVATE PRESS (see 346) and Franklin's THE PRIVATE PRESSES (see 354). Ransom's book presents "a narrative outline of private press history, [with] some considerations of its influence upon printing as a whole, and lists of books produced both in reserved personal endeavor and publicly in the same spirit." Ransom's work does not attempt to be comprehensive but discusses only those "presses distinguished for significant achievements or marked by certain human qualities of slight importance but considerable interest." The unit on private presses is a narrative history of private presses followed by "and Their Books," which is a checklist of their publications. The list is arranged alphabetically by name of press and is "complete and detailed to the limit of the compiler's knowledge and ability." Indexed. In 1945 Ransom published SELECTIVE CHECK LISTS OF PRESS BOOKS, reprinted in 1963 by Duschnes, New York, which was "a compilation of all important and significant private presses, or press books which are collected."

375   Steinberg, S.H. FIVE HUNDRED YEARS OF PRINTING. 3d ed. Rev. by James Moran. Baltimore: Penguin Books, 1974. 400 p.

This book appeared in 1965 and "has established itself as a standard work, being published in a hardback edition and translated into five other languages." This book attempts to trace "the close interrelationships between printing and culture" in a "concise and scholarly but entertaining account of the study of the relation between printing and civilization." (From THE BRITISH PRINTER.) Includes chapters on the first

century of printing, the era of consolidation, and the nineteenth century and after. Has a number of black-and-white
illustrations. There is a brief bibliography, notes, and an
index. A useful paperback for those who are interested in
an introduction to the history of the printed book.

376   Twyman, Michael. PRINTING 1770-1970: AN ILLUSTRATED HISTORY
        OF ITS DEVELOPMENT AND USES IN ENGLAND. London: Eyre and
        Spottiswoode, 1970. 283 p.

        This book is "concerned with the birth of modern printing and
        its development over the last two hundred years." Covers
        the period "toward the end of the eighteenth century, when
        the Industrial Revolution was gathering momentum and shortly
        before the old order began to be shaken by events in France
        and the radical ideas associated with them." Part 1 is the
        text which consists of introductory essays on printing history,
        while part 2 contains the illustrations of examples. Twyman
        has a select bibliography, an index of illustrations, and a
        general index. Unfortunately some of the illustrations are
        very small.

377   Wroth, Lawrence C., ed. "A History of the Printed Book." THE DOL-
        PHIN 3 (1938): entire issue.

        This is one of the best surveys on the history of books and
        printing in a readable and attractive study of the progress
        and development of the book to 1938. The five-hundred-
        page book is divided into four units, starting with the origin
        and development of the book--a chronological statement,
        which includes chapters on the heritage of the book, the in-
        vention of printing, the spread of printing in the fifteenth
        century, and separate chapters on the sixteenth through twen-
        tieth centuries. The second unit is on the printing house,
        tools and practices, a brief and general discourse on type,
        the history of the printing press, papermaking, and the author
        and his book. The third unit is on the adornment of the
        book, with a chapter on the illustration of books. The volume
        concludes with a summary of printing history and the literature
        of printing. Contributors include Lehmann-Haupt, Fuhrmann,
        Johnson, Rollins, Pottinger, Hunter, Hofer, Winship, and
        others. It contains 190 black-and-white illustrations. This
        hardbound issue of THE DOLPHIN might be hard to locate
        in libraries but it is worth the effort. Some of the chapters
        have a list of references. Indexed.

PRINTING IN THE NEW WORLD

Printing in the New World started in Mexico in the sixteenth century, to provide religious materials for the missionaries in the instruction of the natives in
the Christian religion.

In the English colonies, printing began in 1639 at Cambridge, Massachusetts,
with the establishment of a press by Stephen and Matthew Day. The early set-
tlers had left Europe for religious, political, social, and/or economic reasons,
wanting to establish a new life in a new land, and the concerns of these pioneers were with survival. However, as the land became settled and some peace
and stability were established, the press was needed for recording and preserv-
ing their records, for everyday needs, and the printing of books, newspapers,
and pamphlets. The press spread from New England to New York, and then
South and West. At first the material printed was predominately religious, but
there was a growing interest and need for literary works, scientific studies, histories, and political science. The press followed the pioneers in the move
westward, and in America the press became a powerful force in education and
politics.

With the American Revolution, the importance of the printer increased. Many
printers were leading exponents of the growing spirit of independence, and the
pamphlet and the newspaper "prepared America for the War of Independence."
The Industrial Revolution also had a tremendous impact on printing in the United
States with the mechanization of many procedures in the printing and allied industries. The need for more and more materials saw the ever-increasing growth
of printing and publishing to meet these demands. The technological age, started
in 1450 by Johann Gutenberg, continues down to the present day with the needs
of mass communication. Near the end of the nineteenth century, a new technological revolution took place with the emergence of the age of electric and
electronic media, leading to the new technologies and the world of the computer. These developments are still in progress and will bring about new techniques and machines in the continuing evolutionary history of graphic communication.

The unit contains a few items on printing in the Americas, but is primarily concerned with printing in the United States. Most of these items deal with historical developments.

378   Berthold, Arthur B. AMERICAN COLONIAL PRINTING AS DETERMINED
        BY CONTEMPORARY CULTURE FORCES 1639-1763. New York: New
        York Public Library, 1934. Reprint. New York: Burt Franklin, 1970.
        86 p.

        A brief study of colonial culture which examines "the rela-
        tionship which existed between the trends of thought and
        events that animated the colonial mind and the expression
        which they found through the medium of the colonial press."
        It has a bibliography but no index.

379   Blumenthal, Joseph. THE PRINTED BOOK IN AMERICA. Boston:
       David R. Godine, 1977. 250 p.

       The purpose of this book "is to trace the main currents in
       the development of the printed book in America and to pre-
       sent its leading practitioners." This is "the first comprehen-
       sive history of fine printing in America" to "document and
       illustrate the variety and quality of the 'devil's' craft from
       the Bay Psalm Book (Cambridge, 1640) to the numerous ex-
       amples of private press and fine trade books published in this
       century." Blumenthal discusses the work of Franklin, Brad-
       ford, and Thomas, as well as Updike, Rogers, Dwiggins, and
       Ruzicka, and examines the "perennial problem of production
       and distribution and concludes by exploring the condition of
       the typographic arts today." This is a sequel to his ART OF
       THE PRINTED BOOK (see 341). It has a list of plates for
       the seventy black-and-white and color illustrations and con-
       tains a selective bibliography. Indexed.

380   Hornung, Clarence P., and Johnson, Fridolf. 200 YEARS OF AMERICAN
       GRAPHIC ART: A RETROSPECTIVE SURVEY OF THE PRINTING ARTS
       AND ADVERTISING SINCE THE COLONIAL PERIOD. New York: George
       Braziller, 1976. 211 p.

       A work which attempts "to engage the reader and inspire him
       to further studies." This book "presents a selection of re-
       presentative examples and discussion of general trends; offer-
       ing highlights that serve to illuminate the larger subjects."
       There are chapters on colonial prologue, a new nation, growth
       of the Republic, mid-century decades, Civil War and cen-
       tennial era, the Gilded Age, a world power emerges, the
       golden days of advertising, and the contemporary scene. This
       book "delves into the intricacies of modern printing tech-
       niques and technology." It is profusely illustrated and has
       a selective bibliography. Indexed.

381   Lehmann-Haupt, Hellmut. THE BOOK IN AMERICA: A HISTORY OF
       THE MAKING AND SELLING OF BOOKS IN THE UNITED STATES.
       2d ed. New York: R.R. Bowker Co., 1952. 493 p.

       This book is divided into three units written by specialists in
       each period. Lawrence C. Wroth begins with a unit on book
       production and distribution from the beginning to the American
       Revolution. Rollo G. Silver continues with the period of
       American Revolution to the War Between the States. Lehmann-
       Haupt concludes with the period from 1860 to the present
       day. It also contains a rather extensive bibliography com-
       piled by Janet Bogardus of "sources used by the three con-
       tributors." A valuable study by these leading exponents of
       the history of the book in America. No illustrations. In-
       dexed.

382   McMurtrie, Douglas C. A HISTORY OF PRINTING IN THE UNITED
       STATES. Vol. 2: MIDDLE AND SOUTH ATLANTIC STATES. New
       York: R.R. Bowker Co., 1936. Reprint. New York: Burt Franklin,
       1969. 462 p.

       This is a "study of the introduction of the press and of its
       history and influence during the pioneer period in each state
       of the Union." The original plan was to have this history
       of American printing appear in four volumes, however, it
       was never completed and volume 2 is the only one which was
       ever published. McMurtrie's book was to have been "the
       first attempt at a history of American printing for 126 years,
       since the publication in 1810 of THE HISTORY OF PRINTING
       IN AMERICA by Isaiah Thomas," which he envisioned as a
       successor to Thomas. Even though this was the only volume
       published, it is still useful for the study of printing in Penn-
       sylvania, Maryland, New York City, eastern New York,
       New Jersey, Delaware, District of Columbia, old Virginia,
       South Carolina, North Carolina, and Georgia. It contains
       extensive bibliographies and notes, but there is no index
       since that had been planned as part of volume 4. However,
       Emilie Quast prepared AN INDEX AND BIBLIOGRAPHY FOR
       DOUGLAS C. McMURTRIE'S A HISTORY OF PRINTING IN
       THE UNITED STATES (New York: Burt Franklin, 1974), pro-
       viding the index to volume 2.

383   Oswald, John Clyde. PRINTING IN THE AMERICAS. New York:
       Gregg Publishing Co., 1937. Reprint. New York: Hacker Art Books,
       1968. 565 p.

       This book is concerned with printing in a broad sense and
       includes books and newspapers covering the Western Hemi-
       sphere, with emphasis on the United States. Arrangement is
       chronological in this study of the history of printing in the
       Latin-American countries which is limited to the pioneers.
       Contains many illustrations. Indexed.

384   Reilly, Elizabeth C. A DICTIONARY OF COLONIAL AMERICAN
       PRINTER'S ORNAMENTS AND ILLUSTRATIONS. Worcester, Mass.:
       American Antiquarian Society, 1975. 515 p.

       A rather specialized work of interest for its unusual and
       often quaint illustrations used by the colonial American printers
       in this "systematic examination of the ornaments and illustra-
       tions which appeared in books, pamphlets, and broadsides
       printed between 1640 and 1776 in what is now the United
       States." The purpose of this book is to "aid both bibliog-
       raphers and historians in their studies of the colonial period."
       It is arranged by subject, such as Biblical scenes, historical
       and genre scenes, angels, putti, urns, and baskets. Profusely
       illustrated, it also contains an index of printers and an index
       of dates.

385   Silver, Rollo G. THE AMERICAN PRINTER, 1787-1825. Charlottesville: University Press of Virginia, 1967. 189 p.

This book "describes the condition of the American printer
during the years 1787 to 1825, and his methods of work,
the equipment he used, and the policies by which he con-
ducted his business." Silver states that he has not written
a history of printing in America in this period but a "picture
of the craft of printing between the colonial period and the
arrival of mechanization." The six chapters include apprentices, journeymen and master; the printing office; the practice
of printing; printer and author; expansion of the press; and
typography and illustration. There are several black-and-
white illustrations. The appendix gives examples of sizes
of editions. Indexed.

386   _____. TYPEFOUNDING IN AMERICA, 1787-1825. Charlottesville:
University Press of Virginia, 1965. 139 p.

This study attempts "to extend the history of typefounding be-
yond the colonial period and to present a selection from the
specimens of the founders, thereby providing a useful tool for
those who wish to know more about the letter forms cast in
America." It contains information on typefounding as a per-
manent industry, some minor typefounders and punchcutters,
growth and expansion, inventions and patents, and the im-
portation of type and has thirty-six black-and-white illustrations. Indexed.

387   Thomas, Isaiah. THE HISTORY OF PRINTING IN AMERICA, WITH A
BIOGRAPHY OF PRINTERS. 2d ed. 2 vols. Albany, N.J.: J. Mun-
sell, 1874. Reprint. New York: Burt Franklin, 1976.

This is mainly a republication of the 1810 edition "in a corrected copy, left by him [Thomas] for a new edition." The
second edition claims to be with "Author's Corrections and
Additions and a Catalogue of American Publications Previous
to the Revolution of 1776." Although useful for the early
history of printing it is "sometimes inaccurate in its state-
ments." Volume 1 traces the early history of printing in
Spanish, French, Dutch, Portuguese, and English America
(now the United States), "down to the most important event
in the annals of our country--the Revolution," and it continues with the history of printing in the thirteen original
states, the new states, and the British colonies of Halifax
and Quebec. Volume 2 examines the history of newspapers
and magazines. There are no illustrations, but there is an
index at the end of volume 2.

388   Thompson, Susan O.   AMERICAN BOOK DESIGN AND WILLIAM
       MORRIS.   New York: R.R. Bowker Co., 1977.   258 p.

> A study of the impact and influence of William Morris on
> book production in the United States at the end of the nine-
> teenth and beginning of the twentieth century.   The author
> "documents in depth the real extent of Morris' influence on
> American book design."   Thompson contains 111 black-and-
> white "illustrations of bindings, title pages, type, and deco-
> rations," an extensive bibliography, as well as numerous
> footnotes.   A scholarly look at this phase of the revival of
> printing on this side of the Atlantic Ocean.   Indexed.

389   Woodbridge, Hensley, and Thompson, Lawrence S.   PRINTING IN CO-
       LONIAL SPANISH AMERICA.   Troy, N.Y.:   Whitson Publishing Co.,
       1976.   172 p.

> This is a revision and updating of Thompson's work which was
> published in 1962.   A brief but useful study of the earliest
> printers in the New World, it has units on the beginning of
> printing in Mexico, Mexican printing in the second half of
> the sixteenth century, the beginning of printing in Peru,
> printing in the "reducciones" of old Paraguay, the beginning
> of printing in the Rio de la Plata region, printing in Mexico
> and Central America in the seventeenth and eighteen cen-
> turies, the beginning of printing in old Granada, the begin-
> ning of printing in Chile, and the beginning of printing in
> the Spanish Antilles.   It contains forty-eight black-and-white
> illustrations, but no bibliography.   Indexed.

390   Wroth, Lawrence C.   THE COLONIAL PRINTER.   2d ed.   Portland,
       Maine: Southworth-Anthoensen Press, 1938.   Reprint.   Charlottesville:
       Dominion Books, University Press of Virginia, 1964.   368 p.

> A look at the first presses in the colonies which examines
> the printer's activities and attempts a "reconstruction of the
> physical aspects of his establishment as well as to affirm the
> general conditions under which he functioned."   The chapters
> deal with the colonial printer's tools and materials, the press,
> type, ink, and paper, and also examine shop procedure, labor
> conditions, nature of his product, and the remuneration he
> received for his efforts.   It contains twenty-four black-and-
> white plates and six line drawings, and there is an extensive
> list of works referred to in the notes.   Indexed.

Section 5

NONPRINT MEDIA

This section is intended to lend media support to this bibliography by providing data on sources, as well as a listing of nonprint media on the history of books and printing. This unit does not attempt to be comprehensive but to list some items which might be helpful in the study and appreciation of the history of the book.

Inclusion in this list does not imply availability, and each person will have to make that determination. Since quality varies considerably, it is essential to view each item before purchase or use in order to make a decision as to quality, value, and appropriateness of these materials.

The use of nonprint media can be helpful for an understanding of the history, techniques, and processes of books and printing since it presents visually the materials discussed and studied in the sources. This section provides some information on the variety and range of nonprint media for those who are interested in using these materials.

This section is arranged by media (films, filmstrips, slides, micro-publications, reproductions, overhead transparencies, and realia) and includes a listing of some sources, as well as individual items. Within each media unit the listing is arranged by headings and sub-headings, corresponding to the contents of this bibliography. The subject index will be useful in locating specific items.

It is difficult and often impossible to establish a date of publication for non-print media, especially slides and although various bibliographies, catalogs, brochures, and lists were checked for bibliographical information, there are some items which lack such data.

GENERAL NONPRINT MEDIA SOURCES

391   AUDIO-VISUAL MARKET PLACE: A MULTI MEDIA GUIDE. New York: R.R. Bowker Co., 1969-- . Annual.

392   INTERNATIONAL INDEX TO MULTI-MEDIA INFORMATION. Pasadena, Calif.: Audio Visual Associates, 1970-- . Quarterly. Incorporates FILM REVIEW INDEX (see 398).

393   MEDIA REVIEW DIGEST. Ann Arbor, Mich.: Pieran Press, 1972-- Quarterly. From 1970 to 1972 called MULTI MEDIA REVIEW INDEX.

394   NICEM. INDEX TO PRODUCERS AND DISTRIBUTORS. 4th ed. Los Angeles: University of Southern California, National Information Center for Educational Media, 1977.

395   PREVIEWS. New York: R.R. Bowker Co., 1972-- . 9/yr.

FILMS

Film Sources

396   EDUCATIONAL FILM LOCATER OF THE CONSORTIUM OF UNIVERSITY FILM CENTERS AND R.R. BOWKER. 1st ed. Edited by Willard D. Philipson and Emory I. Koltay. New York: R.R. Bowker Co., 1978.

397   FILM EVALUATION GUIDE. New York: Educational Film Library Association, 1946-64. Supplements, 1965-67 and 1967-71.

398   FILM REVIEW INDEX. 2 vols. Monterey, Calif.: Audio Visual Associates, 1970-71 (see also 392).

399   LANDERS FILM REVIEWS. Los Angeles: Landers Associates, 1956-- . Bimonthly.

400   NICEM. INDEX TO 16MM. EDUCATIONAL FILMS. 6th ed. Los Angeles: University of Southern California, National Information Center for Educational Media, 1977.

Materials and Techniques Used in Book Production

401   BASIC REPRODUCTION PROCESSES IN THE GRAPHIC ARTS. Graphic Arts Films, 1963. Color. 24 min.

This is a rather technical film which examines the basic
methods of printing in relief, intaglio, planographic, and
serigraphic techniques, with the emphasis on modern developments and mechanical methods.

402   THE BLACK TAMPON.   Film Images, 1967. Black and white. 26 min.

This film which was made in Holland but is available with
English narrative is a useful historical study of processes and
tools used in graphic art, which depicts the various materials
and techniques in use today and how they emerged from the
past.

403   THE BOOK.   Encyclopedia Britannica Educational Corp., 1955. Black
and white. 20 min.

A study of book production showing the variety of talents
and techniques which are needed in the task of producing a
book is presented.

404   BOUND TO LAST.   Produced for the Binder's Board. Manufactured by
William J. Ganz, 1936. Black and white. 18 min.

A rather out-of-date film for today's printing developments,
this is still useful for how book manufacturing was done. It
examines the stages in the production of a book from the work
of the typesetter, through the various stages, to the final
bound volume.

405   COMMUNICATION: STORY OF ITS DEVELOPMENT. Coronet, 1959.
Color and black and white. 11 min.

This study of the different techniques of communication, examines the history of writing and printing, and traces the history
of the alphabet and of the developments of paper and printing.

406   COMMUNICATION: THE PRINTED WORD. Informational Materials,
1973. Color. 18 min.

This is a presentation of the major developments of communi-
cating by the printed word which also examines the important
people in the history of printing, papermaking, and graphic
art.

407   FROM TYPE TO PAPER. Copley Productions, 1960. Color. 29 min.

This film studies the evolution of written records from ancient
stone carvings to the newspapers of today.

408   LOVE OF BOOKS. British Information Services, 1952. Black and white. 11 min.

    This is a brief look at printing in England from William Caxton to Eric Gill.

409   MAKING A BOOK. Eastman Kodak, n.d. Color. 17 min.

    This film presents the processes of bookmaking from beginning to end.

410   MAKING BOOKS. Encyclopedia Britannica Educational Corp., 1947. Black and white. 11 min.

    This film traces the entire book manufacturing operation from script to printed book, but is now a bit dated for modern developments.

411   A NEW ERA OF PRINTING. International Typographers Union, n.d. Color. 28 min.

    An overview of composition and the printing process is presented.

412   THE WONDERFUL STORY OF BOOKS. Institute of Italian Culture, 1970. Color. 10 min.

    This film examines the history of Italian books from medieval times, to Aldus and Bodoni, and down to the present.

Surfaces and Materials Used

413   GREEK PAPYRI. McGraw-Hill Films, 1970. Color. 45 min.

    This presentation of the history of papyrus also examines its method of production, and methods of treating, restoring, and interpreting the papyrus scrolls of the ancient world.

414   PAPER--GIFT OF TS'AI LUN. Hammermill Paper Co., 1956. Black and white. 33 min.

    Ts'ai Lun or Ts'ai Lung is considered the inventor of the process of papermaking around A.D. 105 in China. This commercial film examines his gift to the world and how it relates to papermaking in the mid-twentieth century.

415   PAPER, PACEMAKER OF PROGRESS. F.C. Huyck and Sons, 1945. Color. 28 min.

    This is an examination of "both the hand and machine processes" of papermaking, as well as tracing its history through the ages.

416   PAPER: THE MESSENGER OF MANKIND. Hammermill Paper Co., n.d.
        Color. 29 min.

> This film "takes viewers on a trip through forest lands, to
> show how trees are grown, how they are cultivated, and how
> the land is protected. Then on to the actual papermaking
> process--from pulp to the finished product--in one of the
> world's finest, most modern paper mills." The Hammermill
> Paper Research Center is also visited to see the testing of
> papers to safeguard quality, and "where scientists ponder new
> products--new ways to put messages on paper."

417   PAPER: THE PROLOGUE. American Paper Institute. Made by Gold-
        shell Associates, 1972. Color. 17 min.

> This fairly up-to-date study of the history of papermaking
> emphasizes its production today.

418   PAPER MAKING. Coronet, 1941. Black and white. 22 min.

> This film explains the papermaking processes by examining
> each operation involved in "turning trees into paper."

419   PAPER MAKING IN CHINA. Beloit Corp., n.d. Color. 25 min.

> Papermaking processes as used in ancient China and the tech-
> niques which were used then and which are used at the present
> time are examined in this film.

420   PAPER WORK. Champion Paper and Fibre Co., 1953. Color. 32 min.

> This is a look at the processes of papermaking and its manu-
> facture as a specialized field.

421   A SHORT COURSE IN PAPER MAKING. P.H. Glatfelter Co., 1948.
        Color. 35 min.

> This commercial film briefly examines the history of paper-
> making and concentrates on its production as a major industry
> in the mid-twentieth century.

The Alphabet and Writing

422   ALPHABET. University of Buffalo, 1970. Black and white. 29 min.

> An attempt is made to study the history of the English lan-
> guage system, as well as other writing systems.

423   THE ALPHABET: MARK OF MAN. McGraw-Hill Films, 1968. Color.
        20 min.

> This is an informative visual study of the history of the

alphabet in the "story of one of man's most important inventions." The film examines pictogram, ideogram, phonogram,
and their development from ancient to modern times, and also
shows examples of materials used at various stages of civilization.

424   DEBT TO THE PAST: LANGUAGE AND COMMUNICATION. Moody
Institute of Science, 1961. Color. 21 min.

An attempt is made to study the evolution of spoken and
written language, as well as to examine a variety of other
contributions of the past, such as mathematics, law and government, and architecture.

425   THE EARLIEST WRITING. Educational Services, 1964. Color. 11 min.

The earliest forms of writing on clay tablets and what they
mean is examined.

426   HISTORY OF WRITING. Encyclopedia Britannica Educational Corp.,
1950. Black and white. 28 min.

This film is a longer version of WRITING THROUGH THE
AGES (see 428) and is a chronological study of writing and
its impact of ancient civilizations.

427   MILESTONES IN WRITING. Department of Cinema, University of Southern
California, 1956. Color. 10 min. each.

This is a series of six films entitled PICTOGRAPHS, PAPYRUS,
THE ALPHABET, MANUSCRIPTS, PAPER, and PRINTING. Processes and techniques in which Frank Baxter narrates and
demonstrates the various production methods is presented.

428   WRITING THROUGH THE AGES. British Information Services, revised
by Encyclopedia Britannica Educational Corp., 1969. Black and white.
10 min.

An abridged version of HISTORY OF WRITING (see 426) was
prepared specifically for American audiences, in a film which
examines the effect of tools on the evolution of writing styles.

429   THE WRITTEN WORD. Department of Cinema, University of Southern
California, released by NBT Film Service, 1956. Black and white.
29 min. each.

This is a series of films showing the development of the book
through the ages. Narrated by Frank Baxter, the film titles
include SIGN AND SYMBOL; BETWEEN THE RIVERS; ALONG
THE NILE; THE BOOK TAKES FORM; KEYS TO THE MYSTERIES;

ABC'S; WESTWARD TO GREECE; THE BEAUTIFUL BOOK;
WOOD BLOCKS AND METAL TYPE; PAPER FROM CHINA;
NEW WORLDS FOR THE BOOK; VENICE, THE PERFECT
BOOK; PRINTING: FUEL FOR THE RENAISSANCE, and
DECLINE AND REVIVAL. It is rather extensive film coverage
of the history of books and printing.

Bookbinding

430 BOOKBINDERS. AFL/CIO, 1959. Black and white. 14 min.

Americans at work at binding and rebinding old books showing the "exceptional skill of the bookbinder" is depicted.

431 A BOOK BY ITS COVER. Iowa State University, 1968. Color. 12 min.

This presentation explains the procedures involved in hand
bookbinding, especially the "art of binding books in leather
with gold inlay."

432 FRITZ AND TRUDI EBERHARDT. Cinema Group Productions, 1970. Color.
27 min.

This film presents the various stages in the bookbinding process and reveals that "the craft of bookbinding is being kept
very much alive in America by a dozen or so bookbinders."

Book Illustration

433 ART IN WOODCUT. BFA Educational Media, 1962. Color. 19 min.

A demonstration by Jakob Steinhardt working on one of his
woodcuts reveals his concept and philosophy of the art of the
woodcut.

434 GRAPHISMES. Societé d'Éditions Photomechanique, n.d. Black and
white. 10 min.

This French film examines the techniques of Chagall, Matisse,
Rouault, Picasso, and de Segonzac in their work on the production of the illustrated "editions de luxe." It is an interesting, if brief, look at the role of these major artists of
the twentieth century and their interest and work in the book
arts.

435 LINES IN RELIEF· WOODCUT AND BLOCK-PRINTING. Encyclopedia
Britannica Educational Corp., 1964. Color. 11 min.

This film demonstrates the techniques of relief printing with
the woodcut, as well as a brief history of the evolution of
woodcut and block printing.

436   PRINTMAKING--FOUR ARTISTS, FOUR MEDIA. BFA Educational Media,
       1968. Color. 17 min.

> A useful film for beginners showing the work of four contem-
> porary artists demonstrating their work in woodcut, lithograph,
> serigraph, and intaglio. The artists are shown at work in
> each media, the process is explained, and the final product
> shown.

The History of Books and Printing—The Ancient World

437   LASCAUX: CRADLE OF MAN'S ART. International Film Bureau, 1950.
       Color. 18 min.

> Cave paintings of Lascaux in southern France depicting the
> art and lives of these prehistoric people is studied in this
> film.

The Medieval World

438   THE BOOK OF KELLS. Ulster TV Ltd., 1974. Color. 20 min.

> The work of the artists and scribes of eighth-century Ireland
> are seen in this film which examines the illustrated pages of
> this national treasure. The narrator examines the elaborate
> and highly decorative pages of the Book of Kells and ex-
> plains the influences, symbolism, and humor in this famous
> book.

439   IMAGES MÉDIÉVALES. AF Films, 1952. Color. 19 min.

> Available in French and English. This film depicts the life
> and times of fourteenth- and fifteenth-century Europe as seen
> through the paintings in the manuscripts of that time. It
> looks at medieval life, customs, traditions, and beliefs. The
> manuscripts are from the collection of the Bibliothèque Na-
> tionale in Paris. Medieval music provides the background
> with an informative narrative.

440   JEAN FOUQUET--CHANTILLY, 1420-1480. Les Films Michel François.
       Distributed in the United States by Time-Life Films, 1970. Color. 15
       min.

> This is an exception to listing an item on an individual since
> this film deals primarily with Fouquet's BOOK OF HOURS
> OF ÉTIENNE CHEVALIER and in his work as a major artist
> of that time.

The Modern World

441 THE COLONIAL PRINTER. McGraw-Hill Films, 1952. Color. 26 min.

This film set in colonial Williamsburg studies the role and place of the early printers in American society and reveals the important place which the printer held during that time. It follows the adventure of an apprentice and his work and activities in the printer's shop.

442 DIARY OF AN AMERICAN PRINTER, 1840. Stuart Roe, 1963. Color. 10 min.

This brief look at the life and work of the nineteenth-century American printer shows the role which the press then "performed as a means of communication."

443 GRAPHIC COMMUNICATION: WE USED TO CALL IT PRINTING. Peckham Productions, E.J. Du Pont de Nemours, 1969. Color. 23 min.

This film examines developments in modern printing and looks at "dimensional printing, computerized and photographic typesetting, color reproduction, printing of tablets, labels, cans, etc."

444 THE HISTORY OF PRINTING. Lennie Blondheim. Don Bosco Films, 1975. Color. 22 min.

Printing from its beginnings to modern times is examined. The film also takes a look at a collection of rare books and old printing presses. A useful overview for the student.

445 IN BLACK AND WHITE. Central Office of Information, London, 1951. Made by World Wide Pictures, 1953. Black and white. 20 min.

This is a history of printing in England which also examines the development of papermaking, typefounding, and the printing industry.

446 THE MAKING OF A RENAISSANCE BOOK. American Friends of the Plantin-Moretus Museum, 1969. Black and white. 20 min.

Filmed at the Plantin-Moretus in Antwerp in an attempt to recreate the world of printing at the time of Christopher Plantin, this film shows the methods which were used in typecasting and printing.

447 THE NUREMBERG CHRONICLE. Wesleyan University, 1967. Black and white. 22 min.

This film examines the NUREMBERG CHRONICLE of 1493

printed by Anton Koberger, revealing how this book reflects
the view of fifteenth-century man toward history and his world.
A showing of this film and an examination of Adrian Wilson's
THE MAKING OF THE NUREMBERG CHRONICLE (see 325)
would make a useful and meaningful unit in the study of
incunabula.

448   PRINTING THROUGH THE AGES. Encyclopedia Britannica Educational
      Corp., 1950. Black and white. 14 min.

      A brief look at printing and papermaking and its historical
      developments comprises this shorter version of STORY OF
      PRINTING (see below) which was made for American viewers.

449   STORY OF PRINTING. Encyclopedia Britannica Educational Corp.,
      1950. Black and white. 40 min.

      This film is a longer version of PRINTING THROUGH THE
      AGES (see above) which traces the history of printing from
      carved wood blocks to the transition from pictures to printing
      with letters and examines the contributions of Gutenberg and
      other leading printers.

450   SUBIACO 1465. Italian Cultural Institute, n.d. Color. 15 min.

      This is a study of the work of the first printers in Italy,
      Sweynheym and Pannartz, who came from Mainz to establish
      the first printing press, in Italy, at Subiaco.

FILMSTRIPS

Filmstrip Sources

451   EDUCATIONAL SOUND FILMSTRIP DIRECTORY. 10th ed. St. Charles,
      Ill.: Du Kane Corp., n.d.

452   NICEM. INDEX TO 35MM. EDUCATIONAL FILMSTRIPS. 6th ed. 3
      vols. Los Angeles: University of Southern California, National Infor-
      mation Center for Educational Media, 1977.

Materials and Techniques Used in Book Production

453   BOOKS--THEIR STORY. Jam Handy Organization, 1967. Color. 7
      filmstrips.

      A brief introduction to the study of the book which includes
      these titles: WRITING AND PICTURES; OUR ALPHABET; THE
      STUDY OF NUMERALS; THE STORY OF PAPER; HANDWRITTEN
      BOOKS; THE HISTORY OF THE PRINTED BOOK; and HOW
      BOOKS ARE MADE. Treatment is superficial.

454 THE GRAPHIC ARTS: AN INTRODUCTION. Educational Audio Visual, 1977. Color. 4 filmstrips with discs and cassettes, automatic or manual.

This set is "designed to introduce students to the technical, commercial and artistic possibilities of the graphic--or printed-- arts" and it "examines the role of the graphic arts on communications throughout history." It includes units entitled TYPOGRAPHY AND DESIGN; ILLUSTRATIONS; PHOTOGRAPHY; and FINE ARTS PRINTS, and has interviews with successful graphic artists which "highlight current trends in the graphic arts." Visuals include "numerous examples of typography and its uses, book and advertising illustration, photography as journalism and as an art form, and fine art prints." It has teacher's notes and the full text of the narration.

455 HOW A BOOK IS MADE. Educational Audio Visual, 1969. Color. 3 filmstrips and 3 records.

This is a presentation of each step "in the creation of a book, from author's manuscript to final production." The book used in Bishop's THE BALLAD OF THE BURGLAR OF BABYLON. It contains information on the book's editorial art, production, printing, and binding, and has a teacher's guide, as well as the full text of the narration, an overview, and glossary of production terms. The unit also contains a copy of the book.

Surfaces and Materials Used

456 PAPER AND BOOKS. Eye Gate House, 1953. Color. 26 frames. Phonotape and 1 cassette.

This is a classroom presentation for young adults on the history of the book from the Greeks to Benjamin Franklin. It also has a teacher's manual.

457 PAPER IN THE MAKING. Society for Visual Education, n.d. Black and white. 51 frames.

School-oriented survey of the history of papermaking.

The Alphabet and Writing

458 THE STORY OF WRITING. Webster Publishing Co., 1959. Color. 36 frames.

A series of drawings studying the history of writing from cave paintings to the dictionary of today is presented. Has a teacher's guide.

459 WRITING: ORIGINS AND DEVELOPMENT. Diana Wyllie. Released by International Film Bureau, 1968. Color. 44 frames.

> This detailed and useful study of the history of writing examines its development from ancient to modern times, and also looks at the changes and evolution of writing implements. The advisor for this set was the late David Diringer. Has a teacher's guide.

460 WRITING AND PRINTING. Curriculum Films, 1950. Color. 27 frames.

> A classroom study of the history of writing and printing and its role in the progress of civilization. Has a teacher's manual.

Type and Typography

461 TYPOGRAPHY TODAY. International Typographic Composition Association, 1973. Color. 115 frames.

> A look at various aspects of type production, its history, and the basic concepts of good typography.

Book Illustration

462 THE ART AND CRAFT OF PRINTMAKING. Educational Audio Visual, 1970. Color. 5 filmstrips with records or cassettes, automatic and manual.

> This is a useful introduction to the various processes and techniques involved in printmaking, giving a step-by-step presentation which examines the tools, equipment, and skills needed in relief printing with the woodcut, intaglio methods, lithograph, and silk screen. Has a teacher's guide.

463 EARLY ITALIAN ENGRAVINGS. Educational Productions, n.d. Black and white. Filmstrip or 20 slides.

> Italian engravings of the Renaissance are presented in this sampling.

464 ETCHING AND ENGRAVING. Educational Audio Visual, n.d. Color. 2 filmstrips with discs or cassettes, automatic or manual.

> This set examines "the history and techniques of this painstaking art." It starts with the fifteenth century and studies "the work of major artists up to the present." There is also a step-by-step presentation giving instructions "for mastering the necessary skills." Contains material on the INTAGLIO PRINT and TECHNIQUES. Has teacher's notes and full text of the narration.

465   A HISTORY OF GRAPHIC ART. Educational Productions, 1963. Black and white. 6 filmstrips.

> This is a companion to James Cleaver's book A HISTORY OF ART (see 167). The filmstrips can be integrated with this book since it is basically a filmstrip set which is identical with the illustrations in the book. The filmstrip titles are THE ROOTS OF BOOK ILLUSTRATION; THE WOODCUTS OF THE EARLY PRINTERS; COPPER-PLATE ENGRAVING AND ETCHING; POPULAR PRINTS, 1775-1825; VICTORIAN BOOK AND PERIODICAL ILLUSTRATION; and 20TH CENTURY ILLUSTRATION. Some of these visuals are small and quality is fair.

466   LINOLEUM AND WOODCUT. Educational Audio Visual, n.d. Color. 2 filmstrips with discs or cassettes, automatic or manual.

> This set studies "the development of relief printing to the present" and "details the evolution of materials, techniques, and styles" and also provides "instruction for creating and transferring images from wood and linoleum blocks to paper and fabric, and a history of man's earliest printing techniques. . . ." The set is in two parts, techniques and history, and also has teacher's notes, and full text of the narration.

467   NORTHERN EUROPEAN WOODCUTS AND ENGRAVINGS. Educational Productions, n.d. Black and white. Filmstrip or 20 slides.

> A companion set to EARLY ITALIAN ENGRAVINGS (see 463) presenting a brief look at the work of the graphic artists of Germany.

468   SILK SCREEN. Educational Audio Visual, n.d. Color. 2 filmstrips with discs or cassettes, automatic or manual.

> Students are introduced first to the tools, materials, and techniques of silk-screen printing, and then to its history in this look at the "development of the silk stencil in the 18th century up to today." Teacher's notes and full text of the narration are included.

The History of Books and Printing—General Works

469   OUR LITERARY HERITAGE. Made by George and Suzanne Russell. Educational Filmstrips, 1970. Color. 6 filmstrips with cassettes. 396 frames.

> Treatment is basic in this set which includes THE ORIGINS OF WRITING, ORIGIN OF THE ALPHABET, CLASSICAL BOOKS AND LIBRARIES, MONASTICISM AND THE BOOK, THE BOOK DURING THE ISLAMIC NAISSANCE AND THE EUROPEAN RENAISSANCE, and THE DEVELOPMENT AND DISSEMINATION OF PRINTING.

Nonprint Media

The Ancient World

470   DEBT TO THE PAST. Moody Institute of Science, 1969. Color. 2 filmstrips. 94 frames.

> This is a basic introduction to the influence of the Egyptians on writing and its spread throughout the Near East, as well as a unit on the Semites and their contribution to the development of the alphabet and writing.

The Medieval World

471   APOCALYPSES. EP Microform, n.d. Color. Filmstrip.

> Selections from the DOUCE APOCALYPSE and other thirteenth-century manuscripts are included.

472   BIBLE. EP Microform, n.d. Color. Filmstrip.

> Visuals from a mid-thirteenth-century English Bible in the Bodleian Library, Oxford, are presented.

473   BURGUNDIAN MANUSCRIPTS FROM CHATSWORTH HOUSE. EP Microform, n.d. Color. Filmstrip.

> A few examples of the magnificent manuscripts produced in the duchy of Burgundy are given.

474   CAEDMON GENESIS. EP Microform, n.d. Filmstrip.

> The manuscript is in the Bodleian Library, Oxford, and this set contains visuals, from that book, on the fall of Lucifer and the incidents of Genesis 1 and 2, with notes.

475   THE CANTERBURY PSALTER. EP Microform, n.d. Color. Filmstrip.

> This manuscript was written "about 1150 at Canterbury by a monk named Eadwine" and is a fine example of the Romanesque style as it developed in England.

476   THE COMING OF CHRIST. EP Microform, n.d. Filmstrip.

> This is from the gospels of Emperor Henry II showing the Incarnation which is "presented as a drama of tremendous import" and also scenes from the Last Judgment are covered. Notes are included.

477   DAVID AND GOLIATH. EP Microform, n.d. Filmstrip.

> Illustrations of the Old Testament from a French manuscript. Includes notes.

478   GOTHIC SCRIPT FROM BODLEIAN MANUSCRIPTS. EP Microform, n.d.
Color. Firmstrip. 25 frames.

"A selection from six mediaeval manuscripts" is presented.

479   ILLUMINATED MANUSCRIPTS. Budek, 1960. Black and white. 40 frames.

This set might be useful for a study of composition and design but reproductions of illuminated manuscripts in black and
white leave something to be desired. It contains examples
of manuscripts from the late antique period to 1400.

480   ILLUMINATED MANUSCRIPTS OF THE ISLAMIC ORIENT: MASTERS,
SCHOOLS AND WORKS. Budek, 1960. Black and white. 3 filmstrips, 42 frames each.

It is unfortunate that the richness of color of these manuscripts
is not reproduced since black and white can hardly reveal
the beauty of the originals. There are units of Arabian manuscripts, Persian manuscripts, and Turkish illuminated manuscripts, with a teacher's manual.

481   LIFE OF ST. ALBAN. EP Microform, n.d. Filmstrip.

This is from the manuscript of Matthew Paris showing the
"exquisite drawings of the great 15th century draughtsman
and historian." Notes are included.

482   THE LIFE OF ST. CUTHBERT. EP Microform, n.d. Color. Filmstrip.

A twelfth-century English manuscript of "vivid pictures illustrating Bede's life of the Saint."

483   LIFE OF ST. EDWARD THE CONFESSOR. EP Microform, n.d. Filmstrip.

This is another manuscript of Matthew Paris. Notes are included.

484   MEDIAEVAL BACKGROUND FROM THE BODLEIAN ILLUMINATED MANU-
SCRIPTS. EP Microform, n.d. Color. 37 filmstrips. 826 frames.

An extensive collection from THE ROMANCE OF ALEXANDER:
ENGLISH ROMANESQUE ILLUMINATION, and BESTIARIES,
as well as selections from manuscripts of individual themes
such as scenes from daily life, sports and pastimes, hawking
and hunting, musical instruments, medieval food and feast-
ing, occupations of the months, herbal and bestiaries, games
and toys, games and children, children, fools, domestic
equipment, dancing, costume, professions, town life, ships
and seafaring, warfare, transportation, symbolism, and build-
ings and architecture. An interesting look at medieval life
through the pages of its manuscripts.

485 MIRACLES AND PARABLES OF OUR LORD. EP Microform, n.d. Filmstrip.

> This is from the gospels of Emperor Henry II which is a German manuscript of the eleventh century. This set contains reproductions of twenty miracles and four parables; has notes.

486 PAGES FROM MS DOUCE 293. EP Microform, n.d. Color. Filmstrip.

> An English Psalter probably executed at Durham. The manuscript is now in the Bodleian Library, Oxford.

487 PSALMS. EP Microform, n.d. Filmstrip.

> Selections from an eleventh-century manuscript.

488 SCRIPTURE PICTURES FROM THE BODLEIAN ILLUMINATED MANUSCRIPTS. EP Microform, n.d. Color. 14 filmstrips. 642 frames.

> This set contains materials from English, Byzantine, and Romanesque manuscripts, as well as from such topics as life of Christ, treasures of Corpus Christi College, Bible iconography, Bible historiale, Bible moralisée, Franciscan missal, miracles of Christ, baptism, Psalter, and Adam and Eve.

489 STORIES OF . . . GIDEON, SAMSON AND RUTH. EP Microform, n.d. Filmstrip.

> These illustrations are from an Old Testament located in a French manuscript. Notes are included.

The Modern World

490 THE INVENTION OF PRINTING. Encyclopedia Britannica Educational Corp. Made by Producers Color Service, 1968. Color. 65 frames.

> This set examines the impact of the printing press on the cultural and intellectual world of western Europe.

SLIDES

Slide Sources

491 De Laurier, Nancy, ed. THE 1976 SLIDE BUYER'S GUIDE. New York: College Art Association, 1976.

492 NICEM. INDEX TO EDUCATIONAL SLIDES. 3d ed. Los Angeles: University of Southern California, National Information Center for Educational Media, 1977.

Other Sources of Slides

COMMERCIAL SOURCES: Dealers such as Prothmann Associates, Sandak, American Library Color Slide Co., and others provide a wide range and variety of 2 x 2 slides for purchase. Check NICEM listing of distributors and producers for more information, as well as the catalogs of these and other slide companies.

LIBRARIES AND MUSEUMS: Many libraries and museums have slides available for purchase. These are usually items from their collections which are made available for general use. Check with each institution for availability and price. See listing of LIBRARIES, SPECIAL COLLECTIONS, AND MUSEUMS (p. 157) for possible sources.

PRODUCTION OF SLIDES: It is possible to make slides from books and plates and to develop a personal collection, especially of items which are not available through commercial or institutional sources. However, the quality of the original will determine the quality of the slide, and even with the best reproduction the resultant slide will be fair. It is extremely difficult, if not impossible, to obtain permission to make slides from original materials because of the fragile nature of many of these items and the professional knowledge of photography needed for such work. Problem of copyright might be involved and should be checked by each individual. The Kodak Ektagraphic Visualmaker is useful for the amateur photographer interested in making slides from books. Actually the production of one's own slides is mainly to supplement materials not available from regular sources.

Materials and Techniques Used in Book Production

493   CALLIGRAPHY AND WRITING MATERIALS. Unit six of FINE EXAMPLES OF CHINESE ARTS AND CRAFTS SERIES. Budek, n.d. Color. 38 slides.

> This is a selection from the National Library at Taipei which is useful for an understanding of Chinese culture and especially the art of the calligrapher.

494   HIEROGLYPHICS AS DECORATION. Visual Media, n.d. Color. 18 slides.

> The decorative nature of the ancient Egyptian writing is discussed.

Book Illustration

495   AMERICAN GRAPHIC ART. Educational Audio Visual, n.d. Color. 12 slides.

496   DEVELOPMENT OF BOOK ILLUSTRATION. Prothmann Associates, n.d. Black and white. 24 slides.

497   GRAPHICS: PRINTING MEDIA AND PROCESSES. Sandak, 1971.
       Color. 90 slides.

> This slide set "illustrates the basic creative procedures of the
> various graphic processes and acquaints the student with the
> visual characteristics of the resulting print." It gives ex-
> amples of leading graphic artists, and examines the relief
> process, intaglio, metal engraving, drypoint etching, hard-
> and soft-ground etching, aquatint, planographic processes,
> and others.

498   HISTORY OF THE WOODCUT. Prothmann Associates, n.d. Black and
       white. 24 slides.

499   HOW PRINTS ARE MADE. Budek, n.d. Color. 75 slides.

> A step-by-step demonstration of three different processes, in-
> taglio, relief, and planographic, is presented.

Bookbinding

500   FRENCH BOOKBINDING FROM THE 16TH CENTURY TO THE PRESENT.
       Society for French-American Cultural Services and Educational Aid, 1959.
       Color. 32 slides, with text.

> Examples of bindings from the collection of the Bibliothèque
> Nationale, Paris, are included.

The History of Books and Printing—The Ancient World

501   THE BOOK OF THE DEAD. American Library Color Slide Co., n.d.
       Color. 10 slides.

> The rituals observed by the ancient Egyptians in this funeral
> papyrus of 1025 B.C. from Thebes are depicted in this set.

502   CAVE PAINTINGS. Sandak, 1973. Color. 30 slides.

> Visuals from the "renowned paintings and reliefs from the
> Spanish caves of Altamira and Castillo, and the caves of
> Lascaux, in France."

503   EGYPTIAN MINOR ARTS--WRITING. American Library Color Slide Co.,
       n.d. Color. 12 slides.

> Examples of Egyptian writing from the Book of the Dead and
> funerary papyrus are included.

504   LASCAUX: PAINTINGS. Visual Media, n.d. Color. 48 slides.

505   MESOPOTAMIAN MINOR ARTS--WRITING.   American Library Color
        Slide Co., n.d.   Color.   2 slides.

        Examples of a cuneiform clay tablet and a Dead Sea scroll
        are included.

506   PALEOLITHIC CAVE PAINTING.   SPAIN.   Educational Audio Visual,
        n.d.   Color.   13 slides.

        Views from the caves at Altamira in Spain.

507   PALEOLITHIC CAVE PAINTINGS.   American Library Color Slide Co.,
        n.d.   Color.   20 slides.

        Examples of the animal paintings at Altamira, Lascaux, Niaux,
        and other caves in Spain and France.   Depicts the art of
        over 20,000 years ago.

508   PAPYRI.   Cultural History Resources, 1969.   Color.   63 slides.

509   STONE AGE SANCTUARY AT LASCAUX.   American Library Color Slide
        Co., n.d.   Color.   20 slides.

        Detailed views of the cows, bison, horses, reindeer, and
        other objects depicted on the caves at Lascaux.

The Medieval World

510   THE BROOKE ANTIPHONAL.   Colour Centre Slides, n.d.   Color.   8
        slides.

511   BYZANTINE MANUSCRIPT ILLUMINATION.   Visual Media, n.d.   Color.
        6 slides.

512   BYZANTINE MINOR ARTS--MANUSCRIPTS (BOOK ILLUMINATIONS).
        American Library Color Slide Co., 1968.   Color.   24 slides.

        The influence of Byzantine illumination on Western manuscripts
        was important and significant and in order to fully understand
        the development of the book in the West, it is also necessary
        to examine the book in the Near and Far East.   This set
        covers the period from the ninth to the fifteenth centuries.

513   CAROLINGIAN ILLUMINATED MANUSCRIPTS.   Visual Media, n.d.
        Color.   36 slides.

514   THE CAROLINGIAN SCHOOLS OF MANUSCRIPT ILLUMINATION.
        American Library Color Slide Co., 1968.   Color.   17 slides.

A few examples of the medieval manuscript during the reign of Charlemagne and the renaissance of the eighth and ninth centuries.

515   CHRONICLE OF THE COUNTS OF HAINAULT.   Educational Productions, n.d.   Black and white.   6 slides.

516   THE CLASSIC TRADITION IN EARLY MANUSCRIPTS.   American Library Color Slide Co., n.d.   Color.   11 slides.

A study of some of the manuscripts of the classical world during the late antique period.

517   DEVELOPMENT OF THE EARLY GERMAN SCHOOLS OF BOOK ILLU-MINATION.   American Library Color Slide Co., n.d.   Color.   17 slides.

Shows the evolution in the development of the medieval manuscript from Carolingian to Ottonian times.

518   DUTCH MINOR ARTS--MANUSCRIPTS.   American Library Color Slide Co., n.d.   Color.   3 slides.

A few examples of Dutch manuscripts of the early Renaissance, namely the fifteenth century.

519   EARLY CHRISTIAN MINOR ARTS (BOOK ILLUMINATIONS).   American Library Color Slide Co., n.d.   Color.

Contains the following units:
Late Classic. 4th-7th centuries. 14 slides.
Celtic-Anglo Saxon. 7th-10th centuries. 16 slides.
Book of Kells. 8th century. Dublin Trinity College Library. 48 slides.
Merovingian. 7th-8th centuries. 5 slides.
Carolingian. 8th-10th centuries. 23 slides.
Ottonian. 10th-11th centuries. 16 slides.
THE GOLDEN GOSPELS OF ECHTERNACH. c. A.D. 1035-40 Nuremberg. 15 slides.

520   ENGLISH ILLUMINATED MANUSCRIPTS.   Visual Media, n.d.   Color. 12 slides.

521   ENGLISH MANUSCRIPTS.   Colour Centre Slides, n.d.   Color.

Contains the following:
AELFRIC'S PENTATEUCH. 10 slides.
THE AMESBURY PSALTER. 19 slides.
AN ANGLO-SAXON CALENDAR AND MARVELS OF THE EAST. 22 slides.

THE BURY BIBLE. 32 slides.
THE CALIGULA TROPER. 17 slides.
THE CHRONICA MAJORA OF MATTHEW PARIS. 61 slides.
THE DOUCE APOCALYPSE. 20 slides.
THE DOVER BIBLE. 50 slides.
THE EADWINE PSALTER. 50 slides.
THE ETON APOCALYPSE. 25 slides.
THE HUNTERIAN PSALTER. 44 slides.
THE LAMBETH BIBLE. 50 slides.
LIBER REGALIS. 10 slides.
THE LIFE OF ST. EDWARD. 46 slides.
MARCO POLO: LES LIVRES DE GRAUNT CAAM. 15 slides.
THE ORMESBY PSALTER. 36 slides.
THE PSALTER OF ROBERT DE LINDESEYE. 15 slides.
THE ST. CHAD GOSPELS. 22 slides.
THE SHAFTESBURY PSALTER. 15 slides.
THE WESTMINSTER BESTIARY. 30 slides.
THE WINCHESTER BIBLE. 50 slides.

522   ENGLISH MINOR ARTS--MANUSCRIPTS (BOOK ILLUMINATIONS).
American Library Color Slide Co., n.d. Color.

10th-11th centuries Romanesque. LIFE OF ST. EDMUND
(XII). New York, Morgan Library. 6 slides.
LAMBETH BIBLE. 11 slides.
PSALTER OF WESTMINSTER ABBEY. 5 slides.
Other Manuscripts. 7 slides.
13th century (Gothic). 5 slides.
14th century (Gothic). 5 slides.
15th century (Late Gothic). BEDFORD HOURS (c. 1420).
Vienna, National Library. 24 slides.
Other Manuscripts. 1 slide.

523   ETHIOPIAN MANUSCRIPT PAINTING. British Library, n.d. Color.
15 slides.

This is a slide booklet containing the slides and commentary
by R.K. Hosking.

524   FLEMISH GOTHIC ILLUMINATED MANUSCRIPTS. Visual Media, n.d.
Color. 18 slides.

525   FLEMISH MINOR ARTS--MANUSCRIPTS (BOOK ILLUMINATIONS).
American Library Color Slide Co., n.d. Color.

Contains units on:
13th century. (Gothic). 1 slide.
15th century. (Early Renaissance). GRIMANI BREVIARY.
Venice, S. Marco Library. 8 slides.

16th century. (Renaissance). BOOK OF HOURS. London, British Museum. 8 slides. DA COSTA BOOK OF HOURS (1515). New York, Morgan Library. 2 slides.

526   FRENCH AND SPANISH MANUSCRIPTS OF THE PRE-ROMANESQUE PERIOD. American Library Color Slide Co., 1968. Color. 14 slides.

Examples of primitive Christian art in France and Spain in the period prior to A.D. 1000.

527   FRENCH MINOR ARTS--MANUSCRIPTS (BOOK ILLUMINATIONS). American Library Color Slide Co., n.d. Color.

An extensive collection which includes:
13th century. (Gothic). 8 slides.
14th century. (Late Gothic). 2 slides.
BOOK OF HUNT OF GASTON PHEBUS. Paris, Bibliothèque Nationale. 2 slides.
GRANDES CHRONIQUES DE FRANCE (1380). Paris, Bibliothèque, Nationale. 5 slides.
Other Manuscripts. 5 slides.
15th century. (Early Renaissance). BELLES HEURES OF DUKE OF BERRY. (1410-16) by Limbourg Brothers. New York, Metropolitan Museum. 32 slides.
CALENDAR, LABORS OF MONTHS. 12 slides.
HOURS OF ÉTIENNE CHEVALIER BY FOUQUET (c. 1415). Chantilly, Musée Condé. 14 slides.
HOURS OF ROHAN. Paris. Bibliothèque Nationale. 4 slides.
HUNT OF CHANTILLY. Chantilly, Musée Condé. 12 slides.
TRÈS RICHES HEURES OF DUKE OF BERRY (c. 1416) by Limbourg Brothers. Chantilly, Musée Condé. 17 slides.
Other Manuscripts. 24 slides.
16th century. (Renaissance). 8 slides.
ROMAN DE LA ROSE. 6 slides.
THE BEDFORD HOURS. 12 slides.

528   GERMAN AND AUSTRIAN MINOR ARTS--MANUSCRIPTS (BOOK ILLU-MINATIONS). American Library Color Slide Co., n.d. Color.

Includes:
12th century. (Romanesque). 1 slide.
13th century. (Gothic). 1 slide.
14th century. (Late Gothic). 9 slides.
15th century. (Early Renaissance). 4 slides.

529   THE GOSPELS OF ST. AUGUSTINE. Colour Centre Slides, n.d. Color. 16 slides.

530   THE GRANDES HEURES OF JEAN, DUKE OF BERRY. (SELECTIONS).
        Visual Media, n.d. Color. 48 slides.

531   HEBRAIC MANUSCRIPTS (MEDIEVAL TO MODERN). American Library
        Color Slide Co., n.d. Color.

            Contains the following sets:
            Medieval Hebrew Illuminations. 20 slides.
            Syro-Egyptian Jewish Manuscripts. 20 slides.
            Early Jewish Printing. 15 slides.
            THE KAUFMAN HAGGADAH. 104 slides.
            THE KAUFMAN HAGGADAH. (Full-page illuminations).
                35 slides.
            THE KAUFMAN HAGGADAH. (Initial word illuminations).
                48 slides.
            THE SARAJEVO HAGGADAH. 8 slides.
            THE DARMSTADT HAGGADAH. 110 slides.
            THE DARMSTADT HAGGADAH. (Full-page illuminations).
                12 slides.
            THE DARMSTADT HAGGADAH. (Initial word illuminations).
                13 slides.
            THE ROTHSCHILD MANUSCRIPTS. 12 slides.
            PASSOVER HAGGADAH by Arthur Szyk. 47 slides.

532   THE HIBERNO-SAXON MANUSCRIPT ILLUMINATIONS. Visual Media,
        n.d. Color. 18 slides.

533   THE HIBERNO-SAXON SCHOOL OF BOOK ILLUMINATION. American
        Library Color Slide Co., 1968. Color. 15 slides.

            A look at the Irish and English influences on the medieval
            book as revealed in the Celtic manuscripts.

534   ILLUMINATED MANUSCRIPTS. AMCO, n.d. Color. 27 slides. Avail-
        able as filmstrip.

            A few examples of manuscripts from A.D. 700 to 1500.

535   ILLUMINATED MANUSCRIPTS: AN INDEX TO SELECTED BODLEIAN
        LIBRARY REPRODUCTIONS, by Thomas Ohlgren, comp and ed.   New
        York: Garland Publishers, 1977. 646 p.

536   ILLUMINATED MANUSCRIPTS FROM IRELAND. Visual Media, n.d.
        Color. 32 slides.

537   ILLUMINATED MANUSCRIPTS FROM THE BRITISH MUSEUM. Visual
        Media, n.d. Color. 20 slides.

538   ILLUMINATED MANUSCRIPTS OF GOTHIC FRANCE. Visual Media,
        n.d. Color. 36 slides.

539 ILLUMINATED MANUSCRIPTS OF THE TWELFTH THROUGH SIXTEENTH CENTURIES. Visual Media, n.d. Color. 72 slides.

540 INDIAN BOOK PAINTING UNDER THE MUGHALS. British Library, n.d. Color. 24 slides.

> This is a slide box containing the slides with commentary by Kenneth Gardner.

541 IRAN--EARLY PERSIAN MINIATURES. IMPERIAL LIBRARY. Prothmann, n.d. Color. 30 slides.

> This is a lecture set.

542 ISLAMIC CALLIGRAPHY AND ILLUMINATION. British Library. Color. 18 slides.

> A slide booklet set with commentary by Martin Lings.

543 ITALIAN MINOR ARTS. 15th century. American Library Color Slide Co., n.d. Color.

> THE BORSO D'ESTE BIBLE. 17 slides.
> THE SFORZA HOURS. 6 slides.
> PLUTARCH'S LIVES. 10 slides.

544 ITALIAN MINOR ARTS--MANUSCRIPTS (BOOK ILLUMINATIONS). American Library Color Slide Co., n.d. Color.

> 9th-11th centuries. (Romanesque). 8 slides.
> 13th century. (Gothic). 15 slides.
> 14th century. (Proto-Renaissance). 41 slides.
> 15th century. (Early Renaissance). 99 slides.
> 16th century. (High Renaissance and Mannerism). 2 slides.

545 JEAN FOUQUET: LE LIVRE D'HEURES D'ÉTIENNE CHEVALIER. Society for French-American Cultural Services and Educational Aid, 1959. Color. 12 slides.

> This slide set would be useful if used together with the facsimile published by Braziller in 1971 (see 296).

546 JUDAIC ILLUMINATED MANUSCRIPTS FROM THE TENTH THROUGH THE SIXTEENTH CENTURIES. Visual Media, n.d. Color. 48 slides.

547 LAMBETH BIBLE, ETC. Lambeth Palace Library, London, n.d. Color. Slides.

> The Lambeth Palace Library contains a number of important medieval manuscripts as the historical library of the arch-

bishops of Canterbury. See MICRO-PUBLICATIONS (p. 142) for a complete listing of what is available in that nonprint media. Transparencies of the LAMBETH BIBLE, LAMBETH APOCALYPSE and the VAUX PSALTER are available, as well as a number of other transparencies on loan for a lending fee. There are a number of published catalogs of the manuscripts and archives of this important collection.

548   LATE GOTHIC ILLUMINATIONS. College Art Association of America, 1974. Color. 30 slides.

549   LE LIVRE DE CHASSE DE GASTON PHEBUS. Society for French-American Cultural Services and Educational Aid, n.d. Color. 33 slides.

550   LIVRE D'HEURES D'ÉTIENNE CHEVALIER PAR JEAN FOUQUET. Musée Condé, Chantilly, France, n.d. Color. 10 slides.

551   MANUSCRIPTS AND BOOKS. Prothmann, n.d. Black-and-white and color.

This is probably "the world's largest single source" containing over 40,000 slides of the medieval manuscript and the book. Obviously, it is not possible to list them all in this bibliography and inquiries should be directed to Prothmann Associates, 650 Thomas Avenue, Baldwin, New York, 11510. The following are a few examples of what is available:
BIBLIOTHÈQUE NATIONALE, Paris. 14-volume set with 20 slides in each, and accompanying booklet in French.
TRINITY COLLEGE, Dublin. Examples from the Book of Durrow and the Book of Kells. A UNESCO slide book with four-language text.
HIRMER FOTOARCHIV, Munich. Representative for many famous libraries and museums which makes available color and black-and-white slides from thousands of manuscripts.
FOTO MARBURG, University of Marburg, Germany. "Each page in each manuscript from all of the major city libraries in Germany is available . . ." from this extensive source offering over 20,000 slides.
BODLEIAN LIBRARY, Oxford. Extensive collection from this world famous source. A useful index to this collection is entry number 535.

552   MEDIEVAL BESTIARIES. British Library, n.d. Color. 12 slides.

A slide booklet set with commentary by Ann Payne.

553 MEDIEVAL BOOK ILLUMINATION. American Library Color Slide Co., n.d. Color. 18 slides.

This is an integrated survey set accompanied by "lecture text for a one-hour classroom discussion," which includes selections from manuscripts from the sixth through sixteenth centuries.

554 MEDIEVAL MANUSCRIPT ILLUMINATION. (FRENCH, FLEMISH, ENGLISH, ITALIAN, AND SWISS). American Library Color Slide Co., n.d. Color.

Includes the following items:
SOMME LE ROY. 6 slides.
LES GRANDES CHRONIQUES DE FRANCE. 18 slides.
GASTON PHEBUS' BOOK OF THE HUNT. 15 slides.
LES HEURES DE ROHAN. 11 slides.
HOURS OF CHARLES VI. 19 slides.
THE LEGEND OF ST. FRANCIS. 8 slides.

555 MEDIEVAL MINIATURES FROM THE ROYAL LIBRARY OF BELGIUM. Visual Media, n.d. Color. 48 slides.

556 MEROVINGIAN MANUSCRIPT ILLUMINATIONS. Visual Media, n.d. Color. 24 slides.

557 MOZARABIC MANUSCRIPT ILLUMINATION. Visual Media, n.d. Color. 18 slides.

Examples of the Christian manuscripts executed in Spain during Moslem rule.

558 OTTONIAN BOOK ILLUMINATION. American Library Color Slide Co., 1968. Color. 14 slides.

Depicts the medieval book in Germany during the reign of the three emperors named Otto who ruled around the tenth to eleventh centuries.

559 OTTONIAN ILLUMINATED MANUSCRIPTS. Visual Media, n.d. Color. 24 slides.

560 PERSIAN MINIATURE PAINTING. Visual Media, n.d. Color. 12 slides.

561 PERSIAN MINIATURES. British Library, n.d. Color. Slide booklet.

Contains:
13th to mid-15th centuries.
late-15th to mid-16th centuries.
mid-16th to 19th centuries.

562   PERSIAN MINOR ARTS--MANUSCRIPTS (BOOK ILLUMINATIONS).
        American Library Color Slide Co., n.d. Color.

        A chronological coverage which includes:
        13th century. 1 slide.
        14th century. 5 slides.
        15th century. 5 slides.
        16th century. 12 slides.
        17th century. 3 slides.

563   LE PSAUTIER DE SAINT LOUIS. Society for French-American Cultural
        Services and Educational Aid, n.d. Color. 84 slides.

564   ROMANESQUE MANUSCRIPTS. Delaware Art Center, n.d. Color.
        20 slides and lecture.

565   SELECTED ILLUMINATIONS FROM THE PETERBOROUGH BESTIARY.
        EP Microform, n.d. Color. Slide set.

566   SELECTIONS FROM THE BOOK OF KELLS. American Library Color
        Slide Co., 1968. Color. 20 slides.

        The Book of Kells is one of the national treasures of Ireland
        and probably one of the most famous of the early medieval
        manuscripts.

567   SPANISH MINOR ARTS--MANUSCRIPTS. American Library Color Slide
        Co., n.d. Color.

        13th century. (Gothic). 1 slide.

568   SWISS MINOR ARTS--MANUSCRIPTS. American Library Color Slide
        Co., n.d. Color.

        15th century. (Early Renaissance). ANTIPHONAL OF
        ESTAVAYER-LE-LAC. 9 slides.

569   TRÈS RICHES HEURES DU DUC DE BERRY. Musée Condé, Chantilly,
        France, n.d. Color. 12 slides.

        Contains the miniatures of the calendar of this famous French
        manuscript.

570   THE WINCHESTER SCHOOL. American Library Color Slide Co., 1968.
        Color. 8 slides.

        A few examples of this English school of illumination which
        was active in the ninth and tenth centuries are presented.

The Modern World

571   GRAPHIC ARTS. 17th–20th centuries. Sandak, n.d. Color. 250 slides.

This is part of a survey set on the arts of the United States.

572   A HISTORY OF THE GRAPHIC ARTS. Budek, n.d. Black-and-white
and color. 400 slides.

These slides "are drawn from the collections of the Metropolitan Museum of Art by Caroline Karpinsky, assistant cu-
rator of prints." The set has forty units with ten slides in
each, covering in chronological order such topics as German
fifteenth-century woodcuts, Italian book illustration, woodcuts
of Albrecht Dürer, etching in the sixteenth century, Hogarth
and Rowlandson, William Blake, Francisco de Goya, Whistler,
and others.

573   LANGUAGE OF THE PRINT. Prothmann, n.d. Color. 81 slides.

From the collection of New York's Museum of Graphic Arts,
contains material by Blake, Dürer, Hogarth, Matisse, Rembrandt, Whistler, and others.

574   MASTER ES AND THE ORIGIN OF ENGRAVING. Prothmann, n.d.
Black and white. 24 slides.

575   SOCIAL COMMENT AND PROTEST IN PRINT. Sandak, n.d. Color.
30 slides.

A selection documenting the 1970 exhibition at the National
Gallery of Art, Washington, D.C., "of response to war,
social evils and human suffering by artists from seven countries, spanning four hundred years. . . ."

MICRO-PUBLICATIONS

There is an ever-growing number of micro-publications available on the history
of books and printing consisting mainly of microfilms of medieval manuscripts and
the printed book. Microfilms are available in black-and-white positive and in
color, providing the student and researcher with a rich source of materials. These
micro-publications have been made from items in various libraries or special
collections which are not usually available to the public but may now be examined and studied on microfilm.

This unit includes a few items to give some indication of the increased availability of micro-publications.

Medieval Manuscripts

576   THE ASHMOLE BESTIARY. East Ardsley, England: EP Microform, n.d.
Color. Microfilm. 70 frames.

> "The Bestiary is an illustrated mediaeval compilation about
> animals." Notes are by W.O. Hassall.

577   BIBLE MORALISÉE. East Ardsley, England: EP Microform, n.d. Color.
7 microfilms. 224 frames.

> From a French Bible executed around 1250 and now in the
> Bodleian Library, Oxford. A booklet is available for each
> film.

578   FRENCH HORAE. East Ardsley, England: EP Microform, n.d. 1 reel.

> Reproduced from a fifteenth-century manuscript at Clare Col-
> lege, Cambridge University.

579   HOLKHAM MANUSCRIPT COLLECTION. East Ardsley, England: EP
Microform, n.d. Various media.

> A series which includes color and black-and-white microfilm,
> colored filmstrips, and slides of a great many manuscripts
> and some books from the Holkham Collection. "This collec-
> tion, the finest in England outside the British Museum, is
> from Holkham Hall, Norfolk and has been filmed by kind
> permission of the Earl of Leicester." The listing follows that
> of W. Roscoe and F. Madden (see 592) and includes fifteen
> items in the field of religion; four in jurisprudence; twenty-
> four in the classics; forty-eight in Italian, French, and Eng-
> lish manuscripts, science, art, and heraldry; and three un-
> classified. It is impossible to list all the items individually
> but some titles are: BIBLE PICTURE BOOK; ILLUMINATED
> BYZANTINE GOSPELS; THIRTEENTH-CENTURY FRENCH BIBLES;
> BRUGES BOOK OF HOURS; VIRGIL; HORACE; OVID; LIVY;
> BOETIUS; DECAMERON PICTURE BOOK; CHRONICLE OF
> THE COUNTS OF HAINAULT; and CHRONICLE OF THE
> COUNTS OF FLANDERS. A wonderful source of nonprint
> media from this world-famous collection.

580   LAMBETH PALACE LIBRARY. THE MEDIEVAL MANUSCRIPTS. London:
World Microfilms Publications, n.d. Black and white. Positive roll
and color microfilm.

> This collection of manuscripts is from "one of the world's
> most celebrated Manuscript collections" to be completed in
> eight sections. At present five are available, including OLD
> ENGLISH, FRENCH, ETC.; LAW MANUSCRIPTS; ILLUMI-
> NATED MANUSCRIPTS; HUMANISTIC STUDIES; and THEOL-
> OGY. The manuscripts are fully described in entry number
> 581.

581   James, M.R. DESCRIPTIVE CATALOGUE OF THE MANUSCRIPTS IN
      THE LIBRARY OF LAMBETH PALACE. Cambridge: 1932.

582   LINCOLN CATHEDRAL LIBRARY. THE MEDIAEVAL MANUSCRIPT COL-
      LECTION. London: World Microfilms Publications, n.d. 83 reels
      (73 are silver positive roll microfilm and 10 are in color).

      A major undertaking, this tremendous collection from "Lincoln,
      one of the world's great Cathedrals," "also possesses one of
      the most significant Manuscript Collections (housed in the
      Wren Library) with examples dating back to the 11th century."
      It contains the following: ILLUMINATED MANUSCRIPTS, (in
      color, all others in black and white); LAW AND ADMINI-
      STRATION; SECULAR MANUSCRIPTS; THEOLOGY; BIBLICAL
      STUDIES; and SERMONS, HOMILES, LITURGY, and SAINTS'
      LIVES. There is an index reel by R.M. Wooley (see 594).

583   ST. JOHN'S BESTIARY. East Ardsley, England: EP Microform, n.d.
      Color. Microfilm.

      This is from Oxford MS. 61 in St. John's College with notes
      by W.O. Hassall.

584   SELECTED ILLUMINATIONS FROM THE MANUSCRIPTS IN THE FITZ-
      WILLIAM MUSEUM. East Ardsley, England: EP Microform, n.d. Color.
      Microfilm.

      This contains THE PETERBOROUGH PSALTER, THE DE BRAILES
      BIBLE, and an ENGLISH PSALTER.

585   THE TRINITY APOCALYPSE. East Ardsley, England: EP Microform,
      n.d. Color. Microfilm.

      This "celebrated Apocalypse" was "produced in England around
      1230. The place of its origin is unknown. Illustrated by
      four artists and exceptionally rich in detail the manuscript
      generally agreed to be the finest of its kind."

586   THE TRINITY COLLEGE "ROMANCE OF ALEXANDER." East Ardsley,
      England: EP Microform, n.d. Color. Microfilm. 154 frames.

      "One of the earliest manuscripts of this text. Probably pro-
      duced at St. Alban's in the first half of the 12th century."

587   THE TRINITY GOSPELS. East Ardsley, England: EP Microform, n.d.
      Color. Microfilm. 19 frames.

      An Anglo-Saxon manuscript made at Canterbury in the late-
      tenth or early-eleventh century.

588   WINCHESTER COLLEGE (WARDEN AND FELLOWS' LIBRARY): MEDIAE-
       VAL MANUSCRIPTS COLLECTION. London: World Microfilms Publi-
       cations, 1978. 16 reels (15 monochrome and 1 color).

       A collection of manuscripts to the year 1600 is in this li-
       brary which dates back to the founding of the college in
       1382 by William of Wykeham. There are many important
       manuscripts in this collection. A BRIEF HISTORY AND CATA-
       LOGUE (1978) is also available.

589   THE YORK GOSPELS. East Ardsley, England: EP Microform, n.d.
       1 reel.

       From a manuscript which dates around A.D. 1000 containing
       the "four Gospels written primarily in Carolingian miniscule."

Books and Catalogs

590   Briquet, Charles M. LES FILIGRANES: A HISTORICAL DICTIONARY
       OF WATERMARKS. 1923. East Ardsley, England: EP Microform, n.d.
       4 reels.

       This standard work is included in this bibliography (see 60)
       and is also available on microfilm.

591   Coxe, H.O. CATALOGUES OF MANUSCRIPTS IN OXFORD COL-
       LEGES. 2 vols. East Ardsley, England: EP Microform, n.d. 2 reels.

       A microfilm from the "annotated copy in the Department of
       Printed Books at the Bodleian Library."

592   Roscoe, W., and Madden, F. HOLKHAM, CATALOGUE OF THE
       MANUSCRIPTS IN THE LIBRARY AT. . . . East Ardsley, England:
       EP Microform, n.d. 3 reels.

       The extensive collection of micro-publications of the HOLKHAM
       MANUSCRIPT COLLECTION (see 579) follows this catalog.

593   Verard, A. WOODCUTS FROM THE ART OF GOOD LIVING AND
       GOOD DYING. East Ardsley, England: EP Microform, n.d. 1 reel.

       This popular book was printed in Paris in 1503 and includes
       notes by F.H. Stebbings.

594   Wooley, R.M. CATALOGUE OF THE MANUSCRIPTS OF LINCOLN
       CATHEDRAL CHAPTER LIBRARY. (London: 1927). London: World
       Microfilm Publications, n.d. 1 reel.

       This item is essential for the proper use of the eighty-three
       reels of microfilms of the Lincoln Cathedral Library.

OVERHEAD TRANSPARENCIES

Overhead transparencies are especially helpful in the study and teaching of the history of books and printing since they can be projected for group viewing, presenting visually what is available in book or text. Most overhead transparencies are black and white, but it is possible to make color transparencies as well as overlays for explanations or commentaries. Some transparencies are commercially produced, but it is quite simple to make an overhead, using a photocopying machine for a carbon-based copy and a thermal copier for the production of the overhead. This can then be mounted and labeled and readily available for showing. Overheads may also be made with the Xerox or Diazo process. The most effective overhead transparencies are of line drawings, with good black-and-white contrast; half-tones are usually less successful.

Transparency Sources

595   NICEM. INDEX TO EDUCATIONAL OVERHEAD TRANSPARENCIES.
       5th ed. 2 vols. Los Angeles: University of Southern California, National Information Center for Educational Media, 1977.

REPRODUCTIONS

Reproductions from pages of manuscripts and printed books are available from a variety of sources, including libraries, museums, and dealers. These include reproductions from famous books, flat pictures, postcards, and facsimiles of various items. This type of material is usually available directly from the institution in which the item is located. Other sources for reproductions are portfolios and prints of reproductions from commercial dealers.

Facsimiles of medieval manuscripts and printed books are also available, and some facsimiles of manuscripts are included in this bibliography. Although there are a number of facsimiles of printed books, they have not been included here because the list would be too extensive.

There is no major source which lists reproductions from books, and each individual will have to write to the particular source to see what is available.

REALIA

Realia includes reproductions, in-the-round, of items which are part of the history of books and printing. These are usually reproductions of artifacts, including examples of cuneiform tablets, hieroglyphic inscriptions, and examples of writing on various materials. Of course, it would be ideal to be able to examine and study original materials, and the student of books and printing must always take every opportunity to see the original. However, this is not always possible and realia can be a substitute. Realia also has value as a teaching aid and for exhibit purposes.

It is difficult to locate realia in the history of the book since there is no locator source. Often libraries and/or museums will have such items for purchase at reasonable cost. The following is a listing of a few sources and some realia items:

Realia Sources

596   Alva Museum Replicas
       Greenwich, Connecticut

597   The University Museum
       Philadelphia, Pennsylvania

Realia Materials

SOURCES AND MATERIALS USED

598   FROM FOREST TREE TO HAMMERMILL PAPER. Hammermill Paper Co.,
       Educational Services, n.d. Realia.

       This is a commercially prepared "College and Museum Exhibit"
       in the form of a plastic wallboard with identification labels
       of ten clear plastic cells containing a wood slice, wood
       chips, cooking liquor, unbleached pulp, bleached pulp, size
       milk, colored pulp, machine pulp, fourdrinier wire, and a
       Hammermill Bond roll. There is also a smaller exhibit en-
       titled "Chemistry and Science Exhibit" with only four of these
       manufacturing stages.

THE ALPHABET AND WRITING

599   THE PICTOGRAPHIC AND CUNEIFORM UNIT. Alva-Class-Research-
       Kit 1/2, n.d. Realia.

       This set examines the "development of pictures into cunei-
       form signs . . ." and contains four replicas of early Su-
       merian pictographic tablets dated around 3000 B.C. and two
       replicas of a cuneiform tablet, each with a two-piece en-
       velope dated about 1800 B.C. It has maps, a teacher's
       manual, and student's programs for student participation "in
       the problems which show the limitations of this form of writ-
       ing."

600   THE ROSETTA STONE UNIT. Alva-Class-Research-Kit 1/1, n.d.

This is part of a series on the origins and development of writing. This unit contains museum replicas for the classroom which "demonstrates with ancient hieroglyphics the transformation of simple picture symbols into a script representing sound." Has a teacher's manual and student programs guide.

601   SCRIPT AND ITS DEVELOPMENT. Compiled by Donald E. Stephan. Hubbard Scientific Co., 1973. Realia/museum artifact reproductions.

This useful set contains eleven examples of writing including pictographic materials, cuneiform, hieroglyphics, runes, and others, covering the time period from the Indus Valley stamp seals of 2300 B.C. to a Germanic runic stone of A.D. 985. It also contains a leaflet giving detailed information on each item, and a time-line chart.

Section 6

PERIODICALS AND ANNUALS

This unit contains a listing of some periodicals and annuals which deal with the history of books and printing and related fields. This is only a selective listing and does not attempt to be comprehensive, or complete. Only basic data are given, and other sources will have to be consulted for more detailed information.

PERIODICAL SOURCES

Some of the other items listed in this bibliography might include a section listing periodicals. The following two books, which have been previously cited, are especially useful for information on journals:

St. Bride Foundation Institute. CATALOGUE OF THE PERIODICALS RELATING TO PRINTING AND ALLIED SUBJECTS IN THE TECHNICAL LIBRARY OF ST. BRIDE INSTITUTE. London: 1950. 35 p. (see 14).

Ulrich, Carolyn, and Küp, Karl. BOOKS AND PRINTING: A SELECTED LIST OF PERIODICALS, 1800-1942. Woodstock, Vt.: William Edwin Rudge, Publisher, and New York: New York Public Library, 1942. 244 p. (see 17).

The following periodical directories might also be helpful:

602   IRREGULAR SERIALS AND ANNUALS: AN INTERNATIONAL DIRECTORY. 5th ed. 1978-79. New York: R.R. Bowker Co., 1978.

603   NEW SERIAL TITLES: A UNION LIST OF SERIALS COMMENCING PUBLICATION AFTER DECEMBER 31, 1949. 1950-70 CUMULATIVE. 4 vols. Washington, D.C.: Library of Congress and New York: R.R. Bowker Co., 1973. Supplements, 1971-- .

604   SOURCES OF SERIALS: AN INTERNATIONAL PUBLISHER AND CORPORATE AUTHOR DIRECTORY. 1st ed. New York: R.R. Bowker Co., 1977.

605   THE STANDARD PERIODICAL DIRECTORY. 5th ed. New York: Ox-
      bridge Communications, 1976.

606   ULRICH'S INTERNATIONAL PERIODICALS DIRECTORY. 17th ed. 1977-
      78. New York: R.R. Bowker Co., 1977. ULRICH'S QUARTERLY is
      a supplement to both ULRICH'S INTERNATIONAL PERIODICALS DIREC-
      TORY and IRREGULAR SERIALS AND ANNUALS.

607   UNION LIST OF SERIALS IN LIBRARIES OF THE UNITED STATES AND
      CANADA. Ed. by Edna Brown Titus. 3d ed., 5 vols. New York:
      H.W. Wilson Co., 1965.

PERIODICALS

608   ALPHABET AND IMAGE. London: Shenval Press, 1946-48. Quarterly.
      Formerly TYPOGRAPHY, 1936-39. Quarterly. Review of typography
      and graphic arts.

609   AMERICAN INSTITUTE OF GRAPHIC ARTS JOURNAL. New York:
      American Institute of Graphic Arts, 1965-- . Quarterly.

610   AMPHORA. Richmond, British Columbia, Canada: Alcuin Society,
      1967-- . Quarterly.

611   APHA LETTER. New York: American Printing History Association,
      1974-- . Bimonthly.

612   ARCHIV FÜR DRUCK UND PAPIER. Berlin, Germany: Buchund-Druck-
      gewerbe-Verlag, KG., 1955-- . Quarterly. Archives for printing,
      paper, and kindred trades.

613   ARS TYPOGRAPHICA. New York: The Marchbanks Press, 1918-34.
      Quarterly.

614   ARTS ET MÉTIERS DU LIVRE. Paris: Éditions Technorama. Formerly
      RELIURE, 1891-- . Monthly.

615   ARTS ET MÉTIERS GRAPHIQUES. Paris: Éditions Arts et Métiers Graph-
      iques, 1927-39. 5/yr.

616   BIBLIOFILIA. Florence, Italy: Olschki, 1899-- . 3/yr.

617   BIBLIOGRAPHICA. London: Kegan Paul, Trench, Trübner and Co.,
      1895-97. Vols. 1-3. Papers on books, their history and art.

618   BIBLIOGRAPHICAL SOCIETY OF AMERICA. PAPERS. New York:
      Bibliographical Society of America, 1904-6-- . Quarterly.

619   BOOK PRODUCTION. New York: Freund Publishing Co., 1954-- .
      Monthly. From 1925 to 1937 called BOOKBINDING MAGAZINE and
      from 1937 to 1954 called BOOKBINDING AND BOOK PRODUCTION.

620   BRITISH PRINTER. London: Maclean Hunter, 1888-- . Monthly.
      Leading technical journal of the printing industry.

621   BYBLIS. Paris: Éditions A. Morancé, 1921-31. Quarterly. Miroir
      des arts du livre et de l'estampe.

622   CARACTERE. Paris: Compagnie Française d'Éditions, 1949-- . Monthly.
      Revue des industries graphiques.

623   CAXTON MAGAZINE. London: Institute of Printers and Kindred
      Trades of the British Empire, 1901-59. Monthly.

624   CODICES MANUSCRIPTI. Vienna: Breuder Hollinek, 1975-- . 4/yr.

625   THE COLOPHON. New York: The Colophon Ltd., 1930-34; new
      series, 1935-38, and the new graphic series, 1939-40. Quarterly. A
      book-collector's quarterly.

626   DOLPHIN. New York: Limited Editions Club, 1933-41. 3/yr. A
      periodical for all people who find pleasure in fine books.

627   FINE PRINT. San Francisco: Fine Print, 1975-- . 4/yr. A review
      for the arts of the book.

628   FLEURON. London: Office of the Fleuron and Cambridge. The Uni-
      versity Press, 1923-30. Annual. A journal of typography.

629   LA FRANCE GRAPHIQUE. Paris: Éditions Plan, 1947-- . Monthly.

630   GARC NEWSLETTER. Rochester, N.Y.: Rochester Institute of Tech-
      nology, Graphic Arts Research Center, 1973-- . Monthly.

631   GRAPHIC ARTS ABSTRACTS. Pittsburg, Pa.: Graphic Arts Technical
      Foundation, Library, 1947-- . Monthly.

632   GRAPHIC ARTS LITERATURE ABSTRACTS. Rochester, N.Y.: Rochester
       Institute of Technology, Graphic Arts Research Center, 1954-- . Monthly.
       An expansion of GRAPHIC ARTS INDEX. Formerly GRAPHIC ARTS
       PROGRESS.

633   GRAPHIC ARTS MONTHLY AND THE PRINTING INDUSTRY. Chicago:
       Magazine Division, Dun-Donnelley Publishing Corp., 1929-- .

634   GRAPHICS. Kissammee, Fla.: Cody Publications, 1953-- . Monthly.

635   GRAPHIS. Zurich, Switzerland: Walter Herdeg Graphis Press, 1944-- .
       Bimonthly. International journal for graphic and applied art. Text in
       English, French, and German.

636   GUTENBERG-JAHRBUCH. Mainz, West Germany: Gutenberg Gessell-
       schaft, 1926-- . Annual.

637   ILLUSTRATOR. Minneapolis, Minn.: Art Instruction Schools, 1916-- .
       Quarterly.

638   IMPRESSIONS. Cardiff, Wales: South Wales and Monmouthshire Master
       Printer's Alliance, 1922-- . 3/yr.

639   IMPRIMATUR. Weimar, East Germany: Gesellschaft der Bibliophilen; and
       Hamburg, West Germany: Gesellschaft der Bücherfreund, 1930-55. Annual.

640   IMPRINT. London: The Imprint Publishing Co., 1913. Monthly.

641   INLAND PRINTER/AMERICAN LITHOGRAPHER. Chicago: Maclean
       Hunter Publishing Corp., 1883-- . Monthly.

642   ITALIA GRAFICA. Milan, Italy: Associazone Nazionale Italiana In-
       dustrie Grafiche Cartotechniche e Transformatrici, 1946-- . Monthly.

643   ITALIX. Fair Lawn, N.J.: Haywood House, 1971-- . Quarterly.
       The calligraphic quarterly.

644   JOURNAL OF TYPOGRAPHIC RESEARCH. Cleveland: The Press of
       Western Reserve University, 1967-70, vols. 1-4. Continued as VISIBLE
       LANGUAGE.

645   THE LIBRARY. London: The Library Association. Series I, 1889-99;
       London: The Bibliographical Society; Series II, 1900-1909; Series III,
       1910-19; Series IV, 1920-46; London: Printed for the Bibliographical
       Society at the Oxford University Press; Series V, 1946-- . Quarterly.
       Transactions of the Bibliographical Society.

Periodicals and Annuals

646 THE LIBRARY QUARTERLY. Chicago: University of Chicago Press, 1931-- .

647 MÉTIERS GRAPHIQUES. Paris: Société des Éditions de l'Imprimerie Nouvelle, 1970-- . Vol. 7-- . 33/yr.

648 NOUVELLES DE L'ESTAMPE. Paris: Bibliothèque Nationale, 1963-- . 6/yr.

649 NOUVELLES GRAPHIQUES/GRAFISCH NIEUWS. Antwerp, Belgium: Internationale d'Impression et d'Éditions, 1950-- . Semimonthly. Editions in Dutch and French.

650 THE PENROSE ANNUAL. London: Lund, Humphries and New York: Hastings House. Title and publisher varies: THE PROCESS YEAR BOOK, 1896-97; PENROSE'S PICTORIAL ANNUAL, 1898-1914; PENROSE'S ANNUAL, 1915-34; THE PENROSE ANNUAL, 1935-- . International review of the graphic arts.

651 PRINT. New York: R.C. Publications, 1939-- . Bimonthly. America's graphic design magazine.

652 PRINT DESIGN AND PRODUCTION. London: Cox and Sharland, 1965-- . Bimonthly. Formerly BOOK DESIGN AND PRODUCTION. London: Thames Publishing Co., 1958-65. Quarterly.

653 PRINTING AND PUBLISHING. Washington, D.C.: Domestic and International Business Administration, Bureau of Domestic Commerce, 1964-- . Quarterly.

654 PRINTING HISTORICAL SOCIETY JOURNAL. London: St. Bride Institute, 1965-- . Annual.

655 PRINTING PAPER QUARTERLY. Westfield, Mass.: Paper Makers Advertising Association. From 1912 to 1964 called DIRECT ADVERTISING and from 1964 to 1977 known as D/A. 1978-- .

656 PRINTING WORLD. London: Benn Brothers, 1878-- . Weekly.

657 PRINT REVIEW. New York: Pratt Graphics Center, 1973-- . Semiannual.

658 PRIVATE PRESS BOOKS. Pinner, Middlesex, England: Private Libraries Association, 1959-- . Annual.

659 PRIVATE PRINTER AND PRIVATE PRESS. Oxford, England: Peter Hoy and Rigby Graham, 1968-- . 2-3/yr.

660   QUARENDO. Amsterdam: Theatrum Orbis Terrarum, 1971-- . Quarterly. A journal from the Low countries devoted to manuscripts and printed books. Text mainly in English, occasionally in French and German.

661   REVIEW OF THE GRAPHIC ARTS. Kissammee, Fla.: Cody Publications. Combined with CRAFTSMEN'S TECHNICAL DIGEST, formerly SHARE YOUR KNOWLEDGE incorporating CRAFTSMEN'S TECHNICAL DIGEST, 1920-- . Bimonthly. International Association of Printing House Craftsmen.

662   SCRIPTORIUM. Ghent, Belgium: Story-Scientia, 1946-47-- . Semiannual. International review of manuscript studies.

663   SIGNATURE. London: Signature. 1st series, 1933-40 and 2d series, 1946-54. A quadrimestrial of typography and graphic arts.

664   TYPOGRAPHICA. London: Lund, Humphries, 1949-70. Semiannual.

665   VISIBLE LANGUAGE. Cleveland: Visible Language, 1971-- . Vol. 5-- . Quarterly. Continuation of the JOURNAL OF TYPOGRAPHIC RESEARCH.

666   ZENTRALBLATT FUER BIBLIOTHEKSWESEN. Leipzig, East Germany: Bibliographisches Institut, 1884-- . Monthly. Text in German, contents page in English, French, German, and Russian.

Section 7

ASSOCIATIONS, SOCIETIES, AND CLUBS

The following is a listing of a few groups which have been formed to encourage and support interest and activities in the history of books and printing, the book arts, and related areas.

667   THE ALCUIN SOCIETY
P.O. Box 94108
Richmond, British Columbia
Canada V6Y 2A

668   AMERICAN FRIENDS OF THE
GUTENBERG MUSEUM
(Mainz, West Germany)
c/o Dr. Robert Leslie
140 Lincoln Road
Brooklyn, N.Y. 11225

669   AMERICAN FRIENDS OF THE
PLANTIN-MORETUS MUSEUM
(Antwerp, Belgium)
c/o Roderick Stinehour
Stinehour Press
Lunenburg, Vermont 05906

670   AMERICAN INSTITUTE OF
GRAPHIC ARTS
1059 Third Avenue
New York, N.Y. 10021

671   AMERICAN PRINTING
HISTORY ASSOCIATION
(APHA)
Box 4922
Grand Central Station
New York, N.Y. 10017

672   BIBLIOGRAPHICAL SOCIETY
OF AMERICA
P.O. Box 397
Grand Central Station
New York, N.Y. 10017

673   BIBLIOGRAPHICAL SOCIETY
OF THE UNIVERSITY OF
VIRGINIA
Alderman Library
Charlottesville, Virginia
22901

674   THE BOOK CLUB OF
CALIFORNIA
545 Sutter Street
San Francisco, California
94102

675 THE CAXTON CLUB
60 W. Walton Street
Chicago, Illinois 60610

676 CENTER FOR BOOK ARTS
15 Bleeker Street
New York, N.Y. 10012

677 CLUB OF ODD VOLUMES
77 Mount Vernon Street
Boston, Massachusetts 02160

678 COLUMBIAD CLUB
c/o Thompson R. Harlow
1 Elizabeth Street
Hartford, Connecticut 06105

679 FRIENDS OF THE
HUNTINGTON LIBRARY
Huntington Library, Art Gallery,
and Botanical Gardens
San Marino, California 91108

680 FRIENDS OF THE PIERPONT
MORGAN LIBRARY
29 East 60th Street
New York, N.Y. 10016

681 THE GOUDY SOCIETY
301 East 48th Street
New York, N.Y. 10017

682 THE GROLIER CLUB
47 East 60th Street
New York, N.Y. 10022

683 INTERNATIONAL ASSOCIATION
OF PAPER HISTORIANS
c/o The Gutenberg Museum
Liebfrauenplatz 5
Mainz, West Germany

684 INTERNATIONAL CENTER FOR
THE TYPOGRAPHIC ARTS
P. O. Box 2438
Grand Central Station
New York, N.Y. 10017

685 THE PHILOBIBLON CLUB
c/o The Secretary
Free Library
Logan Square
Philadelphia, Pennsylvania
19103

686 THE PRINTING HISTORICAL
SOCIETY
St. Bride Institute
Bride Lane, Fleet Street
London EC4 Y8EE, England

687 THE ROUNCE AND COFFIN
CLUB
William Andrews Clark Library
2520 Cimarron Street
Los Angeles, California
90018

688 THE ROWFANT CLUB
3028 Prospect Avenue
Cleveland, Ohio 44115

689 THE TYPOPHILES
c/o Dr. Robert Leslie
140 Lincoln Road
Brooklyn, N.Y. 11225

690 THE WILLIAM MORRIS
SOCIETY
Kelmscott House
26 Upper Mall, Hammersmith
London W69TA, England

691 THE WILLIAM MORRIS
SOCIETY OF NORTH
AMERICA
c/o Joseph Dunlap
420 Riverside Drive
New York, N.Y. 10025

692 ZAMORANO CLUB
Box 465
Pasadena, California 91102

Section 8

LIBRARIES, SPECIAL COLLECTIONS, AND MUSEUMS

The following is a selected listing of some institutions which have collections dealing with the history of books and printing, the art of the book, books about books, and/or related topics. In addition to collections of books about books, many of these libraries also have rare books or special collections containing examples of notable items in the history of the book. For more detailed information on libraries, the following will be helpful:

SOURCES

693   THE AMERICAN LIBRARY DIRECTORY. 31st ed. New York: R.R. Bowker Co., 1978.

694   Ash, Lee, ed. SUBJECT COLLECTIONS. 5th ed. New York: R.R. Bowker Co., 1978.

695   DIRECTORY OF SPECIAL LIBRARIES AND INFORMATION CENTERS. Edited by Margaret L. Young, Harold C. Young, and Anthony T. Kruzas. 4th ed. 3 vols. Detroit: Gale Research Co., 1977. For the subject directory to this work see 699.

696   INTERNATIONAL LIBRARY DIRECTORY. A WORLD DIRECTORY OF LIBRARIES. 3d ed., 1968-70. London: A.P. Wales Organization, 1968.

697   MAJOR LIBRARIES OF THE WORLD: A SELECTIVE GUIDE. Edited by Colin Steele. London and New York: Bowker Publishing Co., and R.R. Bowker Co., 1976.

698   SUBJECT COLLECTIONS IN EUROPEAN LIBRARIES. Compiled by Richard Lewanski. New York: R.R. Bowker Co., 1965.

699   SUBJECT DIRECTORY OF SPECIAL LIBRARIES AND INFORMATION
       CENTERS. 4th ed. 5 vols. Detroit: Gale Research Co., 1977.
       This is a subject arrangement of all entries in the DIRECTORY OF
       SPECIAL LIBRARIES AND INFORMATION CENTERS, (see 695).

700   WORLD GUIDE TO LIBRARIES. 5th ed. 4 vols. New York: R.R.
       Bowker Co., and Munich: Verlag Dokumentation, 1978.

Another source is PRIVATE PRESSWORK: A BIBLIOGRAPHIC APPROACH TO
PRINTING AS AN AVOCATION by Frank J. Anderson, ed., pages 113-36
(see 1).

LIBRARIES, SPECIAL COLLECTIONS, AND MUSEUMS

The following listing is arranged alphabetically by name of institution and provides some data on their areas of specialization which might be of interest and
value to the student of the book. This listing does not attempt to be complete
but to include areas of specialization which are pertinent to this bibliography.

NAME	AREA/S OF SPECIALIZATION
701 AMERICAN ANTIQUARIAN SOCIETY LIBRARY 185 Salisbury Street Worcester, Massachusetts 01609	Americana Juveniles (Early American) Isaiah Thomas Collection History of Printing
702 AMERICAN PHILOSOPHICAL SOCIETY LIBRARY 105 S. Fifth Street Philadelphia, Pennsylvania 19106	Americana Frankliniana
703 ANTIQUARIAN BOOKMAN LIBRARY 1007 Paulison Avenue Clifton, New Jersey	Books About Books History of Printing Binding
704 BANGOR PUBLIC LIBRARY 145 Harlow Street Bangor, Maine 04401	Book Illustrations Limited Editions Club Paper Making and Paper Trade
705 BOSTON ATHENAEUM 10 1/2 Beacon Street Boston, Massachusetts 02108	American Authors Victorian Children's Books

NAME	AREA/S OF SPECIALIZATION
706 BOSTON PUBLIC LIBRARY Copley Square 666 Boylston Street Box 286 Boston, Massachusetts 02117	Americana Benjamin Franklin Collection John Baskerville (Benton Collection) Imprints Before 1850 Early and Important Children's Books First Editions (Connolly Collection) Bookbindings History of Printing Illustrated Books Incunabula Private Presses Engravings and Early Rare Impressions Wiggin Collection of Prints Fore-Edge Paintings
707 BOSTON UNIVERSITY Mugar Memorial Library 771 Commonwealth Avenue Boston, Massachusetts 02215	Private Press Books Americana Art of the Printed Book
708 R.R. BOWKER COMPANY 1180 Avenue of the Americas New York, New York 10036	Books About Books Bookmaking
709 BROOKLYN MUSEUM Wilbour Library of Egyptology 188 Eastern Parkway Brooklyn, New York 11238	Ancient Egypt
710 BROWN UNIVERSITY LIBRARIES Prospect Street Providence, Rhode Island 02912	Americana Incunabula Rare Books
711 UNIVERSITY OF CALIFORNIA LIBRARY Berkeley, California 94720	Rare Books Fine Printing
712 UNIVERSITY OF CALIFORNIA University Library 405 Hilgard Avenue Los Angeles, California 90024	History of Printing Press Books Rare Books Hebraica and Judaica Early Children's Books Western Americana Eric Gill Collection Pickering and Bodoni Imprints

Libraries, Special Collections, Museums

713   UNIVERSITY OF CALIFORNIA   History of Printing
Santa Barbara Library   Bookbinding
Santa Barbara, California   Fine Printing
93106

714   LA CASA DEL LIBRO   History and Art of the Book
Calle Del Cristo 255   Fine Printing
P.O. Box 2265   Incunabula (especially Spanish imprints)
San Juan, Puerto Rico 00901   Calligraphy
                                   Letter Design
                                   Papermaking
                                   Book Illustration
                                   Book Design
                                   Bookbinding

715   CATHOLIC UNIVERSITY OF   Rare Books
        AMERICA   History of Books and Printing
John K. Mullen of Denver   Catholic Americana
        Memorial Library   Celtic
620 Michigan Avenue N.E.   Medieval Studies
Washington, D.C.   20017

716   CERCLE DE LA LIBRARIE   Books About Books
Syndicats des Industires du
        Livre, Bibliothèque Technique
117, Boulevard Saint-Germain
75 Paris 6e, France

717   COLUMBIA UNIVERSITY   Rare Books
        LIBRARIES   Incunabula
535 W. 114th Street   History of Books and Printing
New York, New York   10027   Press Books
                                   Typography
                                   Papyri
                                   Assyrian and Babylonian Tablets
                                   Arthur Rackham Collection
                                   George Macy Memorial Collection

718   DARTMOUTH COLLEGE   Rare Books
Baker Library   Press Books
Hanover, New Hampshire 03755   New England Early Illustrated Books

719   DETROIT PUBLIC LIBRARY   Rare Books
5201 Woodward Avenue   Press Books
Detroit, Michigan   48202   Bookbinding
                                   History of Printing

NAME	AREA/S OF SPECIALIZATION
720 DEUTSCHEN BUCH-UND SCHRIFTMUSEUM DER DEUTSCHEN BUCHEREI 701 Leipzig, Deutscher Platz German Democratic Republic	Books About Books
721 R.R. DONNELLEY AND SONS CO. Central Reference Library 2223 S. Martin Luther King Drive Chicago, Illinois 60616	Printing Archives Printing Technology Private Presses Bookbinding
722 FREE LIBRARY OF PHILADELPHIA Logan Square Philadelphia, Pennsylvania 19103	Children's Literature (Rosenbach Collection of Children's Literature, 1682-1836) Arthur Rackham Collection Howard Pyle and His School Kate Greenway Collection Bibles Americana Horn Books Cuneiform Tablets History of Printing Incunabula European and Oriental Manuscripts Judaica Books and Printing Calligraphy--9th to 20th Centuries
723 FRICK ART REFERENCE LIBRARY 10 East 71st Street New York, New York 10021	Illuminated Manuscripts
724 GEORGETOWN UNIVERSITY Joseph Mark Lauinger Library 37th and O Streets, N.W. Washington, D.C. 20007	Catholic Americana Rare Books Incunabula
725 GROLIER CLUB LIBRARY 47 East 60th Street New York, New York 10022	Bibliography Typography Graphic Arts History of Printing Incunabula Private Presses Miniature Books

	NAME	AREA/S OF SPECIALIZATION
726	GUTENBERG MUSEUM MIT GUTENBERG BIBLIOTHEK Liebfrauenplatz 5 Mainz, West Germany	Printing History Books About Books Johann Gutenberg
727	HARVARD UNIVERSITY LIBRARIES Cambridge, Massachusetts 02138	History of Books Printing and Graphic Arts Classics Rare Books Incunabula Book Illustration
728	HUNTINGTON LIBRARY, ART GALLERY AND BOTANICAL GARDENS 1151 Oxford Road San Marino, California 91108	Illuminated Manuscripts Incunabula Rare Books History of Printing Book Illustration Western Americana Bookbinding
729	UNIVERSITY OF ILLINOIS AT URBANA-CHAMPAIGN LIBRARY Urbana-Champaign Campus Illinois 61801	Rare Books Incunabula History of Printing
730	INDIANA UNIVERSITY LIBRARIES Lilly Rare Book Library 10th Street and Jordan Avenue Bloomington, Indiana 47401	Rare Books Incunabula History of Printing Manuscripts
731	INSTITUTE OF PAPER CHEMISTRY J.A. Kimberly Memorial Library 1043 E. South River Street Box 1048 Appleton, Wisconsin 54911	History of Papermaking Paper Technology Dard Hunter Paper Museum
732	JEWISH THEOLOGICAL SEMINARY OF AMERICA LIBRARY 3080 Broadway New York, New York 10027	Hebraica and Judaica Manuscripts Incunabula Rare Books Bibles

NAME	AREA/S OF SPECIALIZATION

733 UNIVERSITY OF KENTUCKY
Margaret I. King Library
Lexington, Kentucky
40506

History of Books
Broadside Ballads and Chapbooks
Typography
Graphic Arts
Tibetan Manuscripts and Xylography
W.A. Dwiggins Collection

734 THE LIBRARY OF CONGRESS
Washington, D.C. 20540

The CENTER FOR THE BOOK
has been established as part of the
Library of Congress "to organize, focus,
and dramatize our nation's interest and
attention on the book, to marshal the
nation's support--spiritual, physical,
and fiscal--for the book." It was established in 1977 and hopefully will
bring together and sponsor individuals,
programs, and exhibits on "the role of
the book in our society."

Americana
Frankliniana
Bruce Rogers Collection
F.W. Goudy Collection of Type
   Designs
Illuminated Manuscripts
Incunabula
Judaica
Press Books
Rare Books
Orientalia
Hans Christian Anderson Collection
Children's Literature

735 LIBRARY SCHOOL LIBRARIES

(Check THE AMERICAN LIBRARY
DIRECTORY, New York: R.R.
Bowker Co., for a complete
listing of library schools [see
693].)

A few library school library collections are listed in this unit; however,
there are many more and it would
be expected that these collections
would have books and periodicals
on the history of books and printing
and related fields.

736 LONG ISLAND UNIVERSITY
B. David Schwartz Memorial
   Library
C.W. Post Center
Greenvale, New York 11548

History of Books and Printing
Books About Books
Book Arts
History of Children's Literature

737 LOS ANGELES PUBLIC LIBRARY
630 W. Fifth Street
Los Angeles, California 90019

History of Printing

738 METROPOLITAN MUSEUM OF
   ART LIBRARY
Fifth Avenue at 82d Street
New York, New York 10028

Art History
Graphic Arts
Illuminated Manuscripts
Miniature Painting

Libraries, Special Collections, Museums

	NAME	AREA/S OF SPECIALIZATION
739	UNIVERSITY OF MICHIGAN LIBRARY Ann Arbor, Michigan 48104	Papyri Herbals Incunabula Press Books
740	NEWBERRY LIBRARY 60 W. Walton Street Chicago, Illinois 60610	Americana History of Papermaking History of Penmanship and Calligraphy History of Printing Incunabula Rare Books Thomas Bewick Collection Wing Foundation on the History of Printing
741	NEW YORK PUBLIC LIBRARY Fifth Avenue and 42d Street New York, New York 10018	Americana Berg Collection (American and English Literature) Incunabula Rare Books Judaica Orientalia Press Books Wilberforce Eames Collection of Babylonia Spencer Collection (Art of Illustration)
742	UNIVERSITY OF NORTH CAROLINA Louis Round Wilson Library Drawer 870 Chapel Hill, North Carolina 27514	Graphic Arts First Editions Incunabula History of the Book Manuscripts Americana
743	UNIVERSITY OF NOTRE DAME Memorial Library Notre Dame, Indiana 46556	Eric Gill Rare Books Medieval Institute Library First Editions Microfilm copies of the manuscripts in the Ambrosian Library
744	UNIVERSITY OF OREGON LIBRARY Eugene, Oregon 97403	Manuscripts Incunabula Fine Printing

NAME	AREA/S OF SPECIALIZATION
745 UNIVERSITY OF PENNSYLVANIA LIBRARIES 3420 Walnut Street Philadelphia, Pennsylvania 19104	Books About Books
746 THE PIERPONT MORGAN LIBRARY 29 East 36th Street New York, New York 10016	Bookbindings Egyptian, Greek, and Other Papyri Incunabula Later Printed Books Medieval and Renaissance Illuminated Manuscripts Mesopotamian Seals and Tablets Blockbooks Rare Bindings Bibles Rare Books Books About Books History of Books and Printing
747 PLANTIN-MORETUS MUSEUM LIBRARY Antwerp, Belgium	History of Books and Printing Books About Books
748 PRATT INSTITUTE LIBRARY Brooklyn, New York 11205	Book Arts History of Printing
749 PRINCETON UNIVERSITY LIBRARIES Princeton, New Jersey 08540	Elmer Adler (Pynson Printers) Aubrey Beardsley Assyrian and Babylonian Tablets Islamic Manuscripts Papyri Rare Books Incunabula Graphic Arts Americana
750 PRINTING INDUSTRY OF AMERICA LIBRARY Washington, D.C.	History of Printing Printing as a Trade
751 PROVIDENCE PUBLIC LIBRARY 150 Empire Street Providence, Rhode Island 02903	Children's Books Printing (Daniel B. Updike)

	NAME	AREA/S OF SPECIALIZATION
752	PURDUE UNIVERSITY LIBRARIES West Lafayette, Indiana 47907	Bruce Rogers Collection
753	ROCHESTER INSTITUTE OF TECHNOLOGY Wallace Memorial Library 1 Lomb Memorial Drive Rochester, New York 14623	Printing Graphic Arts
754	ST. BRIDE PRINTING LIBRARY Bride Lane, Fleet Street London, England EC4 Y8EE	Technique and Design History of Printing Typography Development of Letter Forms Type Design Printing Machinery Papermaking Bookbinding (Also has a collection of 2 x 2 slides on these topics.)
755	ST. JOHN'S UNIVERSITY Monastic Manuscript Microfilm Library Collegeville, Minnesota 56321	Medieval Manuscripts (Contains microfilm of the holdings of over fifty European libraries of bound handwritten manuscripts. Basically medieval and Renaissance material.)
756	ST. LOUIS UNIVERSITY Pius XII Memorial Library 3655 W. Pine Boulevard St. Louis, Missouri 63108	Rare Books Illuminated Manuscripts History of Printing Vatican Manuscripts Library Microfilm Depository
757	SAN DIEGO PUBLIC LIBRARY 820 East Street San Diego, California 92101	History of the Book Fine Printing History of Children's Literature
758	SAN FRANCISCO PUBLIC LIBRARY Civic Center San Francisco, California 94102	Press Books Bookbinding History of Printing The Development of the Book Fine Printing Illuminated Manuscripts

	NAME	AREA/S OF SPECIALIZATION
759	SMITHSONIAN INSTITUTION LIBRARY Constitution Avenue at Tenth Street, N.W. Washington, D.C. 20560	Americana Hall of Printing and Graphic Arts
760	STANFORD UNIVERSITY LIBRARIES Stanford, California 94305	Press Books
761	SYRACUSE UNIVERSITY Ernest S. Bird Library 222 Waverly Avenue Syracuse, New York 13210	History of Printing Manuscripts
762	UNIVERSITY OF TORONTO LIBRARIES Toronto, Ontario Canada	History of Printing
763	UNIVERSITY OF TORONTO Pontifical Institute of Medieval Studies Toronto, Ontario Canada	Medieval Culture
764	TRINITY COLLEGE LIBRARY 300 Summit Street Hartford, Connecticut 06106	Incunabula Press Books Bibliography History of Printing
765	UNION THEOLOGICAL SEMINARY LIBRARY 3041 Broadway New York, New York 10027	Assyrian and Babylonian Tablets Rare Books Incunabula Bibles
766	VEREENIGING TER BEVORDERING VAN DE BELGANEN DES BOEKHANDEIS Niewe Prinsengracht 57 Amsterdam, The Netherlands	Books About Books

Libraries, Special Collections, Museums

	NAME	AREA/S OF SPECIALIZATION
767	WALTERS ART GALLERY LIBRARY 600 N. Charles Street Baltimore, Maryland 21201	Medieval and Renaissance Illuminated Manuscripts Incunabula Private Presses Bookbindings
768	WILLIAMS COLLEGE Chapin Library Williamstown, Massachusetts 01267	Early Manuscripts Incunabula Rare Books Americana Press Books Bibles Aldine Press
769	YALE UNIVERSITY LIBRARY 120 High Street Box 1603 A Yale Station New Haven, Connecticut 06520	Americana Arabic and Near Eastern Manuscripts Incunabula Rare Books Babylonian Tablets Papyri Bibles Printing History John Baskerville Collection Bruce Rogers Frankliniana Press Books Illuminated Manuscripts Judaica Bibliography

Section 9

BOOK DEALERS

There are a number of book dealers who specialize in books on books, as well as in other areas in the history of books and printing. It would be impossible to list them all, but the following reference tools might be helpful in locating dealers and their areas of specialization. Rare book and antiquarian book dealers, as well as second-hand book dealers often have items on the history of the book, in addition to their regular stock of rare books. Visits to exhibitions, antiquarian book dealers, book auctions, antiquarian book fairs, and bookshops will be helpful in obtaining a firsthand knowledge of these materials. The following sources can provide information.

BOOK DEALER SOURCES

770   ABAA. MEMBERSHIP LIST. New York: Antiquarian Booksellers' Association of America, 1979.

771   AMERICAN BOOK TRADE DIRECTORY. 24th ed. New York: R.R. Bowker Co., 1978.

772   THE ANTIQUARIAN BOOKTRADE: AN INTERNATIONAL DIRECTORY OF SUBJECT SPECIALISTS. Compiled by B. Donald Grose. Metuchen, N.J.: Scarecrow Press, 1972.

773   BOOKDEALERS IN NORTH AMERICA: A DIRECTORY OF DEALERS IN SECONDHAND AND ANTIQUARIAN BOOKS IN CANADA AND THE UNITED STATES OF AMERICA. 1976-78. 7th ed. London: Sheppard Press, 1976.

774   BOOK TRADE OF THE WORLD. Edited by Sigfred Taubert. 3 vols. New York: R.R. Bowker Co., 1972-78.

Book Dealers

775   EUROPEAN BOOKDEALERS: A DIRECTORY OF DEALERS IN SECOND-
      HAND AND ANTIQUARIAN BOOKS ON THE CONTINENT OF EUROPE.
      3d ed. London: Sheppard Press, 1971. Triennial.

776   INTERNATIONAL DIRECTORY OF ANTIQUARIAN BOOKSELLERS.
      London: International League of Antiquarian Booksellers, 1977.

In addition a list of thirty-one book dealers in books about printing, private
presses, bookbinding, and related graphic arts topics can be found in PRIVATE
PRESSWORK: A BIBLIOGRAPHIC APPROACH TO PRINTING AS AN AVOCA-
TION, by Frank J. Anderson, editor, pages 155-58 (see 1).

AUTHOR INDEX

This index includes authors, editors, and compilers of works cited in the text. The alphabetization is letter by letter. The number after each item is to the entry number in the bibliography.

A

Aeschlimann, E. 240
Aldis, Harry G. 338
Alexander, J.J.G. 233, 234, 301
Allen, Agnes 208
Allen, Edward M. 21
Anderson, Donald M. 89
Anderson, Frank J. 1
Appleton, Tony 3
Arnold, Edmund C. 33
Artz, Frederick B. 329
Ash, Lee 694

B

Baab, Clarence T. 155
Bader, Barbara 161
Baird, Russell N. 56
Baltimore Museum of Art 150
Banister, Manly 139
Bartram, Alan 136
Basso, Carlo 244
Baumfield, Brian 339
Beatson, Elizabeth M. 282
Bennett, Paul A. 116, 340
Berry, W. Turner 23
Berthold, Arthur B. 378
Besterman, Theodore 4, 5, 312
Bibliothèque Nationale, Paris 551
Biggs, John R. 117, 118

Bigmore, Edward C. 6
Binns, Norman E. 209
Bischoff, Bernhard 323
Bland, David 135, 162, 163
Bliss, Douglas P. 164
Blum, André 59
Blumenthal, Joseph 341, 379
Boase, T.S.R. 311
Bodleian Library, Oxford 551
Bouchot, Henri 342
Bradley, John W. 235
Branner, Robert 236
Brassington, W.S. 140
Brewer, Roy 34
Briquet, Charles M. 60, 590
Brown, Horatio F. 343
Brunner, Felix 35
Bühler, Curt 313
Burdett, Eric 141
Burns, Aaron 119
Butler, Pierce 314

C

Cameron, George G. 220
Carter, Harry 120
Carter, John 338, 344
Carter, Thomas F. 345
Cave, Roderick 346
Cazelles, Raymond 307
Chappell, Warren 347

Author Index

Chatto, W.A. 165
Chiera, Edward 220
Cianciolo, Patricia 166
Clair, Colin 24, 348, 349, 350
Clapperton, R.H. 61
Clark, A.C. 237
Cleaver, James 167
Clodd, Edward 91
Cockerell, Douglas 142
Cockerell, Sydney C. 303
Cohen, Marcel 92
Cole, E.J. 63
Comparato, Frank E. 143
Corderoy, John 144
Coxe, H.O. 591
Craig, James 36, 121
Craig, Peggy 244
Crosland, Margaret 262
Crutchley, E.A. 338
Curwen, Harold 37

D

Dain, A. 239
Dair, Carl 122
Dalphin, Marcia 188
D'Ancona, Paolo 240
Darley, Lionel S. 145
Davenport, Cyril 38
Day, Frederick T. 62
Day, Kenneth 123, 365
Delaissé, L.M.J. 241
De Laurier, Nancy 491
Denham, Frank 124
Deuel, Leo 221
De Vinne, Theodore L. 315
Diehl, Edith 146
Diringer, David 93, 94, 222, 242
Doblhofer, Ernst 95
Dowding, Geoffrey 125
Dupont, Jacques 243

E

Ede, Charles 351
Egbert, Donald D. 306
Eppink, Norman R. 168
Escarpit, Robert 352
Esdaile, Arundell 210

F

Fairbank, Alfred 96, 97
Febvre, Lucien 353
Fontana, John M. 316
Formaggio, Dino 244
Forman, B. 223
Forman, W. 223
Foster, J. 189
Foto Marburg, University of Marburg 551
Fraenkel, Gerd 98
Francastel, P. 245
Franklin, Colin 354

G

Gaehde, J.E. 259
Gardner, Kenneth 540
Gaskell, Philip 39
Geanakoplos, Deno John 330
Gelb, Ignace J. 99
Gentry, Helen 27
George, M. Dorothy 169
Gerber, Jack 9
Gerulaitis, Leonardas V. 317
Getlein, Dorothy 170
Getlein, Frank 170
Gilbert, Stuart 243
Glaister, Geoffrey A. 26
Gnudi, Cesare 243
Goldschmidt, E.P. 331, 332
Goodrich, L. Carrington 345
Gordon, Cyrus H. 100
Goudy, Frederic W. 126
Grabar, André 246, 247
Grannis, Chandler 355
Gray, Basil 261
Greenhood, David 27
Grevel, H. 342
Grose, B. Donald 772
Gross, Henry 147

H

Haas, Irvin 356
Haebler, Konrad 318
Haller, Margaret 28
Hamilton, Edward A. 40
Handover, P.M. 357

Author Index

TITLE INDEX

This index includes titles of books, as well as of nonprint media cited in the text. The alphabetization is letter by letter. In a few cases the title has been shortened. The number after each item is to the entry number in the bibliography.

A

Title Index

H

Title Index

Title Index

SUBJECT INDEX

This index contains topics covered in the text. Underlined numbers refer to main areas of emphasis within the topic. The alphabetization is letter by letter. The number after each item is to the entry number in the bibliography.

Subject Index

Apocalypse, in manuscript illumination 269. See also names of Apocalyptic writings (e.g. CLOISTERS APOCALYPSE, THE)

Apostolis, Michael 330

Aquatint, slides about 497

Arabs
illuminated manuscripts of 480
library collection devoted to 769
influence on Spanish manuscript illumination 281
See also Egypt

Art
influence on book design 358
micropublication of manuscripts on 579

Ashendene Press 354

ASHMOLE BESTIARY, THE, micropublication of 576

Asia
the book in 218
illustration in 162
library collections devoted to 722, 734, 741
manufacture of paper in 59
manuscripts and records of 221
See also names of Asian countries (e.g. China)

Asia, Southeast, papermaking in 74. See also Thailand

Assyria. See Clay tablets; Cuneiform inscriptions

Australia, history of printing in 350

Austria, wood-engraving in 172

Austrian National Library, illuminated manuscripts of 274, 299

Authors
bibliographies on 7
influence on printing 42
the printer and 385

Autographic reproduction 37, 201-2

B

Babylonia, library collections devoted to 741. See also Clay tablets; Cuneiform inscriptions

Ballads, broadside, library collections devoted to 733

Baltimore Museum of Art 150, 275

Bangor (Maine) Public Library 704

Bark, as a writing surface 221

Baroque period, book illustration in the 173

Baskerville, John 22
Library collections devoted to 706, 769

BAY PSALM BOOK 379

Beardsley, Aubrey, library collections devoted to 749

BEDFORD HOURS, slides of 522, 527

BELLES HEURES OF JEAN, DUKE OF BERRY, THE
facsimiles of 282-83
slides of 527

BENEDICTIONAL OF ST. ETHELWOLD, THE, facsimile of 284

Beneventan writing 104

Berbers, influence on Spanish manuscript illumination 281

Berry, Jean de. See de Berry, Jean

Bestiaries, in manuscript illumination 269, 484, 521, 552, 565, 576, 583

Bewick, Thomas
Library collection devoted to 740

Bibles
facsimile of a Greek O.T. manuscript 308
filmstrip of an 11th century Psalms manuscript 487
filmstrip of an O.T. French manuscript 477, 489
filmstrip of a 13th century English 472
library collections of 722, 732, 746, 765, 768-69
micropublication of manuscripts of 577, 579
prevalence of manuscript N.T. examples 221
printing of in London 357
See also Apocalypse; Gospelbooks; Psalters; names of Bibles (e.g. DOVER BIBLE, THE)

Bibliography, library collections devoted to 725, 764, 769

Bibliothèque Nationale
examples of bindings from 500
illuminated manuscripts of 180, 303, 439, 551

printer-publishers of 264
wood-engraving in 172
See also Roman Empire; Rome;
    Subiaco, Italy; Venice

J

Japan
  beginning of literature in 227
  papermaking in 71, 76
Jewish Theological Seminary of
  America. Library 732
Jews
  early printing of 531
  influence on Spanish manuscript
    illumination 281
  See also Hebrew books; Hebrew
    manuscripts
Judea, beginning of literature in 227
Jurisprudence, micropublication of
  manuscripts on 579-80, 582
Juvenile literature. See Children's
  literature

K

KAUFMAN HAGGADAH, THE, slides
  of 531
Kelmscott Press 354. See also
  William Morris
Kent, Rockwell 199
Kentucky, University of. Margaret
  I. King Library 733
Kingman, Lee 176
Koberger, Anton 325, 336, 369,
  447
Kollwitz, Käthe 170
Korea, papermaking in 76

L

LAMBETH APOCALYPSE, transparencies of 547
LAMBETH BIBLE, THE
  slides of 521-22, 547
  transparencies of 547
Lambeth Palace. Library
  catalog of the manuscripts of 581
  micropublication of the manuscripts
    of 580

Language, vernacular, role of printing
  in establishing 353
Lascaux, France. See Cave paintings
Latin America, history of printing in
  383, 389
Latin literature, preservation of 265
Latin paleography 228-29
Law. See Jurisprudence
LEGEND OF ST. FRANCIS, THE,
  slides of 554
Lehmann-Haupt, Hellmut 219, 319
LIBER REGALIS, slides of 521
Libraries 252, 342
  ancient 226
  bibliography of in the incunabula
    period 312
  directories and lists of 1, 693-
    769
  filmstrip on classical 469
  Hebrew 216
  history of 211
  of the Middle Ages 217
Library of Congress 734
Library science
  bibliography on 7
  general information sources devoted
    to 25
  history of 211
LIFE OF ST. ALBAN, filmstrips of
  481
LIFE OF ST. CUTHBERT, THE, filmstrips of 482
LIFE OF ST. EDWARD THE CONFES-
  SOR
  filmstrip of 483
  slides of 521
Limbourg brothers 255, 282, 527
Limited Editions Club, collections of
  books by 704
Lincoln Cathedral. Library
  catalog of manuscripts of 594
  micropublications of the manu-
    scripts of 582
Lindeseye, Robert de. See PSALTER
    OF ROBERT DE LINDESEYE,
    THE
Linoleum block printing 207
  filmstrip about 466
Literacy, the spread of 107
Literary forgeries. See Forgeries,
  literary

Subject Index

Subject Index

Readers and reading
  in ancient Greece and Rome 225
  bibliographies on 7, 12
  in the incunabula period 317, 323
Reformation, role of the printing
    press in 353
Religion
  influence on book design and format
    214, 358
  micropublication of manuscripts on
    580, 582
  See also Bibles; Psalters
Rembrandt, van Rijn 170, 573
Remington, Frederic 186
Renaissance period 221
  the book in 146, 219, 264,
    329-37
    films about 429, 446
    filmstrip about 469
    filmstrip of Italian engravings of
      the 463
  handwriting during 97, 114, 136
  illuminated manuscripts of 233
    slides of 525, 527-28, 544,
      568
  preservation and transmission of
    literature in 265
René (King). See CUEUR D'AMOURS
    ESPRIS, LE
Rhode Island, history of papermaking
    in 66
Rochester Institute of Technology.
    Wallace Memorial Library
    753
Rockwell, Norman 186
Rococo period, book illustration in
    the 174
Rogers, Bruce 379
  Library collections devoted to 734,
    752, 769
ROHAN BOOK OF HOURS, THE
  facsimiles of 304-5
  slides of 527, 554
Roman alphabet and writing 105,
    110, 136
ROMANCE OF ALEXANDER, micro-
    publication of 586
ROMAN DE LA ROSE, slides of 527
Roman Empire
  the book in the 212, 225, 227
  manuscript illumination in the
    235, 246, 276

publishers and bookshops of the
    226
reading in the 225
Romanesque period, illuminated manu-
    scripts of 234, 247, 258,
    263, 266, 268-69
  filmstrips of 475, 484, 488
  slides of 528, 544, 564
Roman type 128
Rome, printing of incunabula in 328
Rosenback Fellowship in Bibliography
    313, 328
ROSSANO GOSPELS, THE, facsimile
    of 276
ROTHSCHILD MANUSCRIPTS, THE
    slides of 531
Rouault, Georges 170, 434
Rowlandson, Thomas 169, 572
Royal Library of Belgium, illuminated
    manuscripts of 241, 555
Rubrishers 192
Runes, exhibits and examples of 601
Ruzicka, Rudolph 379

S

St. Bride Foundation Institute 754
  catalog of periodicals in the 14
  catalog of the Technical Reference
    Library 15
ST. CHAD GOSPELS, THE, slides of
    521
ST. JOHN'S BESTIARY, micropublica-
    tion of 583
St. John's Monastic Manuscript Micro-
    film Library 755
St. Louis University. Pius XII Memo-
    rial Library 756
San Diego Public Library 757
Sandys, John Edwin 219
San Francisco Public Library 758
SARAJEVO HAGGADAH, THE, slides
    of 531
Satire, as exemplified by the art of
    printmakers 169-70
Scandanavian countries, "fine
    printing" in 351
Schoeffer, Peter 369
Science, micropublication of manu-
    scripts on 579. See also
    Technology